HISTORY, CRITICISM & FAITH

Four exploratory studies

GORDON J. WENHAM
F.F. BRUCE
R.T. FRANCE
COLIN BROWN

EDITED BY COLIN BROWN

INTER-VARSITY PRESS

© INTER-VARSITY PRESS, ENGLAND

Universities and Colleges Christian Fellowship
38 De Montfort Street, Leicester LE1 7GP, England

Inter-Varsity Christian Fellowship
Box F, Downers Grove, Illinois 60515, USA

First edition December 1976

ISBNs: UK 0 85111 315 X
       USA 0 87784 776 2

Printed in the United States of America

CONTENTS

PREFACE

CHIEF ABBREVIATIONS

I HISTORY & THE OLD TESTAMENT

1. HISTORY & THE OLD TESTAMENT *13*

GORDON WENHAM MA PhD

Lecturer in the Department of Semitic Studies,
The Queen's University of Belfast

II HISTORY & THE NEW TESTAMENT

2. MYTH & HISTORY *79*

F. F. BRUCE DD FA

Rylands Professor of Biblical Criticism and Exegesis
in the University of Manchester

3. THE AUTHENTICITY OF THE SAYINGS
OF JESUS *101*

R. T. FRANCE MA BD PhD

Librarian of Tyndale House, Cambridge

III HISTORY & THE BELIEVER

4. HISTORY & THE BELIEVER *147*

COLIN BROWN MA BD PhD

Lecturer at Trinity College, Bristol

INDEX

PREFACE

The four studies in this volume on *History, Criticism and Faith* are exploratory in a double sense. It is their aim to explore certain crucial areas where history and faith meet. They seek to probe this ground in the light of current critical thinking, and to give a positive, constructive statement of their conclusions. Three main areas have been selected for investigation: the Old Testament, the New Testament and the philosophical questions that arise for a faith that is grounded in history. Within these wide areas attention is focused on a series of issues which are of decisive importance to Christian faith today.

Dr Wenham was given the task of undertaking a broad survey of history and the Old Testament. In particular, he discusses the relationship between biblical theology and history, methods of Old Testament criticism, and the bearing of archaeology on the conquest of Canaan.

The two studies which come under the heading of 'History and the New Testament' focus attention on two subjects which have been at the centre of fierce debate for the past quarter of a century and which are of vital importance to the whole fabric of Christian faith. Professor Bruce's study of 'Myth and History' examines the contention that the New Testament accounts of the origins of Christianity were shaped by the mythological notions of the ancient world, and that hence any modern view of Jesus and the Christian gospel needs to be demythologized. Dr France examines the sayings of Jesus. He does so against the background of the arguments of recent form and redaction critics that the sayings attributed to Jesus by Matthew, Mark and Luke were not really the utterances of Jesus himself but the pious fabrication of the early church for the edification of the faithful.

The final chapter, by Dr Brown, is entitled 'History and the Believer'. Its theme is the triangular debate between historians, philosophers and theologians on the problems raised by the idea of God acting in history. It looks at the meaning and implications of the idea, and at miracles, historical criteria and explanations, and the role of history in revelation.

There is a second sense in which these studies are exploratory. Because all explorations have to have defined and limited objectives, it is inevitable that much of great interest and importance has to be passed by. No attempt has been made to work out a Christian philosophy of history or to compare such a philosophy with a Marxist philosophy of history. It would have been illuminating to have made a critique of thinkers such as Hegel and Heidegger. Some of the ideas of contemporaries such as Van Austin Harvey and Wolfhart Pannenberg are discussed at various points. But the temptation to undertake a full-scale assessment of their thought as a whole has had to be withstood. The study of the sayings of Jesus has been restricted to the synoptic Gospels. The complex issues raised by the Fourth Gospel require a separate companion study. While the two New Testament essays in this volume are a contribution to the debate on the 'new quest of the historical Jesus', no attempt has been made to chart the course of this quest so far. These are all important issues, but they must remain subjects for further explorations.

It remains to be said that Professor Bruce's study appeared in embryonic form under the title of 'Myth and the New Testament' in *TSFB* 44, 1966, pp. 10-16. The section by Dr France is an amended version of a paper read to the New Testament Study Group of the Tyndale Fellowship for Biblical Research in July 1971. The chapter by Dr Brown has grown out of the Tyndale Biblical Theology Lecture for 1972 which was delivered at Tyndale House, Cambridge. Sections of it have subsequently been delivered before various audiences including the Theological Forum of the University of British Columbia, Vancouver. The authors wish to express their gratitude to numerous friends for their constructive comments.

CHIEF ABBREVIATIONS

APhQ	*American Philosophical Quarterly*
AThR	*Anglican Theological Review*
BA	*Biblical Archaeologist*
BASOR	*Bulletin of the American Schools of Oriental Research*
BZAW	*Beihefte zur Zeitschrift für die alttestamentliche Wissenschaft*
CBQ	*Catholic Biblical Quarterly*
CThM	*Concordia Theological Monthly*
EQ	*Evangelical Quarterly*
ExpT	*Expository Times*
HThR	*Harvard Theological Review*
HUCA	*Hebrew Union College Annual*
IEJ	*Israel Exploration Journal*
JBL	*Journal of Biblical Literature*
JNES	*Journal of Near Eastern Studies*
JPh	*Journal of Philosophy*
JR	*Journal of Religion*
JTS	*Journal of Theological Studies*
NTS	*New Testament Studies*
PhR	*Philosophical Review*
RS	*Religious Studies*
SJT	*Scottish Journal of Theology*
TB	*Tyndale Bulletin*
TLZ	*Theologische Literaturzeitung*
TSFB	*TSF Bulletin (journal of the Theological Students Fellowship*
TU	*Texte und Untersuchungen*
VT	*Vetus Testamentum*
VTS	Supplement to *Vetus Testamentum*
ZNW	*Zeitschrift fur die Neutestamentliche Wissenschaft*
ZThK	*Zeitschrift für Theologie und Kirche*

I
HISTORY &
THE OLD
TESTAMENT

1. HISTORY & THE OLD TESTAMENT

GORDON WENHAM

1. BIBLICAL THEOLOGY AND THE QUESTION OF HISTORY

To the casual reader most of the Old Testament appears to be tales of an ancient and undistinguished people, of little interest to any save antiquarians. Whether the stories it contains are true or the events it records really happened does not concern him at all. But for Jews and Christians the Old Testament is of great importance. It is the Jewish Bible and describes the origins of Judaism and its development over more than a millennium. Naturally, then, most Jews have been concerned to defend the authenticity of the biblical account, viewing any attempt to cast doubt on its reliability as an attack on the integrity of the Jewish faith.

The church, too, has customarily set great store by the Old Testament. In a real sense it was the church's Bible before the New Testament was written. The New Testament was never intended to replace the Old, but to complement it. The Old Testament was regarded by the church as more than interesting background reading to the New; it described God's dealings with his people in the past and his plans for the future, plans that were now being fulfilled in Christ and in the church. In short, the Old Testament was held to be true and inspired like the New Testament and, therefore, authoritative in questions of doctrine and practice. But in spite of this theoretical position the church has, in practice, never been quite sure how to deal with the Old Testament.

The most glaring problem was that of interpreting Old Testament laws under the changed circumstances of the new covenant. How far did they apply to the new Israel, the church? Old Testament history also posed problems. Quite early, from about the third century, the church began to sit light to Old Testament history. The relevance of many of its narratives was obscure, and a number were not immediately very edifying. Hence allegorical interpretation was introduced and remained very popular until the Reformation. By this means, preachers attempted to preserve and make relevant the religious value of the Old Testament.[1]

The modern church is again confronted with the problem of the Old Testament. There are a few who would discard it completely or at least reduce it to the status of any other religious document. Most Christians, however, feel bound by the teaching of Christ and of the early church to regard the Old Testament as in a real sense the Word of God. But how can this be reconciled with the conclusion of some critical scholarship that many of the Old Testament books purporting to relate the history of Israel were in fact written long after the events they describe, and that if they are not deliberate forgeries, they at least give us a very distorted account of what really happened? How is the Christian to reconcile the apparent historical errors of the Bible with its spiritual truth?

One solution is to deny the importance of the biblical history. It is said that what really matters is the Old Testament's teaching about God, man, sin and redemption. The religious teaching of the Old Testament is still valid even if the writers were quite wrong about the history. In this way we can still use the Old Testament as a devotional aid and preserve our intellectual integrity intact. Biblical scholars can continue to read the Old Testament on Sundays as the Word of God, but on weekdays treat it as a human production full of all kinds of errors.

Attractive as this solution to the problem of the Old Testament may be to some, it is, I believe, inadequate. The religious teaching of the Old Testament cannot be divorced from the history, for the theology of the Old Testament depends on the history. If certain events did not happen, the Old Testament writers are simply wrong in what they teach about God. The heart of the Old Testament gospel is that God saved his people from Egypt: without the exodus, the central article of the Old Testament creeds is lost. Yet it is precisely in this area of the early history of Israel that there are most doubts and uncertainties. It is little surprise, therefore, that there have been a number of recent discussions of this question. In what follows I shall first try to explain why the history of the Old Testament is as vital to the Christian as it is to the Jew, and in precisely what way Old Testament theology depends on Old Testament history. Different attempts to resolve the tension between Old Testament criticism and Old Testament theology will be discussed. Then the value of different types of criticism will be explored in general. Particular attention will be focused on the importance of historical criticism, especially with regard to the earliest period of Israel's history and how far archaeology can be used to support or disprove the biblical traditions. Here the tension between theology and criticism is sharpest, because it touches on events that are at the heart of Old Testament faith. It also illustrates very clearly the nature of the critical method and the sort of problem it raises for the theologian. The essay concludes with some suggestions for the direction in which historical and theological investigation of the Old Testament might proceed in the future.

The authority of the Old Testament
Before turning to the history of the Old Testament, we must ask a more fundamental question: What authority does the Old Testament have? Various answers to this question are discussed by John Bright in his book *The Authority of the Old Testament*. He concludes that the attempts to remove the Old Testament from the Christian canon of Scripture, whether by the second-century Marcion or by nineteenth-century liberals, were misguided. He argues that if the Christian church is to be faithful to its Lord it must accept the Old Testament as canonical Scripture:

> I am quite unable to get around the fact ... that the Old Testament *was* authoritative Scripture for Jesus himself. Jesus knew no Scripture save the Old Testament, no God save its God; it was this God whom he addressed as 'Father'. True, he used the Scriptures with sovereign freedom, as befitted him. But never once did he suggest that in the light of his

work they might safely be discarded. On the contrary, he regarded the Scriptures as the key to the understanding of his person; again and again he is represented as saying that it is the Scriptures that witness to him and are fulfilled in him. At no place did he express himself as shocked by the Old Testament, nor did he adopt . . . a polemical attitude toward it (though often enough toward the religious leaders of his day and their interpretations). I find it most interesting and not a little odd that although the Old Testament on occasion offends our Christian feelings, it did not apparently offend Christ's 'Christian feelings'! Could it really be that we are ethically and religiously more sensitive than he? Or is it perhaps that we do not view the Old Testament—and its God—as he did? The very fact that the Old Testament was normative Scripture to Jesus, from which he understood both his God and (however we interpret his self-consciousness) himself, means that it must in some way be normative Scripture for us too—*unless we wish to understand Jesus in some other way than he himself did and the New Testament did.*[2]

To state that the Old Testament is authoritative for the Christian does not, of course, solve the problems of its interpretation and application. Bright thinks these are little different from those presented by the New Testament, because there is a fundamental unity of theological outlook linking the Testaments. Though the perspective of the Old Testament on a number of issues differs from that of the New, its theology still has authority and relevance for the modern church.[3]

The relationship of history, history of religion and Old Testament theology

If it is the theology of the Old Testament that matters, why bother about the history? Can we not just get on with studying the message of the Old Testament and forget about its history? This is another area of recent keen controversy. It brings us right into the question of the relationship between Old Testament theology, the history of Old Testament religion and ordinary history. We cannot here go over the whole debate, but we shall simply set out some of the characteristic positions.[4] The first point that must be clarified is the nature and scope of Old Testament theology. What is the task of an Old Testament theologian? Is it to compare and contrast the theological views current in Israel at various periods with those of other religious systems and then to write a history of the development of theological outlooks within the Old Testament? Or must the Old Testament theologian sit light to comparative study and simply study the Old Testament on its own terms and seek to bring out the distinctive views of the different writers? Should prophets, wise men, and historians be allowed to speak with their own voice on their own terms and express their experience of God? Or is there a third way of writing Old Testament theology, one in which the theologian not only seeks to understand what the Old Testament writers were saying but also seeks to go on to appropriate their message for himself and to reinterpret the Old Testament in the light of his understanding of Christ?

The majority of modern Old Testament theologies seem to fall into the first category, and would seem to be more appropriately described as works of comparative religion or history of religion than of Old Testament theology. Even the second type, best represented by the *Old Testament Theology* of von Rad,[5] is really closer to being a history of Old Testament religion (at least a history of its religious ideas) than to an Old Testament theology. The only adequate understanding of the Old Testament theologian's task is the third. No-one who takes the authority of the Old Testament seriously can be satisfied with a theology of the Old Testament which leaves the ideas of the Old Testament suspended in mid-air and fails to relate them to the further revelation in Christ and the subsequent development of Christian dogma. The task of Old Testament theology has been well expressed by the eminent Roman Catholic scholar, Roland de Vaux: 'Theology is the science of faith.'[6] That is, theology seeks to understand the meaning of the faith from the standpoint of faith.

> As a Christian theologian I accept the Old Testament as the Word of God, the Word of *my* God, addressed to his chosen people but destined also for *me* as their spiritual descendant.
> The Old Testament contains the revelation of *my* God.[7]

Bright agrees with this view:

The two Testaments have to do with one and the same God, one history, one heritage of faith, one people. Since this is so, the Christian must claim the Old Testament, as the New Testament did, for it belongs to him no less than it did—and does —to Israel. Indeed, the Christian has through Christ in the truest sense been made an Israelite, grafted onto Israel like a wild branch onto a tree (Rom 11:17-24). He must therefore see the Old Testament's history as *his* history, the history of his own heritage of faith, its God as *his* God, its saints and sinners as men who had to do with that God. The Christian who refuses to see it so flies in the face of the New Testament's witness and does no less than reject his own past. The unity of the Testaments within a single redemptive history must at all times be affirmed.[8]

If this is the proper understanding of the Old Testament theologian's task, how is it related to the history of Old Testament religion and to the political history of Israel? According to de Vaux,[9] the three are interrelated like three concentric circles. Old Testament theology presupposes the conclusions of the historian of Old Testament religion, while the latter presupposes the results of the ordinary historian, who is concerned with the development of Israel's political, economic and religious institutions.

An example will perhaps clarify the situation. Isaiah 7 relates how the kings of Syria and Israel came in alliance to besiege Jerusalem. Ahaz, King of Judah, scared by the combined onslaught, was contemplating signing a treaty with the king of Assyria. But Isaiah the prophet violently opposed such a move and did all in his power to dissuade Ahaz from allying himself with a foreign king. The passage records some of Isaiah's remarks on this occasion, including his prophecy of Immanuel. The chapter contains material of interest to a secular historian, to a historian of religious ideas, and to an Old Testament theologian. The secular historian is interested in the light the passage sheds on the course of events in about 735 BC. He will compare it with other accounts of the same period, Assyrian and biblical, and endeavour to build up a detailed picture of the course of events in this year, of the external and internal problems facing King Ahaz and of his motives in concluding an alliance with Assyria.

The general historian will also be interested in what this incident discloses about the policy of the states of Israel, Syria and Assyria and about their relative strengths. In his study of this episode, the Near Eastern historian will use much the same sort of evidence and much the same sort of methods as a historian of any other period. He will pay particular attention to the literary sources and attempt by means of textual, literary and historical criticism to extract as much information as possible from them. He will also use whatever archaeological or other non-literary evidence may be available to fill out the historical picture obtained from the literary sources.

The religious historian will focus on different aspects of this episode. He will be primarily concerned with the beliefs of the principal actors in the story, Ahaz and Isaiah, as well as with those of the narrator, if the narrator is to be distinguished from Isaiah. He will attempt to discover what they believed from their explicit statements and from what is implied by their actions. To grasp the significance of their actions he will have to relate them to the official Jerusalem theology expressed in a number of psalms. To determine whether the promise of Immanuel is to be construed as a curse or a blessing, he will have to take into account the references to 'curds and honey' in verses 15 and 22, as well as the rest of Isaiah's teaching about the covenant. It will be necessary for the religious historian to ask a whole range of questions, before he can be confident of what Isaiah believed in 735 BC.

It is evident that the religious historian is heavily dependent on the work of the ordinary historian, if he is to achieve any sure results himself. Without a clear understanding of the course of events that formed the background against which Isaiah was speaking, many of his remarks are very cryptic and could be taken in several different ways. More important still, the religious historian has to rely on the techniques of the ordinary historian in order to establish the text of Isaiah's oracles and then to date them. If the religious historian attempts to date them simply by the religious views they contain, he is in great danger of arguing in circles rather than writing a reliable history of Israel's theological development. It is clear then that the religious historian presupposes the results and work of the ordinary historian. The history of religious ideas is, in this sense, therefore, an outer circle which includes ordinary history.

The theologian is naturally most interested in the Immanuel prophecy. He will note how Isaiah reverts to this theme in the following chapters and expands on it. He will want to know what justification Matthew and subsequent generations have for seeing this prophecy as fulfilled in Christ. But to solve this problem he depends on the findings of the historian and religious historian, for only their methods are capable of discovering who Isaiah thought Immanuel was. Though a Christian would claim that any text of Scripture may mean more than it meant in the mind of its human author (since it is at the same time the Word of God as well as a human word), without further revelation in Scripture, later human exegetes can go no further than discovering the meaning the human author intended. Did Isaiah believe that Immanuel was to be born in a few months, perhaps to a woman present in the court, or was he expecting this special child to be born in the more distant future? If we affirm the former, namely that Immanuel was to be born within a few months of the prophecy, it is hard to see in the birth of Jesus its literal fulfilment. At best, the Christian theologian could say that the birth of Immanuel was a type of the birth of Christ. Certainly Matthew uses typology to link other passages with the life of Christ (*e.g.* Ho. 11:1; Mt. 2:15). But if the religious historian concludes that Isaiah was not anticipating the birth of Immanuel straight away but in a later but unspecified period, the theologian may well have less difficulty in seeing Isaiah's words as a real prophecy of the birth of Christ.[10]

It is not my purpose to discuss the rival interpretations of this text but simply to point out how in interpreting it the Old Testament theologian is dependent on the findings of the religious historian, while the latter is in turn dependent on the findings of the ordinary historian. To adapt a biblical image: if biblical theology is honey, its religious ideas are the honeycomb, and history is the hive in which both are created. We cannot understand Old Testament theology without getting to grips with the different religious ideas of its authors, and we cannot understand these ideas without knowing something about the period in which they lived. In this sense, then, history is basic to Old Testament theology.

Biblical theology: a theology of history

At a deeper level, theology and history are linked in the Bible by their content. Biblical theology may be crudely described as a theology of history. This is even clearer in the Old Testament than in the New. But both Testaments are primarily concerned with telling us what God has done, is doing and will do in history. It is unnecessary to read very far in Genesis to see how the Bible affirms the dependence of world history on the will of God. God created the world and everything in it. He was not interested in creating a satisfactory total effect, but in getting the details just right. Adam's need of a wife is just as much the Creator's concern as the arrangement of the sun and stars. The wickedness of man in general prompts God to send a universal flood, but as he destroys the rest of the human race he spares Noah and his family because they are upright. These opening chapters of Genesis set out very clearly the presuppositions held by all the writers of the Old Testament about the relationship of God to the world. They declare that God controls not only the forces of nature but also the affairs of men. He is not concerned simply with the fate of nations but with individuals too. He is a God who hates sin to such a degree that he is almost prepared to spoil his creation in order to eliminate it. Yet he is a God of grace who remembers those who are faithful to him.

These themes which are so clear in Genesis 1-11 keep reappearing throughout Scripture. The writers constantly affirm that God's hand is to be seen working out his purpose in human history. And it is to these later writings that we must turn for verifications of this biblical theology of history. The period from the call of Abraham (c. 1800 BC) to the fall of Jerusalem (AD 70) constitutes the great proving-ground for the Bible's theology of history. Inevitably some parts of the story are more susceptible to test than others. We should be surprised to find archaeological evidence for the existence of just one man, such as Abraham, unless he had been an important king. The movements of peoples might have attracted more attention among extrabiblical writers and might be expected to have left traces for the archaeologist. This is one reason why the exodus and conquest occupy such a vital place in the discussion of Old Testament history.

But first we must spell out in more detail the exact significance and character of the biblical view of history. In the words of John Bright:

> The genius of the Old Testament faith does not lie in its idea of God or in the elevation of its ethical teachings. Rather, it lies in its understanding of history, specifically of Israel's history, as the theatre of God's purposive activity. The Old Testament offers a theological interpretation of history. A concern with the meaning of history, and of specific events within history, is one of its most characteristic features. It records a real history, and it interprets every detail of that history in the light of Yahweh's sovereign purpose and righteous will. It relates past events—the stories of the Patriarchs, the Exodus, the covenant at Sinai, the giving of the Promised Land—in terms of his gracious dealings with his people, his promise to them and its fulfilment. It continually sets forth the response that Yahweh requires of his people, and interprets their fortunes in the midst of events, in terms of their obedience or disobedience to his demands. And it announces what Yahweh will yet do, in the judgment of Exile and beyond, for the accomplishment of his purpose. The Old Testament consistently views Israel's history as one that is guided on to a destination by the word and will of her God.[11]

Biblical history versus critical history

Von Rad would agree that this fairly represents the views of the writers of the Old Testament, at least of the historical and prophetic books.[12] But he believes with many other scholars that what actually happened in Old Testament times was very different from what Old Testament writers say occurred, particularly with regard to the earliest period in Israel's history, *i.e.*, from the patriarchs to the conquest. He believes that the critical study of Old Testament history leads to the following conclusions: there was no united people of Israel prior to the settlement in the promised land; different tribes invaded, or more accurately, infiltrated, Palestine at different times; a few had come from Mesopotamia, a few had been in Egypt, yet another group had visited Sinai; Moses' role as a national leader is greatly exaggerated in the Old Testament; he did few if any of the things with which the Pentateuch credits him.[13]

Von Rad believes that, though the Old Testament writers profess to be relating history, they are in fact setting out a theology which bears very little relation to what actually happened. This belief comes to formal expression in the arrangement of his work. The first 100 pages are entitled 'A History of Yahwism and of the Sacral Institutions in Israel', i.e., what von Rad believes really happened. The next 350 pages are taken up with 'The Theology of Israel's Historical Traditions', i.e., what Old Testament writers thought happened. The division between the two parts includes a short section entitled 'Methodological Presuppositions', in which von Rad sets out his own views of the relationship of Old Testament theology to history:

> These two pictures of Israel's history lie before us—that of modern critical scholarship and that which the faith of Israel constructed—and for the present, we must reconcile ourselves to both of them. It would be stupid to dispute the right of the one or the other to exist. It would be superfluous to emphasise that each is the product of very different intellectual activities. The one is rational and presupposing the similarity of all historical occurrence, it constructs a critical picture of the history as it really was in Israel.[14]

> The other activity is confessional and personally involved in the events to the point of fervour. Did Israel ever speak of her history other than with the emotion of glorification or regret? Historical investigations searches for a critically assured minimum—the kerygmatic picture tends towards a theological maximum. The fact that these two views of Israel's history are so divergent is one of the most serious burdens imposed today on Biblical scholarship.[15]

But though von Rad thinks that the critical reconstruction of Israel's history often conflicts with the Old Testament writers' view, he thinks that they must somehow be connected. The Old Testament story-teller, when he relates a story, should be regarded not so much as handing on information about God's action in the past as passing on his own experiences and belief in God. The story-teller may give us a garbled account of some past event, but in so doing he gives a clear picture of his own theological convictions. Only when the story-teller's purpose is grasped can the stories of Balaam (Nu. 22-24) be correctly understood. If one asks what is historical in these tales, von Rad replies:

> Certainly some definite but very elusive particular event which stands at the primal obscure origin of the tradition in question —but what is also historical is the experience that Jahweh turns the enemy's curse into blessing, and that he safeguards the promise in spite of all failure on the part of its recipient, etc. Israel did not dream up this confidence, but came to it on the basis of rich and wide experience, of her history in fact; and symbolising it in a person, she illustrated it in a story. This of course occasions another and rather severe clash with our critical way of thinking about history. Did the historical Balaam actually curse, or did his mouth really utter blessings? We may assume that it was only in the story that that which was given to Israel's faith became presented as a visible miracle. This process of glorification is quite clear in many of the stories about the Conquest—the events are depicted with a splendour and a strong element of the miraculous which are impossible to square with older strands in the report.[16]

In his *Old Testament Theology* von Rad has spotlighted the dilemma that faces any Jew or Christian who studies the Old Testament critically, yet who at the same time believes it to be in some sense the Word of God. If there are so many serious errors in the Bible at those points where it is subject to test, *i.e.*, in its history, can it still be relied on where it is not possible to test it, *i.e.*, in its theology? A few would answer Yes. Even if biblical history is haywire, its theology is admirable. Many more would take this attitude in practice, if not in theory. By resorting to superficial moralizing or spiritualizing, they try to escape the difficult historical problems—problems which must be faced if the truth of the Old Testament is to be meaningfully affirmed. Von Rad's position, however, has been fiercely rejected by various scholars.

Eichrodt picks on three aspects of von Rad's position to which he takes particular exception.[17] First, it wrenches apart the critical reconstruction of history and the salvation-history of the Old Testament writers so drastically that it is impossible 'to restore any inner coherence between these two aspects of Israel's history'.[18] Because of the gulf between salvation-history and real history, the former has but a 'spurious factuality' and 'possesses a claim to validity only for the man who is prepared to "ask the same sort of questions and accept the same sort of answers" '.[19] It means that 'any genuine historical foundation for a confession of faith in Yahweh, the God of Israel, must always be out of the question'.[20] Secondly, because von Rad believes that there is no unity between the different statements of faith within the Old Testament, one cannot talk of 'any constant factor in God's relations with Israel'.[21] Thirdly, and this arises from the previous point, the only link between the different revelations of God in the Old Testament, or more precisely, between the different descriptions of religious experience in the Old Testament, is typological. The same event is understood by different writers in different ways, and so there can be no normative interpretation of the Old Testament.[22] Eichrodt believes that these three aspects of von Rad's theology all derive from one root, '*the conviction that the existentialist interpretation of the biblical evidence is the right one*. If what matters in both the Old and New Testaments is the existential understanding of the professing believer, and not the presuppositions or individual content of his belief, then obviously the relation of his convictions to history becomes immaterial.'[23] Put more simply, according to von Rad what really matters is not the event but the reader's reaction to the story. Even if the event never occurred, provided that the story-teller had some indefinable experience which prompted him to tell a story it makes no difference to the present-day believer.

Eichrodt insists that von Rad's approach is unsatisfactory:

> First, the basic assumption that existential illumination constitutes the proper revelatory function of the testimonies of Scripture seems to the present writer quite invalid. It involves an intolerable cramping of the far more comprehensive vision of the biblical preaching, and totally obscures the importance for the faith of the congregation of God's sovereignty in the universe and in the history of mankind. Hence the sacrifices required if this approach is to be carried out without restriction must be rejected as too severe. There must be an absolute re-

fusal to surrender a real historical foundation to the faith of Israel, or to interpret the conflicts between the statements of the Old Testament version of history and that discovered by critical scholarship in a merely negative way as proof of the unimportance of the historical reference of religious statements. This denigration is to be all the more vigorously resisted when it is realized that in the Old Testament we are dealing not with an anti-historical transformation of the course of history into a fairy tale or poem, but with an interpretation of real events inspired by contact with the mysterious Creatorhood of the God who controls history, and from continual experience of his saving action.[24]

De Vaux has criticized von Rad from a slightly different point of view:

> This revelation took place in history and Von Rad was right to insist on the 'historical fact' of the faith of Israel. That faith rested on the interpretation of events in which Israel saw at work the hand of its God. But if such an interpretation is to command the faith of Israel and my own faith, it must be true and it must originate from God himself. But in Von Rad's terms neither of these conditions holds. In his view 'sacred history' is not 'true' history, it is the changing and false interpretation—as far as the historian is concerned—which the holy men of Israel gave to the events of history. The only conclusion which we can draw from this standpoint . . . is that the faith of Israel is an 'erroneous faith.' When Von Rad subsequently proposes that Christians might seek in the same way to find a 'charismatic' interpretation (which would be equally subjective and fallible) of what the people of Israel believed in throughout their history, he destroys the certainty of our own faith by rejecting its very foundation, which is the truthfulness of God.[25]

God reveals himself in history. His choosing of the people of Israel, their salvation, the promises made to them and the punishments imposed upon them are reported as *facts*. In the New Testament, the Incarnation is a *fact*, and the Resurrection is a *fact*. These facts have to be true, because as St Paul says, 'If

Christ has not been raised to life, our faith is in vain.'[26]

De Vaux goes on to expound the way in which he sees the relationship between the description of historical events that a secular historian would give and the description that the biblical writers supply. Partly by accepting that there is an absolute dichotomy between the methods and assumptions of secular historians and those of the biblical writers, von Rad was led to the conclusions outlined above. 'Presupposing the similarity of all historical occurrence'[27] means for von Rad that, first, only secular explanations of events are truly valid and, secondly, that no miracles are possible, since they are without analogy in our experience.[28] De Vaux goes on to query both these assumptions; he admits, however, that the only explanation that a historian can give of events (since he is not a prophet, but human, and has no private source of special revelation) must inevitably be a natural or human one:

> The paradox of faith, which flows from its very essence, is that these facts of history are incapable of being grasped by historical methods. They are the objects of faith, facts interpreted. Perhaps we should enlarge on this. The whole of History (with a capital 'H') is a process of interpretation. One bare, singular, isolated fact taking place at a point in space and time is of no significance to the historian as long as it stands in isolation. Rather it is a stone which the historian must fit into the edifice he is trying to build, and it cannot be identified as a foundation stone, or part of a supporting wall or as the keystone of the vault until it has been compared with many other facts and seen in relation to them. If this interpretation is purely human, and even if it is also true, it has no power to command my faith, which is an allegiance to divine truth. To say that God reveals himself in history does not simply mean that God instigates events which he leaves man to interpret nor does it mean that he merely endows events which he has not ordained with a significance they would not otherwise possess. God is at once master of the events of history, which he controls, and master of their interpretation. It may happen that the intervention of God in history suspends or modifies the natural sequence of cause and effect, but this is not necessary, nor even usual, since

God orders natural causes to produce the event he desires. And it may happen that the divine interpretation of the same events differs from that which man may give, since man explains them solely in terms of their natural causes.

Now to ensure that these facts and their interpretation should be recognized as vehicles of Revelation and that this Sacred History should command not only the faith of Israel but my faith as well, it is essential that it should be communicated with a guarantee from God. The Bible is accounted Sacred Scripture not just because it contains Sacred History but principally because it is written under the inspiration of God to express, preserve, and transmit God's revelation to men.[29]

Since God is at once master of the events of history and master of their interpretation, then it follows that there can be no contradiction between the two and that there must be a link between them. Once we admit that the kerygma is not founded on fact and that the historical confession of Israel's faith does not have its roots in history, then we empty our faith of its content. We have already seen quite clearly that there is a world of difference between the history of Israel as it is reconstructed by modern historical science and the salvation history written by the authors of the Bible. But salvation history depends on facts which the historian with his positive methods should be able to check. Von Rad doubts whether this is possible and believes that in any case it does not make any difference. It makes all the difference in the world, since it involves the truthfulness of God and the foundation of our faith.[30]

Eichrodt, de Vaux and Bright[31] all argue strongly that the substantial historicity of the Old Testament narratives is important. They believe that, if the events related there never occurred, the claim that the Old Testament is the Word of God is disproved or meaningless. In their historical studies, therefore, they try to close the gap between a critical account of Israel's history and the biblical account. But they recognize that the Old Testament writers are not trying to do quite the same things as modern historians, and therefore that the gap between the two accounts will never be completely eliminated.

De Vaux rightly insists, for example, that in the case of the fall of Jerusalem there is no conflict between the account given by a modern historian and that given by Kings. But the levels of explanation are different. A modern historian would explain the events of 587 BC in terms of great power politics and the particular circumstances of the time. The author of Kings also mentions these factors, but he does not regard them as the real explanation. This is to be found in the mind and will of God. God had made a covenant with his people, which stipulated the kind of behaviour he required and warned them in a series of curses how he would deal with them if they were disobedient. Kings explains how they had disobeyed and consequently experienced military defeat and deportation as predicted in the covenant curses.[32]

The differences between a modern history of Israel and the biblical account are not to be explained merely in terms of the difference between a secular and a religious view of life. A pious Old Testament believer living at the beginning of the sixth century might well have wondered whether the calamities befalling his nation were to be explained in terms of punishment on his nation's sins. But without the preaching of Jeremiah, he would not have been sure that his surmise was correct. The author of Kings definitely accepts the prophetic explanation of the nation's plight. He is writing not just moral history, but prophetic history. He states categorically that the fall of Jerusalem was the result of national apostasy. It seems to me that this is beyond the realm of verification by historians. A Christian today might try to explain the rise and fall of the British Empire in terms of the moral or religious health of the nation. In this case he would be a moralizing historian. But unless he was inspired by the Spirit, he could never write a prophetic history relating the decline of the Empire to the purpose of God. His moralizing must for ever remain his personal opinion open to challenge by other historians. In this sense then the gap between the interpretation of events in Kings and a modern historian's interpretation is unbridgeable. The historian can say that all the events described in the book of Kings happened just so, but he will never be in a position to prove that the explanation in Kings is correct.

This does not mean that, in principle, historians could not disprove the theological explanations of events related in the Bible. If, for example, the modern historian could show that Naaman never had leprosy or never existed, this would invalidate the theological point of including the story in Kings—to show the power of God at work in Elisha. To disprove the broader principles expounded by the book of Kings, e.g., that the capture of Samaria by the Assyrians was due to the persistent disobedience of the nation and its kings, the historian would have to prove that the account of events given in Kings was seriously in error, not just in its details. If he could show that when Samaria was taken not Hoshea but (say) Menahem was king, this would not enhance the reputation of Kings as a historical source, but neither would it invalidate its broader interpretation of the history of Israel. If, however, the modern historian could show that Samaria was not captured by Assyria, or alternatively that Israel had followed the prophets' advice very carefully, the whole thrust of Kings would be undermined.

In the light of modern study the above examples are hypothetical. They are given merely to show that although the theology of the biblical writers is not proved by the historicity of their narrative, it would be invalidated if the events or situations it professes to explain could be shown never to have occurred. Thus, modern historians cannot prove the biblical theologies of history, but they can, in principle, disprove them. An analogous situation prevails in science. Experiments in science cannot positively prove a hypothesis but they can disprove it. If a hypothesis predicts that something should happen under certain experimental conditions, and experiment shows it does not, this means that the hypothesis needs revision. If, however, the experiment works as predicted by the hypothesis, this does not prove that the hypothesis is the only or the complete explanation. Further data may be found which require the hypothesis to be modified.

Today it is generally agreed that the books of Kings give a substantially accurate account of the history of Judah and Israel from the accession of Solomon to the fall of Jerusalem. Whether you accept the theological explanation which Kings gives of this history depends on your view of revelation and biblical inspiration. In the case of the early history of Israel, the period of exodus and conquest, the situation is not so simple. According to von Rad, the actual course of events was so different from that described in the Old Testament that it is very hard to see how the theological conclusions of the Old Testament writers can be justified. This is the burden of the complaint of Eichrodt and de Vaux against von Rad. If the people of Israel were not as a group present in Egypt and therefore never experienced an exodus, what right had they to affirm in song and creed that God had saved them from the slavery of Egypt? De Vaux is prepared to accept that there are mistakes in the details of the early history, but not in its fundamentals. He believes that if these are surrendered, the theology of the Pentateuch must also be surrendered. The Christian scholar appears to face an awkward dilemma: must he abandon either his theology or his criticism?

The necessity of criticism
There are two approaches to solving this problem. The first is to suspend judgment about the validity of Old Testament theology until criticism has decided whether the records on which the theology rests are reliable. But as we have seen, proof of the historicity of the Old Testament does not involve acceptance of their theology. This approach is possible for a non-Christian, though before long even he will have to decide what he thinks of the theology of various Old Testament writers if he wishes really to appreciate what they are saying. But for a Christian this option is not really open. A Protestant such as Bright finds himself committed by the teaching of Christ to accepting the authority of Old Testament theology. Others would affirm with the Roman Catholic de Vaux that the Old Testament is the inspired Word of God.

Should criticism, therefore, be dismissed as an irrelevancy, a red herring introduced by unbelieving scholars which should be ignored? Though few say as much, many laymen feel this way. Bright and de Vaux, by their detailed study of critical problems, have shown their disagreement with this attitude. Bright criticizes those who, whenever they meet a problem, resolve it 'by appeal to presuppositions regarding the reliability of Scripture'.[33] Van A. Harvey has set out the inadequacy of this approach in *The Historian and the Believer*. He points out that if an orthodox scholar tries to allay the doubts of a sceptical layman simply by appeal to the dogma of Scripture he will probably have the opposite effect:

Theologians do not often realize to what extent this problem deeply troubles theological students and informed laymen. Faced with a plurality of views defended by learned men, they find themselves unable to give any convincing grounds why they should choose one rather than another. Nor do more conservative theologians sense the ironic dilemma they face in their attempts to allay the anxiety of those who want to know whether the traditional historical claims can stand the acids of reasoned argument. If the Christian apologist simply assumes the doctrine of inspiration and accepts the principle of supernatural intervention, he begs the issue and arrives at 'conclusions' which were in the premises from which he started. This practice inevitably breeds suspicion in the minds of those he is most trying to convince. If, however, the doctrine of inspiration and the principle of supernatural intervention are set aside, the apologist necessarily employs the canons of those with whom he is in debate.[34]

We may put Harvey's point another way. Christians before the nineteenth century believed in the truth of the Old Testament because Christ taught them to regard it as the Word of God. Then in the nineteenth century it came to be generally accepted that there were many errors in the Old Testament. This in turn threw doubt on the reliability of Christ's teaching. His attitude to the Old Testament was proof that he was no more than a man of his time. That he shared the misapprehensions of his contemporaries showed the full extent of his incarnation. Previously, writers on the incarnation had speculated whether his humanity limited Christ's knowledge but had not suggested that it actually involved him in error. The suggestion that incarnation meant error represented a big departure in Christian thinking. If Christ was wrong in what he taught about the Bible, might he not be wrong about other matters—the character of God, his own person, sin and salvation, heaven and hell, forgiveness and ethics? In fact, why should Jesus' views be regarded as any more trustworthy than those of any other first-century Jew? After all, on most of the above subjects many of his contemporaries agreed with him.

It is evident that if Jesus was mistaken in what he taught about the Old Testament we are going to be hard pressed to demonstrate that any of his teaching should be accepted, where it does not accord with current ideas. Therefore, unless we are obscurantists, we cannot escape discussion of the problems raised by Old Testament criticism. Suppose it could be shown that Christ's discussion[35] of Psalm 110 depends for its validity on the Davidic authorship of the psalm, but that critical considerations make it unlikely that David wrote the psalm. If we then say 'Jesus affirmed the Davidic authorship of Psalm 110, therefore the critical view is wrong', we miss the point. It is because people believe that criticism has disproved Jesus' view of the Old Testament that they also believe his teaching cannot always be trusted. So it is no good appealing to Jesus' teaching to authenticate the Old Testament as if that eliminated the problem. It is the alleged errors in the Old Testament that cast doubt on Jesus. It is only by taking Old Testament criticism seriously that we may hope to answer both the believer's doubts about the truth of the Old Testament and about the reliability of Christ as a teacher. It should be noted that it is the believer's doubts that we are primarily concerned with here. But a thoroughly honest criticism is also of inestimable value in removing the obstacles to faith in an unbeliever. Harvey appropriately compares the work of a biblical critic with that of a lawyer defending his client:

> A lawyer may have faith that his client is innocent, but his arguments in court are logically independent of this trust. The lawyer will have to show why his inner trust is justified, and he will have to appeal to data and warrants that are acceptable to those who remain to be convinced.[36]

Though the Christian is committed by the teaching of his Lord to affirming the truth and inspiration of the Old Testament, I do not believe that this means he must believe that every narrative in the Old Testament must necessarily be regarded as a record of a historical event. If Christ was a traditional Jew in his view of the Old Testament's authority, he was radical in his interpretation of it.[37] In the Sermon on the Mount he casts aside Pharisaic tradition that had attempted to limit the meaning of the law to outward actions. Jesus points out that the lawgiver's original intention went much further than deeds: it covered words and thoughts as well. His insistence on the original meaning of the law is crucial. When this is applied to narrative and other literature, it means that the exegete's task is to discover the author's understanding of what he wrote. Where the Old Testament writer thought he was writing history, the modern reader must take it as history; but where he was writing poetry or fiction the reader must take it in that way.

2. METHODS OF OLD TESTAMENT CRITICISM

So far we have talked about criticism in very general terms, perhaps even giving the impression that it is a necessary evil rather than a positive theological exegesis of the Old Testament. The most unwavering believer in biblical inspiration requires the techniques of criticism to interpret the Bible. At present it is customary to distinguish six main branches of biblical criticism: textual criticism, literary or source criticism, form criticism, tradition criticism, redaction criticism, and historical criticism. Though it is convenient to distinguish these as separate disciplines, in practice there is considerable overlap between the different branches.[38] To clarify the scope of each type of criticism, I will discuss each one separately and give examples of its use in discussions of the Pentateuch.

Textual criticism

Textual criticism is concerned with recovering the original text of a document. Mistakes are liable to creep into every document copied by hand, and it is the task of the textual critic to spot these errors and then to eliminate them by suggesting plausible emendations. Study of numerous manuscripts has led to the formulation of principles of textual criticism that are applicable to many different sorts of document. For the most part the scribes who copied the Pentateuch were very careful and the number of errors that crept into the Hebrew text would appear to be very small. Nevertheless, the gap of well over a thousand years between the composition of the Pentateuch and the earliest complete manuscripts of it makes some corruption inevitable. In other books of the Old Testament, notably Samuel and Jeremiah, there is more difficulty in establishing the original text.[39]

But if the original intention of the author is to be discovered, his original text is a necessary prerequisite. Thus, without textual criticism, accurate exegesis is impossible.

Source criticism

Source criticism, the attempt to discover and define the literary sources used by the biblical writers, can also be a valuable aid to biblical interpretation. This is a difficult undertaking, but an important one, for its conclusion has a great bearing on the historical value of the biblical writings.

For instance, the books of Kings cover the period from the accession of Solomon to the fall of Jerusalem—a period of about four hundred years. It is evident that Kings cannot have reached its present form until after the last event it records, namely the release of Jehoiachin from prison. If we suppose that the author of Kings was writing shortly after this event, it would be reasonable to trust his account of the imprisonment and release of Jehoiachin, since he was either an eye-witness or could have had access to eye-witness reports. But what about earlier events, forty or four hundred years earlier? How did our author know about these? How was he able to give such precise figures for the length of each king's reign? I suppose an unthinking believer in biblical inspiration might claim that the author was directly told by God what happened, and that is the source of his information. This view of biblical inspiration has to my knowledge never been advocated by scholars, for the simple reason that it is contradicted by the texts themselves. The authors of Kings and Chronicles both refer the reader who wants further details to various sources, most often 'the book of the chronicles of the kings of Judah and/or Israel', but also to various books of the prophets. These remarks clearly suggest that the authors of Kings and Chronicles were using the works they cite as the source of their information. If 'the book of the chronicles of the kings of Judah' was the royal annals of the Judaean kingdom, we may assume on the analogy of contemporary Near Eastern documents that the annals were written up shortly after the events concerned and are therefore trustworthy historical records.[40] In as far as the account of Solomon's accession in 1 Kings 1ff. is taken from a contemporary or even eye-witness source, usually referred to as the 'court history of David', we can use it as a historical source with as much confidence as the latest parts of 2 Kings.[41] In this respect, literary criticism helps to make credible the historical narratives in the Old Testament. Faith in them cannot then just be dismissed as credulity. Or to use a metaphor, the leap of faith is reduced to a step.

Careful literary criticism can also prevent historical misinterpretation. An example of great moment for the criticism of the Pentateuch is to be found in 2 Kings 22 and 23, the account of Josiah's reign and various reforms he enacted. A parallel account is to be found in 2 Chronicles 34 and 35. This account at many points coincides with that of Kings but it places some of the events in a different order. As Kings was written before Chronicles, however, its chronology has generally been preferred. Kings relates (in 2 Ki. 22:3—23:3) how a law book was found in the temple in the eighteenth year of Josiah. It then lists (23:4-20) a number of cultic reforms which took place at an unspecified time. Then (23:21-23) it refers to a passover celebrated in the eighteenth year of King Josiah. It has therefore been concluded that all the reforms mentioned in 2 Kings 23 took place in the eighteenth year of Josiah's reign.[42] Since they are mentioned after the finding of the law book, it has been assumed that the reforms were prompted by the law book. Historians then go on to try to identify the law book by matching the reforms listed in 2 Kings 23 with parts of the Pentateuch. The most interesting of Josiah's measures was the limitation of all worship to Jerusalem, the so-called 'centralization of worship'. It is widely held that Deuteronomy limits all worship to a single shrine,[43] and therefore it has become customary to argue that Deuteronomy was the book found in the temple. Since centralization was a novelty in the seventh century BC, it seems likely that Deuteronomy was written to secure a reformation along the lines of Josiah's. Stated very baldly, this is the basic argument for dating Deuteronomy in the seventh century.

Had biblical scholars paid more attention to the literary criticism of this passage, however, they would not have arrived so hastily at this conclusion. This is not the place to unpick the argument in detail, but simply to draw attention to one major flaw. The style of 2 Kings 22 and 23 is not at all homogeneous. For a long time it has been recognized that 2 Kings 22:1, 2 and 23: (24-27?) 28ff. are comments typical of the editor of Kings. But, more important, the section 2 Kings 22:3—23:23 is not homogeneous. At least two different sources can be discerned; the first an expansive account of the discovery of the law book in the eighteenth year of Josiah designed to demonstrate the king's piety (2 Ki. 22:3—23:3, 21-23), and the second a list of undated reforms in 2 Kings 23:4-20. If we have two different sources, it is at best an open question whether they are referring to exactly the same series of events, even if they are juxtaposed as in 2 Kings 22 and 23.[44] Indeed, further considerations suggest that they are not referring to the same series of events. Intrinsically, it is more probable that some cultic reforms preceded the discovery of the law book in the temple. The law-book account tells us that the book was discovered while the temple was being repaired (2 Ki. 22:5), *i.e.*, the reformation had already begun. This is corroborated by 2 Chronicles 34:3 ff. which places a number of the reforms, including centralization of worship, before the discovery of the law book (verses 8 ff.). Thus, literary criticism is an essential tool for anyone seeking a historical understanding of the Bible.

Having insisted on the propriety and utility of literary criticism of the Old Testament, it is necessary to re-emphasize its difficulty. Were it not for confirmation provided by Chronicles, I would be sceptical about the validity of the above analysis. It could be correct, but I would not be sure. Unless we know that a modern book is by a number of authors, we find it extremely difficult to detect changes of authorship. Yet we think, speak and write English every day. How much more difficult is it when the documents we are studying are nearly 3,000 years old, and their culture is always foreign to us! C.S. Lewis has stated this trenchantly in his essay 'Modern Theology and Biblical Criticism'. Reviewers often tried to guess how his own or his friends' books were written, but their guesses were always wrong. If critics are so prone to err about the literary composition of works within their own culture, how much less likely is it that they will hit on the truth when they are dealing with those that are remote?

The reconstruction of the history of a text, when the text is ancient, sounds very convincing. But one is after all sailing by dead reckoning; the results cannot be checked by fact. In order to decide how reliable the method is, what more could you ask for than to be shown an instance where the same method is at work and we have facts to check it by? Well, that is what I have done. And we find, that when this check is available, the results are either always, or else nearly always, wrong. The 'assured results of modern scholarship', as to the way in which an old book was written, are 'assured', we conclude, only because the men who knew the facts are dead and can't blow the gaff. The huge essays in my own field which reconstruct the history of *Piers Plowman* or *The Faerie Queene* are most unlikely to be anything but sheer illusions.[45]

Lewis's words are a timely reminder of the subjectivism of much literary criticism. Yet literary criticism is essential if faith is to be based on thought rather than ignorance. How can criticism be improved to counter these strictures? First, by not claiming that critical hypotheses are anything more than possibilities. A little study of the history of critical ideas will show how transitory most of them are.[46] Criticism is subject to fashion. Often what one generation believes to be the unquestioned truth is rejected by the next as absurd. Secondly, by much more attention to comparative method, literary criticism can be made more objective. Literary criticism can reach a fair degree of probability only where we have both part of the source as well as the later document incorporating the source.

In the Old Testament we are fortunate in having a number of parallel documents which may be compared with each other to see which used which. The best known are the two versions of the Ten Commandments and the parallel histories of Judah found in Kings and Chronicles. It has been widely held that Chronicles is little more than an imaginative rehash of Kings by a later priestly Judaean intent on boosting the prestige of Jerusalem and its cult.[47] But Chronicles differs from Kings at too many points to make even the hypothesis that it used the present text of Kings a certainty.[48] It is clear that the chronicler had other sources besides Kings, and it is possible that he may have used some of those used by the author of Kings.[49]

Where we do not have parallel compositions the art of literary criticism becomes even less certain, and it becomes essential that the criteria for literary analysis should be of wide applicability; not just *ad hoc* formulations to explain awkward points in the text, or *a priori* views of what the original text contained. Thus, some help can be derived from other Near Eastern legal collections in distinguishing Israelite laws in Exodus 21-23. Where a law in Exodus coincides or at least overlaps with an earlier Mesopotamian law in its form and content, it seems probable that the Exodus law comes from a cuneiform source. If enough laws can be found that fall into this category, it should be possible to reconstruct the source.[50]

In the case of extended narrative in the Pentateuch, it has become customary to distinguish four main sources (J, E, D and P). Differences in style, vocabulary and outlook are claimed to distinguish them. And it is certainly right and proper to attempt to determine what sources were used in the composition of the Pentateuch. But the accepted source-critical theories of the Pentateuch first gained currency in the nineteenth century when very little was known about the conventions of prose style apart from the Bible; and although the criteria for separating the sources may have seemed reasonable to a scholar familiar with the convention of German or English prose style, it by no means followed that these conventions were the norm in Old Testament times. Less charitably, W. Kaufmann in his *Critique of Religion and Philosophy* argues that the methods of pentateuchal-source criticism could not even be applied to the works of Goethe or Shakespeare without arriving at absurd conclusions.[51]

With modern knowledge of Near Eastern stylistic conventions, it becomes increasingly difficult to accept the validity of traditional source-critical criteria. Several scholars have argued that a new approach to pentateuchal criticism is now imperative,[52] but regrettably no full-scale (let alone definitive) work has yet appeared. Until such a work is produced, the whole edifice of pentateuchal criticism is open to question; for, as we shall see, literary criticism is fundamental to the other branches that have yet to be discussed.

Form criticism

Form criticism is concerned with the study of form in the Bible. Different writings have different forms. An essay differs in form from a poem. The form of a law differs from that of a psalm. Often the form of a piece of literature can tell us a good deal about the nature of the piece and its background, or, as it is technically termed, its life-setting (*Sitz im Leben*). The basic method of form criticism is to compare like with like, to determine the characteristic features of a type of literature, and then to suggest reasons for these features.

Form criticism has been most profitably used in the study of the psalms.[53] They fall into different categories, such as hymns, thanksgivings, laments, royal psalms, pilgrimage songs, *etc*. As a result of form criticism, it is now recognized that most of the psalms were used in the worship in the temple in Jerusalem before it was destroyed in 587 BC. Before the advent of form criticism it had often been supposed that the psalms were personal poems, the work of pious Jews in the exilic and post-exilic period.

Form criticism has also been used in the study of the Pentateuch. If fixed forms can be discovered, they obviously help the work of literary criticism in defining literary units within the books. Recently most attention has been focused on the covenant form of passages in Exodus and Deuteronomy.[54] Sometimes form-critical studies are marred by the doctrinaire assumption that early forms must be short and later forms longer,[55] but, in general, form criticism has been of great benefit to biblical interpretation.

Tradition criticism
Tradition criticism is primarily concerned with the history of traditions before they are recorded in writing and incorporated into literary sources. The stories of the patriarchs, for instance, were probably handed on by word of mouth either in the tribe or in a sanctuary, until such time as they were written down to form a continuous narrative. The alternative would be to suppose that the stories in Genesis are based directly on the diaries of Abraham and others, but there is no evidence of this. Assuming that the patriarchal traditions were transmitted orally for a considerable period, it is likely that at least the presentation of the stories changed in the retelling. It is obviously of great interest to the historian to know what these changes were and how the later tradition, now enshrined in a literary source, differed from the earliest oral one; for the earliest is the one likely to give the most reliable view of events, other things being equal. It is the task of tradition criticism to trace this history.

Tradition criticism is therefore important, but its results are inevitably even less secure than those of literary criticism. This is for two reasons. First, tradition criticism begins where literary criticism leaves off. The conclusions arrived at by literary criticism about the scope and content of various literary sources form the starting-point for tradition-critical investigations. But as we have seen, the conclusions of literary criticism are uncertain, and therefore the conclusions of tradition criticism must be doubly uncertain. Secondly, it is very difficult to check the hypotheses about the development of ancient oral tradition. We do not have tape recordings of how contemporary Assyrian traditions changed and developed in speech. We have only the end product—literary documents. If it is claimed that ancient Hebrew traditions developed in the same way as Arab or even western traditions, this introduces another unverifiable assumption. It therefore seems to me that the results of traditio-historical investigation must be viewed with great scepticism. They could sometimes be right, but we have no means of knowing.

Redaction criticism
Like tradition criticism, redaction criticism is at present enjoying a great vogue in Old Testament study. But it is less open to the charge of subjective speculation, because it is more firmly tied to the text. The task of redaction criticism is to determine how the editor (redactor) utilized his sources, what he omitted and what he added and what his particular bias was. Absolute certainty can be achieved in redaction criticism only when the critic has all the sources which were at the disposal of the editor. At best, in the Old Testament, the critic has only part of the sources (*e.g.*, the book of Kings used by the Chronicler), and elsewhere the sources must be reconstructed out of the edited work itself. Then redaction criticism becomes much less certain as a literary exercise, but its methods do help to bring out the special interests and tendencies of the editor and so lead into a full appreciation of the theology of the work in question. Thus it is very difficult to reconstruct the sources used in the books of Deuteronomy or Joshua, but with the aid of redactional critical methods it is possible to see what the editors of these books were trying to say.[56]

Historical criticism

Historical criticism is a very broad term which can cover a variety of disciplines. Here its sense will be restricted to three. First, the techniques of dating documents and traditions. How do we know when a historical source was written? Secondly, the verification of information about past events contained in such sources. When a document says something happened, how do we know it is telling the truth? Thirdly, historical criticism is concerned with the writing of history, the reconstruction of events and their explanation. It is concerned with describing the exact course of the conquest: which cities were captured, and when and how and by whom and why. It is with historical criticism that we arrive at the heart of our discussion. Granted that the exodus was vital to the faith of Israel, how do we know it happened as described in the Bible, or (more radical still) how do we know that it happened at all? In a very real sense all the other types of criticism I have mentioned are subsidiary tools in the all-embracing discipline of historical criticism. In order to keep the discussion within manageable limits, I will concentrate on the first two aspects of historical criticism, namely dating a source and verifying its assertions; though inevitably these cannot be dealt with in complete disregard of the third aspect.

How is a historical document dated? There are two problems here: the date of composition and the date of writing. Unless we are dealing with an autograph, the date of composition always precedes the date of writing. The latter is relatively easy to determine with modern methods in palaeography and archaeology.[57] The earliest extant pentateuchal manuscript (4QEx^f), however—part of the book of Exodus found near the Dead Sea—dates from about 250 BC. All agree that the book of Exodus must have been composed some time before this, and that this text from Qumran is not the autograph but a late copy. To discover the date of composition of the book of Exodus is a much more involved process. If its author's name were stated in the text this would be an important fact to be considered, but the question would still arise whether the statement were true. A statement about authorship could be designed to deceive the reader. A forgery could claim to be written by Moses in the same terms as an authentic Mosaic document. In fact, only part of

Exodus appears to claim to be directly written by Moses, though if the narrative is accepted as substantially authentic it could well be that he had an important role in the composition of other parts. A second indication of the date of a book is the events it records. Obviously its composition must be later than the last event mentioned. In the case of Exodus, the last event is the erection of the tabernacle. But obviously this provides only a *terminus a quo*, not *ante quem*. A book written in 1976 about early mediaeval England might conclude with the Norman conquest, but no-one would be deceived by its subject matter into thinking that the book was written in 1067.

If one distrusts the information about the author found on the title page or (in the case of a biblical book) within the text itself, one must rely on indirect indications of authorship; namely the language, style and assumptions of the author. Unfortunately we have very few inscriptions in biblical Hebrew, so it is very difficult to write a history of the Hebrew language and then to date the books of the Bible by reference to it. Besides, it is quite likely that the language was modernized in the process of copying; we know that the spelling was,[58] so language and style are by themselves an inadequate guide to the date of composition. It can, at best, tell us when the text was finally revised. It is, therefore, necessary to uncover the assumptions of the author if we are to have a reliable basis for dating the books of the Bible and the sources used in them.

Thus, in practice, Old Testament historical criticism tends to rely largely on the historical and theological presuppositions of the different writings to determine their date of composition. This is especially true in pentateuchal criticism, but more weight is attached to the explicit statements about date and authorship within the text where other Old Testament books are concerned. The reason for this will become apparent shortly. Reliance on the historical and theological assumptions of the writers is not free from difficulty. The problem in both cases is similar to that in arguing from language and style to the date of composition. How is it possible to date documents with reference to a history, if the only source of knowledge about that history is those documents? Unless special care is exercised, the critical historian will find himself arguing in circles.

An example may perhaps clarify the issue. Several parts of the

Old Testament contain the idea of holy war: that is, that the conquest of Canaan was ordained by God, and that God was with Israel in her wars, at once frightening the enemy and giving victory to Israel. Whatever we as Christians make of this idea, the notion is clearly present in the Old Testament. The theological problem is not here our concern, but rather the use to which the notion is put in historical criticism. Since the doctrine of holy war is very prominent in Deuteronomy, it seems likely that the book was written in a period when holy war was regarded as an important doctrine. The argument usually runs as follows: holy war was important in the days of the judges (see Judges and 1 Samuel). It was forgotten in the days of the kings, who had professional armies and, therefore, little use for the doctrine of holy war. In the latter days of the Judaean monarchy, however, when Judah was hard pressed financially and militarily and therefore could not afford to support a standing army, the doctrine of holy war was revived in order to promote enthusiasm for war among the tribal levies. Isaiah and Chronicles make use of holy-war ideology, so these books may be claimed as evidence that these ideas were revived in the late monarchy period. Deuteronomy could be regarded as a document designed to promote holy war, and so it should be connected with the holy-war revival of the seventh century BC.[59]

The fragility of this sort of argument is open for all to see. There is no clear evidence that the holy-war ideology ever really died out, let alone was revived in the seventh century. But, more germane, why associate Deuteronomy with holy-war concepts of the late monarchy period and not with those of the judges' period? And why is it necessary to believe that Deuteronomy was written in either of these periods? Could it not have been written earlier than the judges' period (there is evidence in Exodus of holy-war ideology antedating the conquest), or later in the post-exilic period (see Chronicles and the Dead Sea Scrolls)? At best, then, arguments from the history of theology are indecisive.[60] We just know too little about streams of thought in ancient Israel to say dogmatically that the Israelites could not have believed this or that in any given period.

With historical assumptions we are on somewhat surer ground. If a book about the early Middle Ages compared the Holy Roman Em-

pire with the Common Market, we should feel fairly safe in concluding that the book must have been written after 1958. Similarly, the
refrain in the book of Judges, 'In those days there was no king in
Israel; every man did what was right in his own eyes',[61] suggests that
the author of Judges was writing in a time that knew the benefits of
ordered government under the monarchy. Another passing reference which discloses when a passage was composed is Genesis 36:31,
'These are the kings who reigned in the land of Edom, before
any king reigned over the Israelites,' suggesting that at least this section was written after the accession of King Saul. In both these cases
the historical facts are so well known that there can be little quarrel
with the conclusion drawn. But in other cases we are not so well
placed. If our knowledge of more obscure details of Israel's history
is found only in one book, the book itself obviously cannot be dated
by reference to this detail without the argument becoming circular.
Very strict critical tests have been applied to the Pentateuch and
have led to the conclusion that much of it was written long after the
events it relates. It is arguable that if such rigorous demands had
been made on other biblical writings, they too would have been pronounced of little historical value. But in this case we would have to
admit to complete agnosticism about the whole course of Israelite
history. To avoid this very negative result, it has been generally
accepted that in the prophets and poetry we are close to firsthand
material and that the historical witness of these documents can be relied on. Subsequent discoveries of Mesopotamian historical texts
have led to much more trust being placed in all the biblical books
dealing with the period after 1000 BC, *i.e.* from the reign of David.
The earliest period, especially the exodus and conquest, however, is
evaluated very differently by different scholars. To understand why
there is no consensus among historians about this period, current
theories of pentateuchal criticism must be briefly sketched.

Current theories of pentateuchal criticism
Pentateuchal criticism is highly complex and has been the subject of
immensely detailed study for more than a century. It is impossible
here to go into the intricacies of the arguments, but it is necessary to
say something about the basic principles so that the theological issues

involved may become clearer. In order to set these in sharp perspective, gross oversimplification is unavoidable. Only one line of argument among very many will be followed, but those who are familiar with the topic will realize that similar considerations apply to other areas of the subject.[62]

Although there is considerable divergence in scholarly evaluations of the exodus and conquest, there is a broad consensus of opinion about the literary sources and how they should be dated. As has already been indicated, there are those who disagree with the standard literary analysis of the Pentateuch into four sources. There are others who disagree with the dating of these sources. But it is not my purpose to go into these by-ways here, only to expound the typical scholarly view, which in its essentials has changed very little since the beginning of the century.

This is that the Pentateuch consists of four main sources which have been distinguished by the methods of literary criticism. The first source is known as J or the Yahwist because it uses the name Yahweh (the LORD, AV and RSV) for God. It is a narrative source covering the history of mankind from the creation of man to the conquest of Canaan. The second source is the Elohist, after its designation of God, 'Elohim'. This is again a narrative source, beginning with the call of Abraham and closing with the conquest of Canaan. The third source is the Deuteronomist, which is named after the book which contains the bulk of it, Deuteronomy. It is characterized by a prolix rhetorical style, as might be in place in sermons. Elements of D have been found in Genesis to Numbers, but it is found mainly in Deuteronomy and Joshua. The fourth source is P, the priestly source, so called because it contains material that priests might be interested in—genealogies, cultic regulations, and the like. It is said to use a dry and dull style. It also contains a certain amount of narrative, and it again covers the history from creation to the conquest.

These sources are found all jumbled up in many parts of the Pentateuch, especially in Genesis and Exodus, but elsewhere there are long stretches each belonging to one source. It is believed that these sources were composed at different times and were gradually amalgamated by a series of editors (redactors).

The sources are distinguished by means of literary criticism; they are dated by means of historical criticism. Though all four sources contain numerous references to Mosaic authorship and some parts claim to have been written down by him or at his dictation, little credence is afforded these statements by modern scholars. This is because these sources are believed to conflict with the historical situation in the Mosaic era, but to agree with that of later periods. Hence it is argued that they were written not by Moses but by unknown later authors.

Probably the most important of the areas in which there is apparent conflict between the explicit assertions of the sources and their implicit assumptions is that of worship. From Judges, Samuel and Kings we can obtain an outline picture of the development of worship over some six centuries. One of the most interesting changes concerned the place of worship. In the early period, the centre of national worship was the ark and later the temple at Jerusalem in the southern kingdom, and the bull-calves at Bethel and Dan in the northern kingdom. Throughout this period, however, everyday sacrifices were permitted at local altars. After the destruction of the northern kingdom, Hezekiah (c. 700) and Josiah (c. 630) attempted to limit all worship to Jerusalem. They destroyed all the altars outside Jerusalem and insisted that all worship must take place in the temple. This step may have been taken owing to the difficulty of stopping Canaanite rituals at local sanctuaries. It was certainly a drastic move—it was as though all the parish churches in the land were removed and people were allowed to worship only in one big cathedral—and it naturally met with opposition in Hezekiah's time. Josiah tried to reintroduce it, but he too was not completely successful and local altars were re-established after his death. The exile in Babylon followed soon after, and this had such a traumatic effect on Jewish thinking that when the exiles returned they built an altar and temple only in Jerusalem. Though there are some queries about details, the main outline given above is clear and agreed by all.

Now it has to be explained how the different sources correlate with this history of worship. In J and E the patriarchs Abraham, Isaac and Jacob are said to worship at various different sites in Canaan, building altars, making vows and offering sacrifice. A legal text associated with JE (Ex. 20:24) seems to presuppose that there are a number of places at which God will reveal himself and where altars may be built. It is, therefore, argued that the sources J and E were written in a period before all worship was centralized in Jerusalem. But Deuteronomy repeatedly insists that all Israel must worship at 'the place which the Lord will choose'. To this unnamed place all tithes are to be brought and all Israelite men are to come three times a year for the national feasts of passover, weeks and booths (Dt. 16).Deuteronomy also insists that all the Canaanite shrines and their paraphernalia are to be destroyed. It is, therefore, agreed that Deuteronomy was written as part of a campaign to centralize or limit all worship to Jerusalem. Finally, the priestly document P talks about only one sanctuary, the tabernacle. Without laying very much emphasis on it, P just assumes that all sacrifice and cultic activities will take place in or near the tabernacle. This suggests that P was written in a period when centralized worship was already an accepted fact. This occurred only in the post-exilic age.

Worship tends to be conservative and changes come only gradually, so the different attitudes to the central sanctuary cannot precisely date the various sources. Other considerations have led to a common acceptance of the following dates for the sources: J, about 950 BC; E, about 850 BC; D, about 622 BC (Josiah's reformation) and P, about 500 BC. The different sources were successively combined by a series of redactors. In the eighth century J and E were combined to form JE; in the sixth century JE and D were combined to form JED, and in the fifth century our present Pentateuch was created out of JED and P.[63]

What bearing does this dating of the sources have on their value as historical records? By the normal standards of historical criticism it should have a very profound effect. The further a writer is from the events he is describing, the less his witness is usually to be trusted. On these grounds, the material found in P should be less reliable than that in D, which in turn would be less reliable than that in J and E. If, therefore, we want to write a historical account of the exodus and conquest, we can rely only on the earliest source J. This means that we must reject D's account of the invasion of Canaan as a fierce military conquest in favour of J's picture of a quiet and gradual infiltration.[64] But how reliable is J for this purpose? The exodus and conquest are generally reckoned to have taken place in the thirteenth century BC, some three hundred years before J was written. If we suppose that the stories were handed down orally for these three hundred years, almost anything might have happened to them in the process. Ancient historians of Greece and Rome are generally prepared to trust oral traditions up to a hundred years old, that is about two generations, but beyond that they would be very sceptical. The traditions of the exodus span a period at least three times as long, however, so that the only rational conclusion would be deep agnosticism about the earliest period of Israel's history.

Early twentieth-century historians of Israel were strangely inconsistent in this respect; although their dating of the pentateuchal sources should have led them to thorough scepticism, in practice they tended to accept the earliest sources' view of the history. Roman Catholics who accepted the critical dating of the sources, tended on the basis of their belief in divine inspiration of Scripture to accept the statements of each source as equally true. Though evangelicals may feel inclined to adopt the latter solution, it would, I believe, be misguided. Biblical faith is not a faith that goes against the facts, but a faith that goes beyond them to see the hand of God at work in them. Similarly, faith in Scripture is not a faith in the divine truth of Scripture even though Scripture were untrue on the human level, but a faith that goes beyond the human truth of Scripture to recognize its divine inspiration. It is, therefore, no good ignoring the results of criticism; they should be either accepted or challenged.

Faced with the problem of the time gap between the biblical sources and the events they purport to relate, different scholars have come to different conclusions. Noth developed the art of tradition criticism in which he tried to show how historical traditions change and develop over a long period of time. Though his investigations have done little to disperse the fog of historical scepticism hanging over the traditions of the exodus and conquest, they are the only thorough attempt to deal with the problem. His work must therefore be briefly outlined in the same oversimplified way in which we have discussed classical pentateuchal criticism.[65]

His first step was to find a yet earlier source underlying J and E.[66] These two sources have a good deal in common. For instance their narratives overlap at a number of points. Where this occurs, Noth believes we have evidence of an earlier source being used, which he called G (from *Grundlage*, basis). There are five main themes in G— the promise to the patriarchs, the exodus from Egypt, the revelation at Sinai, the wilderness wanderings and the conquest of the promised land. Since G is used by J and E it must be earlier than either, and therefore Noth dates it to the period of the judges (*i.e.* the twelfth to the eleventh century BC).[67] This is almost within striking distance of the exodus and conquest. Noth believes, however, that in two centuries separating the event from the earliest source, such great changes have occurred in the tradition that its present form bears little resemblance to its earliest form.

Though the five themes are connected in the G source, Noth believes this connection to be secondary.[68] Originally they were independent themes. Just as the idea that the settlement was a rapid military conquest was imposed on the earlier sources J and E by the Deuteronomist, so the author of G has introduced ideas into themes which originally did not belong there at all. For instance, the figure of Moses who appears in most of the themes is secondary.[69] The original stories contained no mention of him, but his name was used to link the stories together. According to Noth, the real historical Moses was not the leader of the Israelite tribes, but a transjordanian sheikh whose grave some of the invading tribes came across on their way into the promised land. His name then became mixed up with a story of a conquest and somehow he became regarded as the leader of it.[70] By a similar process of confusion, Moses' name was attached to three of the other four themes. Similarly, the themes originally concerned different tribes, and it represents a later adaptation of the tradition that they now all appear to refer to the same group of people. In its primitive form, the exodus theme spoke of a group of slaves who had escaped from Egypt. As the story was retold, this group of slaves was identified with another tribal group who had been to Sinai. In this way 'all Israel' was made to participate in the whole set of events related in the five themes. The apparent chronological sequence of the end product is illusory. The historical reality was that different groups had entirely independent traditions about their history which were later amalgamated to create a joint history applying to them all.[71]

Noth, however, is not prepared to ascribe much historical worth to the primitive traditions that were later modified to make them into stories about all Israel. As he sees it, many of the stories have grown out of a desire to explain religious customs or landmarks; that is, they are aetiologies. For example, the story of the capture of Ai arose in answer to the question: Why is this mound called Ai, which means 'a ruin'? The story of the hanging of the five kings (Jos. 10:16-27) grew up as an explanation of why there are five trees near Makkedah.[72] Age-old customs in worship also required explanation. The special importance of the sanctuary at Bethel was justified by creating the tradition of Jacob's journey from Shechem to Bethel (Gn. 35).[73] In the stories Noth regards as aetiological, there is often a reference to the fact that something mentioned in the story is still visible 'today'. This, he believes, shows that the story was first told to explain the existence of the object to which it refers.

The net result of Noth's traditio-historical study is that he regards most of the traditions about the early history of Israel as popular legend rather than sober history. In view of the lack of hard information about the pre-settlement period, it is not surprising that Noth declined to discuss it in his *The History of Israel*.[74] For him the patriarchs and the exodus are not subjects that the historian can deal with. Like earlier scholars, he believes that Israel came to occupy the land of Canaan gradually and not by a concerted military campaign. Indeed, Israel really came into existence as a distinct political group only after the different tribes, who were not related by blood, had all settled in Palestine. There they came together to form a religious federation of tribes bound together by covenant and pledged to defend the league in holy war. This tribal league called itself Israel. In the subsequent period of rapprochement and cultural integration there was also a merging of the 'historical' traditions, which were eventually incorporated in the source 'G'. Thus Noth's reconstruction of the history of Israel's traditions mirrors his view of the way the nation Israel came into being.

If Noth is correct in his view of the early history of Israel, there is a yawning gulf between it and the Old Testament's own representation of the facts; and it is the contradiction between the two that gave rise to von Rad's attempt to reconcile them by means of existentialist interpretation. This was rejected on the ground that it makes no sense to affirm belief in a God who saves his people when as historians we know that this people was quite wrong in thinking that God ever did save them from Egypt or give them the land, let alone promise these things to their ancestors. Such a faith cannot be said to be based on truth but on error.[75]

As has already been mentioned, Bright is one of a number of scholars who believe that theology must grow out of history. Not surprisingly, therefore, he has sharply attacked Noth's views, maintaining that they are theologically unsatisfactory and historically unwarranted. In his monograph *Early Israel in Recent History Writing*, Bright states: 'Noth's method leads him to a mistrust of the early traditions of Israel which is little short of nihilism.'[76] It is Noth's tradition criticism that Bright finds unacceptable. Bright accepts the classical source-critical analysis and dating of J, E, D and P. He also approves of Noth's discovery of G—the common base of J and E—and tries to turn it against him.[77]

In countering Noth's arguments Bright makes four main points. First, he points out that four of the five themes that make up G are already combined in the earliest Old Testament creeds found in Deuteronomy 26:5-11 and Joshua 24. This casts doubt on Noth's contention that the themes were all once independent.[78] Secondly, Bright challenges Noth's assumption that the need for an aetiology can create a story.[79] There were many trees and desolate tells in Palestine, so why should anyone feel it necessary to explain the presence of a few of them? Bright insists that it is necessary to examine other examples of oral traditions containing aetiological features to see how far aetiology gave rise to them. We can do this only with relatively modern stories, where we can check the popular story against known history. He therefore refers to Arab and American aetiological tales, and finds no case of aetiology creating a story. Rather, historical tales attract to themselves aetiological elements. In so far as history does explain the existence of familiar local objects, it is natural for a good story-teller to point this out. It creates a link between the event and the hearer. '*Where historical tradition is concerned*, not only can it be proved that the aetiological factor is often secondary in the formation of these traditions, *it cannot be proved that it was ever primary.*'[80]

Thirdly, Bright argues that Noth quite fails to explain why the tribes ever came together to form a nation, especially as on his theory there were no pre-existing ties of blood or faith. If there was no common faith in Yahweh and no shared historical experience, it is hard to see any reason why they should ever have come together in a religious covenant.[81]

Finally, Bright maintains that archaeological evidence tends to confirm the authenticity of the biblical narrative. Though the bones of Moses have not been discovered or Abraham's deeds been chronicled in extrabiblical sources, archaeology does make the biblical narratives credible. The patriarchal narratives accurately reflect the customs of upper Mesopotamia in the early second millennium BC, the period in which the conquest probably took place. So although the personal details of the biblical narratives cannot be substantiated by archaeology, their general character can be.[82] Bright admits that these arguments do not 'prove' the historical truth of the biblical narratives, if by 'proof' one means an incontrovertible demonstration. This is not the sort of evidence the historian ever possesses; he always works on the basis of probability. 'The trouble is that one cannot by direct argument prove Noth wrong. That is why arguments such as the above have been resorted to. But neither can Noth prove himself right. We move in a realm where we can no longer lay hold of objective evidence; we can only contradict one another. But the burden of proof is definitely on Noth.'[83]

Other scholars have backed up Bright's arguments at various points. Bright appealed to Israel's earliest creeds to demonstrate his view that the five main pentateuchal themes originally belonged together. P.C. Craigie, in an article entitled 'The Conquest and Early Hebrew Poetry'[84] examined the earliest Hebrew poetry for its statements bearing on the exodus and conquest. The 'Song of the Sea' (Ex. 15), the 'Balaam Oracles' (Nu. 23, 24), the 'Blessing of Moses' (Dt. 33) and the 'Song of Deborah' (Jdg. 5) are generally regarded as some of the most ancient parts of the Old Testament, composed soon after the events they relate, as is shown not only by their content but by the number of archaic spellings and forms they contain.

These poems say a good deal about the events of the exodus and conquest, and they may be usefully compared with the prose narratives in the Pentateuch and with critical histories of Israel. For instance, Exodus 15 relates the destruction of the Egyptian army in the Red Sea as they were pursuing Israel. It goes on to tell how divine terror has fallen on the inhabitants of Canaan at the prospect of the Israelite invasion. It lists in order the nations who will have to fight Israel—Philistia, Edom, Moab, Canaan. Similarly, the 'Balaam Oracles' state that God has brought Israel out of Egypt and portrays the people as a mighty horde threatening to overwhelm Moab. The 'Blessing of Moses' mentions Israel and its constituent tribes, Moses, Sinai and various events in the wilderness. The whole poem breathes an atmosphere of war and looks forward to a time when Israel as a whole will enjoy prosperity in the promised land. Not surprisingly, Craigie concludes: 'The historical information which these sources (poems) contain was noted to be compatible with the prose account of the conquest, taken at face value. The implications of the study call into question some recent reconstructions of Israel's origins in the writing of modern historians.'[85]

Bright's contention that aetiology is not important in the creation of tradition has also been endorsed by others. B.S. Childs [86] showed that the formula 'to this day', which Noth thought was a sure sign of an aetiology,[87] has, in most cases, been introduced as an editorial comment. For example, the story of Achan (Jos. 7) was not made up to explain the heap of stones or the name of the valley of Achor. But the editor of the book of Joshua may have added the phrase 'to this day' (verse 26) as his personal testimony to the truth of the story he has related in the preceding verses.

As for Bright's belief that the people of Israel existed before the conquest of Canaan, this also has been supported by other scholars. De Vaux argued that the Hebrew word for people (^{c}am) implies blood relationship. A mere covenant bond between tribes would not have constituted an ^{c}am.[88] Extrabiblical evidence, in the shape of the Merneptah stele (c. 1220 BC), also supports the view that Israel was a nation which was present in Canaan before the judges' period. The stele mentions a campaign in Canaan and states that 'Israel' (written with a determinative for people) 'is laid waste'.[89]

But it is in the area of archaeology that most discussion has taken place since Bright wrote his monograph. Since the relationship of archaeological discovery to the Bible is of wide interest and also shows up very clearly the essential character of historical study, it will be discussed more fully. On the one hand, because archaeology in many instances apparently offers proof of the biblical account, many scholars have been seduced by the chance of an easy archaeological solution and try to by-pass the essential work of literary and historical criticism of the texts which is vital to good history-writing.[90] On the other hand, archaeological discovery sometimes presents the biblical scholar with harder problems than those posed by literary and historical criticism. Because of the subjective nature of literary criticism, awkward results are more easily dismissed as pseudo-problems, the product of the brains of perverse critics. But the empirical archaeological fact that there was no city at Et-Tell (usually identified with biblical Ai), when Joshua is said to have captured it, is more difficult to cope with. But it is just this that makes archaeology important. Here the truth of the Bible as a historical document is most easily subject to test. In the period we are considering we would not expect to find archaeological remains of the crossing of the Red Sea or the wilderness wanderings. For one thing the sites where these events occurred are most difficult to pinpoint; and for another, if the biblical account is correct, the Israelites never settled down in the wilderness. But if the conquest of Canaan was anything like the description in the book of Joshua, it ought to have made a considerable impact on the archaeological record of the land. The coming of the Israelites should be marked by the ashes of burnt-out cities and by a different type of culture in the new Israelite settlements that succeeded the previous Canaanite levels.

3. ARCHAEOLOGY AND THE CONQUEST OF CANAAN

The differences between Noth on the one hand and Bright and other disciples of Albright on the other come to a head in their evaluation of archaeology. Both sides agree that contemporary epigraphic archaeological evidence (*i.e.* inscriptions and similar documents) must have pride of place in historical reconstruction. Unfortunately there is very little evidence of this sort bearing on the exodus and conquest. Both agree that the biblical texts can be evaluated as historical documents only after literary analysis. They disagree, however, about the processes that lie behind the formation of these documents. As we have seen, Noth believes that the cult and aetiology were responsible to a large extent for the creation of features in the tradition, while the Albright school is prepared to give the tradition the benefit of the doubt unless there is evidence to the contrary. The merits of these different positions have already been discussed, and we have seen that none of the evidence adduced by either side was conclusive. We are therefore left with ordinary archaeological evidence as a basis for adjudicating between the two positions. Can the remains of walls, broken pottery and such objects tell us enough about their owners for us to find out whether there was a concerted conquest of Canaan or merely a peaceful invasion?

It is widely agreed that the Israelite conquest, if that is what it was, took place in the second half of the thirteenth century BC (*i.e.* at the end of the Late Bronze Age).[91] Both sides agree that a number of new villages were established in the inland hill country. Albright claimed that these new Iron Age settlements were Israelite and that it is also reasonable to ascribe the destruction of the various towns to Israelite assault.[92] But Noth argued that this involves reading too much into the archaeological evidence; that there are other reasons for the destruction of cities in this era; and, finally, that a critical study of the biblical material suggests that the Israelites entered the land gradually and peacefully.[93] We have already examined the last arguments. We must now look at the strictly archaeological debate.

Noth's position has recently been restated in considerable detail by M. Weippert in *The Settlement of the Israelite Tribes in Palestine*. He first points out that some of the archaeological evidence does not square with the biblical account of the conquest, especially with regard to the cities of Jericho and Ai, whose capture is described in most detail in Joshua 1-11. At Jericho there is no evidence of occupation between 2200 and 1200 BC, *i.e.* from the end of the Early Bronze Age to the beginning of the Iron Age. It seems likely, therefore, that the stories of the capture of these towns have an aetiological origin; that is, they were made up to explain to later generations why these impressive sites were in ruins.[94] Weippert admits that there are certain features of these stories that are hard to explain as aetiological; for instance, the Israelite defeat at Ai at the first attempt and the subsequent strategy.[95] Though field archaeologists have put forward other explanations of the absence of appropriate archaeological deposits at Jericho, Weippert finds these unconvincing.[96]

This brings him to the fundamental criticism of the Albright school and its use of archaeological data. 'Archaeological finds are essentially silent evidence.'[97] He recognizes that there is an obvious parallelism between the destruction of various cities in the thirteenth century and the biblical account of the conquest, but he insists that the historian must ask for clear-cut evidence that the Israelites were responsible. 'Such proof would be simple if the conquerors had left their victory steles behind on the ruins of the Late Bronze Age Canaanite cities.'[98] But unfortunately they did not. Archaeologists are in danger of identifying a site in advance and projecting the history of the site as known from other evidence on to the archaeological evidence. Much more care is required because archaeological results are not 'facts' which speak for themselves. Archaeological evidence is meaningful to a historian only when it is interpreted, and in the interpretation subjective bias may enter in. Cities may have been burnt by the Canaanites warring among themselves.[99] Changes in pottery styles do not necessarily imply a change in population. These phenomena just witness to the social and cultural upheavals associated with the dissolution of the city-state system in the late thirteenth century.[100] Finally, he concludes: 'The only archaeological fact which can, with a great degree of probability, be connected with the settlement of the "Israelite" tribes is the colonization of the Palestinian hill country which is clearly seen in numerous small country settlements of the early Iron Age I. And that is precisely what one expects on the basis of the settlement theories of the "school" of Albrecht Alt.' (Noth is the most eminent representative of this school.) 'Obviously, here too, one cannot decide definitely in individual cases whether we are dealing with an "Israelite" village or a Canaanite one; but there is, nevertheless, a stronger probability in favour of "Israelites".'[101]

In the same year in which Weippert's book appeared in Germany,

P.W. Lapp, one of the most distinguished of American field archaeologists until his untimely death, published an article entitled 'The
Conquest of Palestine in the Light of Archaeology'.[102] In it he defends the approach of Albright against the criticisms of Noth. He
first reviews the available archaeological evidence of the main sites in
Palestine from the Late Bronze and Early Iron Ages. He then turns
to discuss the evaluation of this evidence for historical purposes, the
methods that can be employed and the conclusions that may be
drawn. He says that Noth was right to point out the limitations of
archaeological evidence and that it does not speak for itself. Furthermore, he acknowledges that early excavators did tend to date their
archaeological discoveries by reference to the Bible and then claim
that archaeology proved the Bible. But though this method was
highly questionable in view of the scepticism about the early biblical
accounts at the time, Lapp maintains it has proved very fruitful in
the development of Palestinian archaeology.[103] There have now
been so many excavations, however, that archaeology is much less
dependent on biblical material for establishing its chronology. And
though most archaeological evidence is silent and needs interpreting, Lapp believes that interpretation is much less subjective than
previously. Careful digging with precise stratification enables a very
accurate history of each site to be written. By bringing together the
evidence from a number of sites, it is possible to arrive at a picture of
historical development over a much wider area. The cumulative evidence in Lapp's view makes the idea of a peaceful infiltration very
hard to sustain.

There are a number of large towns in Palestine that were violently
destroyed at the end of the Late Bronze Age. They include Tell Beit
Mirsim (Debir?), Lachish, Ashdod, Tell el Hesi (Eglon?) and Beth
Shemesh, which are all west of Jerusalem; and Bethel, a few miles
north of Jerusalem; Deir Allah in the Jordan valley and Hazor in
upper Galilee. The Late Bronze Age was characterized by a relatively high cultural level, well-fortified cities and fine pottery. After
their destruction at the end of the Late Bronze Age, however, many
of these sites were reoccupied by inhabitants of a much less advanced culture.[104] For instance, the first settlement of Hazor following the destruction of the Canaanite city was described by its excava-

tor as follows: it 'can best be described as the temporary dwelling of a semi-nomadic people. Its only remains consisted of rubble foundations of tents and huts, numerous silos dug into the earth for the storage of pottery and grain and crude ovens sometimes made of disused storage jars.'[105] Though in some respects there is inevitably some continuity in pottery design between one period and the next, there are several clear differences in style and in manufacturing technique between Late Bronze Age and Early Iron Age pottery.[106] This suggests that the Iron Age inhabitants of these sites used a different kiln technique from that of their predecessors. Another difference between twelfth-century Iron Age and thirteenth-century Late Bronze Age pottery is that no imported wares are found in twelfth-century strata.[107]

Careful stratification of these sites shows that the people responsible for the destruction of the Late Bronze Age cities were not the Sea Peoples (Philistines), who are known to have invaded Palestine in the mid-twelfth century.[108] Egyptian records tell how the Egyptians repelled the invasion of the Sea Peoples, who then turned their attention to Canaan. From the point of view of archaeology these Sea Peoples, among whom were the Philistines, are distinguishable from the previous conquerors of Canaan by their different pottery with distinctive painted designs. This Philistine pottery has been found at a good number of Palestinian sites in twelfth-century and thirteenth-century strata. We have in fact two distinct types of pottery from the first phase of the Iron Age. It seems reasonable therefore to postulate two waves of invaders. We know about the second group, the Sea Peoples, from Egyptian sources, and we can reasonably identify the first group with the Israelite invaders described in the Bible.[109]

This is the essence of Lapp's argument. Is the evidence compatible with Noth's theory of peaceful infiltration? Lapp argues that it is not.

> The stratigraphic picture, however, does not indicate a peaceful period; and if the pre-Philistine major destructions are not to be attributed to the Israelites, to whom are they to be attributed? The cities destroyed in the last half of the thirteenth (and perhaps the beginning of the twelfth) century, including the

vast site of Hazor, the resettled towns with new patterns of occupation, the settlement of many unoccupied sites—these can hardly be disassociated and attributed to random tribal movements. How is the destruction of the Canaanite fortress at Lachish at nearly the same time as Tell Beit Mirsim C to be explained? The Philistines had not yet arrived on the scene... A small tribe looking for *Lebensraum* would hardly have attempted to take so strong a fortress and could hardly have succeeded. The most satisfying explanation of the problem of the destruction of Lachish, Hazor, and other towns similarly destroyed is a concerted effort on the part of a sizable group of Israelites.[110]

Finally, Lapp asks why the biblical tradition of a violent military conquest should ever have been invented, if in fact it was a very peaceful business. The biblical evidence, although it comes from different sources and periods, 'is consistent in indicating a substantial conquest in rather a short period of time. To deny the Joshua tribes the destruction of a site such as Hazor, when there is such a striking coincidence of literary and archaeological evidence, would seem to involve a highly questionable methodology.'[111]

Lapp claims, then, that most of the archaeological evidence is clearly in favour of the biblical tradition. Concerning Jericho and Ai, he thinks there are special reasons why the archaeological discoveries do not immediately substantiate the book of Joshua. In the case of Jericho, he holds that the final phase of Late Bronze Age Jericho, the city that Joshua would have captured, has been completely washed away. 'A tell abandoned in the Early Iron Age must inevitably have suffered considerable erosion in three millennia. This is an especially strong possibility where the tell is almost entirely a mudbrick site located in an area that receives occasional heavy rains. In fact, most of Mid- and Late Bronze-Age Jericho was eroded away before the arrival of modern excavators.'[112] As for Ai, he refers in a footnote to Albright's suggestion that the story of Ai originally concerned the neighbouring town of Bethel, but in course of time was transferred to the ruined site of Et-Tell.[113] He also quotes Callaway's earlier view that 'nothing in the present evidence warrants an identification of the village [of Et-Tell] with the city of Ai captured by

Joshua.'[114]

These are the rival views about the implications of archaeological evidence for the biblical account of the conquest. Though the bulk of recent discovery supports the positive evaluation of Lapp, the finds are not of such a character that it is impossible to interpret them differently. The chief objection to his view is the lack of thirteenth-century Late Bronze Age strata at Jericho and Ai. Erosion would seem to be the most plausible suggestion for the lack at Jericho. But the problem of Ai remains intractable. The recent excavations have failed to resolve the problem satisfactorily for anyone who takes the biblical account literally. It may be that Ai has not yet been correctly located, but this seems a desperate last resort. *Prima facie* then, the account of the capture of Ai does look like an aetiological tale designed to explain the presence of this ruin.

But this explanation also has its difficulties. Since Et-Tell = ? Ai was occupied from 1200 to 1000 BC, the story must have been invented after 1000 BC; and presumably some time after, or else the true reason for its ruin would have been known.[115] This would put its creation, even on Noth's theory, within the period when the stories were first being committed to writing. But aetiological tales are usually reckoned to be the product of folklore, not of literary historians.

There is a second and, to my mind, more substantial obstacle to regarding the story of Ai as aetiological in its content. Why should popular story-tellers invent the story of a defeat of Israel? All other stories in Joshua 1-11 recount the swift and miraculous capture of great cities, and the fear and terror that the Israelite campaign produced in the Canaanite population. The story of the ignominious defeat at Ai is quite out of character with the other traditions about the conquest and is, therefore, the more likely to be genuine.[116]

But when all is said and done, on the basis of archaeological evidence now available we can say only that the balance of probability lies with the biblical account of a violent conquest led by Joshua. As yet we do not possess clear-cut proof. It may be hoped that as archaeological techniques are refined and more discoveries are made, the picture will clarify. Only then would archaeology be in a position to corroborate or disprove the biblical account of the conquest. But even if future archaeological discoveries were to support the biblical narrative in every detail, the theological interpretation of the events described in Joshua will for ever be beyond the archaeologist's power to confirm. An archaeologist is a historian, not a prophet.

4. CONCLUSIONS

This discussion of archaeology brings us up to date on the current debate about early Old Testament history. As in other aspects of Old Testament criticism that we have examined, the results of archaeology are seen not to be quite so clear-cut and decisive as they are sometimes made out to be or even as the devout believer would like them to be. Whatever branch of criticism one is dealing with, one must recognize that there is an element of subjectivity. Archaeology and textual criticism may involve less subjective judgments than literary or tradition criticism, but in every branch we must acknowledge that our results are at best probable, not certain.

But if the results of critical enquiry and therefore our interpretation of Israel's history are at best probable, have we any sure basis for faith? The relationship between faith and reason has been much discussed in theology and here I can but allude to the wider issues which have a bearing on this discussion. Faith is sometimes represented as a leap in the dark, or as something that goes against the facts. Then biblical criticism is regarded as antithetical to biblical theology. I believe this to be a mistaken concept of faith and an erroneous view of the relationship between faith and criticism. De Vaux was closer to the mark when he insisted that the Old Testament must be true if it is to summon us to faith.[117] In the Bible, faith means going beyond the bare facts to see God at work and to respond to him. The Old Testament's theology of history is beyond the scope of critical verification, but its historical record can be tested. And it is important that where the Bible is open to being tested in this way, it should be shown to be probably true. One hundred per cent proof of the truth of the Old Testament's history is unattainable, but such a degree of proof is not necessary to summon us to faith. In everyday life we regularly exercise faith in making decisions without our knowing for sure whether we are right.

Anyone who reads the Bible is brought face to face with a record of God's revealing himself in history, and he must ask himself what his relationship to this God is. A few may be prepared to turn to God immediately without consulting anyone or reading any other books about the Bible to see if other people think it is true. Such people would be like someone who sees a car in a showroom and goes in and buys it on the spot. It is an almost blind act of faith. A more cautious man would act differently. Having decided that he needed a car of a particular size, he would seek independent advice from his friends and from technical journals such as *Motoring Which?* This would no doubt make his decision much more complicated, since they would point out snags he had never thought of. After long consideration and a trial run he might eventually decide that a certain model was a good buy. So far, he has been guided largely by reason. Now he has to make an act of faith. Is he prepared to part with the money? Does he trust the *Which?* reports, his friends' advice and his own judgment? His final decision to buy will be the result of critical reflection and faith. Only after he has used the car for several months will he really come to know whether his decision was a wise one.

Although faith in God is of a different order from that required in car-buying, it seems to me that there are some similarities. In particular, criticism of the Bible acts rather like a *Which?* report. It shows up the strengths and weaknesses of the Christian case. Like biblical criticism, *Which?* reports seldom conclude the debate. They show only that one or more brands are probably to be preferred to others. Just as cautious people considering a large purchase will consult a *Which?* report, so serious seekers after truth will be interested in the conclusions of biblical criticism. Those who already believe should also be interested in criticism, not solely for the sake of intellectual integrity, but because if criticism reaches negative conclusions it will tend eventually to undermine belief.

A Christian believes that the biblical history can be shown to be probable at a large number of points, partly on the basis of his own judgment and partly on the claims of Scripture itself inwardly confirmed by the Holy Spirit. But if the believer's claim to spiritual enlightenment is not to be dismissed as conceit, he must do all in his power to demonstrate that from a human point of view his beliefs are probable. This of necessity involves him in some form of biblical criticism. Moslems and Mormons also believe that their scriptures are divinely inspired, but the refusal of devout adherents of these faiths to allow their scriptures to be subject to criticism makes them suspect. Believers in the truth and inspiration of the Bible, whether they be evangelical or catholic, therefore, must realize that they cannot afford to neglect criticism. It is part of what 'faith seeking understanding' means. The theologian's task is to explain the faith to the faithful and to attempt to justify it to outsiders. Biblical criticism is therefore central to his calling.

We have seen that biblical criticism covers a variety of disciplines all of which are valuable for elucidating the original meaning of the biblical text. Only in the realm of literary and historical criticism is there serious possibility of tension between the claims of the texts themselves and the conclusions of critical scholarship. It is in the area of the early history of Israel that the problems are most acute. It is clear, for example, that the exodus and the covenant were fundamental to mainstream religious thought in Israel. Yet scholarship has most doubts about the reliability of these normative traditions. The scholar who has committed himself to the truth of the Bible, however broadly he defines it, thus finds himself in a dilemma. Does he stop proclaiming that God fulfilled his promises to Abraham, because he now believes that these promises were little more than the pious retrojections of later Israel? Or does he take refuge in dogmatic assertions about the truth of the Old Testament, because this is the historic faith of the church?

In practice the choice is not quite so stark. In my judgment the Albright school has shown that the main outline of the biblical story is probable. But the gap between the events and the written sources is still troubling. Noth's scepticism does not seem so unreasonable, if oral tradition had to transmit the story for hundreds of years. This gap is more serious when Christ's teaching is taken into account, since he seems to treat the details as well as the main outline as historical. But in the course of time it is just the details that would be expected to get confused, or forgotten, or even invented. Faith in the truth of the whole Old Testament seems, humanly speaking, less likely if there was this very long period of oral transmission. For the believer, however, these considerations are not conclusive; for God is greater than we are and could have preserved his truth over many centuries in oral tradition.

Even so, it is very hard for the believer to shed his beliefs and look at critical theories objectively. As we have seen, criticism bears so closely on faith that the believing scholar wonders whether he is being intellectually honest if he questions its findings. It would be too convenient if some of the established theories were wrong and the Pentateuch was seen to have been composed closer to the events it describes. Traditional scholarly caution and a proper respect for the learning of former generations inhibit us further from reopening old problems. Nevertheless, in this essay I have drawn attention to certain areas of critical study where current theories are ripe for reappraisal. The doubts expressed by men such as C.S. Lewis and W. Kaufmann give me some confidence that my queries are not merely the result of theological prejudice.[118] Literary, tradition and historical criticism could and should be made more exact with the aid of new evidence from the Near East and modern advances in linguistics.

This is no plea for a return to old pre-critical views of the Old Testament which leave no room for any advance in our understanding of its history and message. What is required is criticism that takes with equal seriousness the claims of the biblical writings as well as their problems. Furthermore, if criticism is to be the true servant of faith, it must show some degree of detachment so that it cannot be accused of fudging the answers for the good of the cause. Where problems are unsolved they must be recognized, not covered up.

St Augustine well compared biblical study to mountaineering. He thought Jerome's invitation to come and 'play harmlessly in the fields of the Scriptures', a most inapt description of the task, 'as if studying the Scriptures were a matter of romping around on level ground, not puffing and panting up a steep mountain-face'.[119] Biblical scholars have often been content to wander on the easier slopes such as biblical theology. But as I have tried to show, a full interpretation of the Bible requires us to tackle the more difficult faces of history and criticism. Though some may have come to grief in studying the Bible, this should not deter future generations from making fresh attempts to reach the summit.

To change the analogy, the process of scriptural interpretation can be compared to the formulation of scientific theories. Hypotheses are propounded to explain a given set of facts. When one hypothesis is shown to cover these facts, it then becomes the basis of further investigation in an effort to relate the first set of facts to fresh data. The scientist then tries to formulate a new hypothesis to cover the old hypothesis and the new data. So science proceeds, each new theory becoming more comprehensive than the old. As far as one can tell there is no end to this process. But this does not mean the basic principles of science are becoming uncertain. In fact, as they are incorporated into an ever-widening context their significance becomes more and more clear.

So too, in the interpretation of Scripture, certain truths are already fairly clear. But this means neither that there is little more to be discovered nor that they are uncertain. What is required is a determination to relate these truths to various outstanding and unexplained facts in Scripture in order to arrive at a fuller understanding of the truth. From this new perspective further problems will become apparent which will demand fresh thought in order to be overcome. As we climb higher, the significance of the basic truths from which we started should become clearer. Progress in our understanding of Scripture thus depends on two things: adherence to the insights already gained (the old hypothesis), and openness both to new data and to new problems. Unless interpretation takes care of both, it is as likely to represent a step backwards as forwards.

This approach to Scripture is demanding. Most people would prefer to think that they had more or less arrived at the final truth, and would prefer to settle down into a cosy obscurantism oblivious to new facts and theories. Certainly there are some fundamental truths about God and his revelation that are so clear that a Christian will not expect to see any changes in them except in detail. But in other areas we can be much less certain. God, who has given us Scripture and other historical records, has also given us minds. It is therefore likely that he intends to keep us thinking until in his new creation our faith gives way to sight.

NOTES

[1] For the history of biblical interpretation, see *The Cambridge History of the Bible* (Cambridge University Press; vol. I, ed. by P.R. Ackroyd and C.F. Evans, 1970; vol. II, ed. by G.W.H. Lampe, 1969; vol. III, ed. by S.L. Greenslade, 1963). On allegorical interpretation see R.P.C. Hanson, *Allegory and Event* (SCM Press, 1959). On the moral problems posed by the OT see J.W. Wenham, *The Goodness of God* (Inter-Varsity Press, 1974).

[2] J. Bright, *The Authority of the Old Testament* (SCM Press, 1967), pp. 77 f.

[3] *Ibid.*, pp. 112 ff.

[4] See G.F. Hasel, *Old Testament Theology: Basic Issues in the Current Debate* (Eerdmans, 1972).

[5] G. von Rad, *Old Testament Theology*, I and II (Oliver & Boyd, 1962-5).

[6] R. de Vaux, 'Is it Possible to Write a "Theology of the Old Testament"?', in *The Bible and the Ancient Near East* (Darton, Longman & Todd, 1972), p. 56.

[7] *Ibid.*, p. 57.

[8] *The Authority of the Old Testament*, pp. 199 f.

[9] In J.P. Hyatt (ed.), *The Bible in Modern Scholarship* (Carey Kingsgate Press, 1966), pp. 15 ff.

[10] For detailed discussions of the various interpretations of this passage see O. Kaiser, *Isaiah 1-12* (SCM Press, 1972), pp. 86 ff.; R. Kilian, *Die Verheissung Immanuels* (Katholisches Bibelwerk, Stuttgart, 1968); M. Rehm, *Der königliche Messias im Licht der Immanuel-Weissagungen des Buches Jesaja* (Butzon & Bercker, Kevelaer, 1968), pp. 30 ff.; J.A. Motyer, 'Context and Content in the Interpretation of Isaiah 7:14', *TB* 21, 1970, pp. 118-25; H. Wildberger, *Jesaja 1-12* (Biblischer Kommentar, Neukirchen, 1972), pp. 262 ff.

[11] *The Authority of the Old Testament*, pp. 130 f.

[12] Cf. *Old Testament Theology*, I, p. 106.

[13] *Ibid.*, pp. 3 ff.

[14] *Ibid.*, p. 107.

[15] *Ibid.*, pp. 107 f.

[16] *Ibid.*, pp. 110 f.

[17] W. Eichrodt, 'The Problem of Old Testament Theology', in *Theology of the Old Testament*, I (SCM Press, 1961), pp. 512-20.

[18] *Ibid.*, p. 512.

[19] *Ibid.*, p. 513.

[20] *Ibid.*, p. 513.

[21] *Ibid.*, p. 514.

[22] *Ibid.*, p. 515.

[23] *Ibid.*, p. 515.

[24] *Ibid.*, p. 516.

[25] R. de Vaux, 'Is it Possible to Write a "Theology of the Old Testament"?', p. 57.

68 ———————————————————————————— HISTORY, CRITICISM AND FAITH

[26]*Ibid.*, p. 57.
[27]G. von Rad, *Old Testament Theology*, I, p. 107.
[28]For a discussion of miracles and the principle of analogy see pp. 156 ff., 171 ff.
[29]R. de Vaux, 'Is it Possible to Write a "Theology of the Old Testament"?', pp. 57 f.
[30]*Ibid.*, p. 59.
[31]J. Bright, *Early Israel in Recent History Writing* (SCM Press, 1956), pp. 11 ff.
[32]R. de Vaux, 'Is it Possible to Write a "Theology of the Old Testament"?', p. 59.
[33]*Early Israel in Recent History Writing*, p. 27.
[34]*The Historian and the Believer* (SCM Press, 1967), p. 19.
[35]Mk. 12:35-7 and par.
[36]*The Historian and the Believer*, pp. 112 f.
[37]*Cf.* W.D. Davies, *The Sermon on the Mount* (Cambridge University Press, 1966), pp. 139 ff.
[38]For a fuller discussion of the different aspects of biblical criticism see K. Koch, *The Growth of the Biblical Tradition* (A. & C. Black, 1969).
[39]The numerous fragments of biblical manuscripts near the Dead Sea are proving most important for OT textual criticism, since they are so much older (third century BC to first century AD) than those known hitherto. See F.M. Cross, 'The Contribution of the Qumran Discoveries to the Study of the Biblical Text', *IEJ* 16, 1966, pp. 81-95; R.W. Klein, *Textual Criticism of the Old Testament* (Fortress Press, Philadelphia, 1974); P.W. Skehan, 'Texts and Versions', in R.E. Brown *et al.* (eds.), *The Jerome Biblical Commentary*, II (Geoffrey Chapman, 1969), pp. 561-80; S. Talmon, 'The Old Testament Text', in P.R. Ackroyd and C.F. Evans (eds.), *The Cambridge History of the Bible*, I, pp. 159-99.
[40]T.N.D. Mettinger (*Solomonic State Officials*, Gleerup, Lund, 1971, p. 39) suggests that the annals of Judah also dealt with affairs of the northern kingdom. The records were kept in two columns; events in Judah were recorded in one, and events in Israel in the other. This would explain how events in one kingdom could be dated by reference to events in another. Assyrian historical records in this form are attested.
[41]For further discussions see J. Liver, 'The Book of the Acts of Solomon', *Biblica* 48, 1967, pp. 75-101; B. Porten, 'The Structure and Theme of the Solomon Narrative (I Kings 3-11)', *HUCA* 38, 1967, pp. 93-128; R.N. Whybray, *The Succession Narrative* (SCM Press, 1968); M. Noth, *Könige* (Biblischer Kommentar, Neukirchen, 1968).
[42]E.W. Nicholson (*Deuteronomy and Tradition*, Blackwell, 1967, pp. 2 ff.) defends this view.
[43]This is the virtually unargued presupposition of M. Weinfeld in *Deuteronomy and the Deuteronomic School* (Oxford University Press, 1972).
[44]This or a similar analysis of the material is to be found in M. Noth, *Überlieferungsgeschichtliche Studien*, I² (Kohlhammer, Stuttgart, 1957), p. 92; N. Lohfink, 'Die Bundesurkunde des Königs Josias', *Biblica* 44, 1963, pp. 261-88, 461-98; and J. Gray, *I and II Kings²* (SCM Press,

1970), pp. 713 ff. But only Lohfink realizes its implications for the criticism of Deuteronomy.

[45]*Christian Reflections* (Bles, 1967), pp. 160 f. reprinted in *Fern-Seed and Elephants* (Fontana, 1975), pp. 116 ff.

[46]H.-J. Kraus, *Geschichte der historisch-kritischen Erforschung des Alten Testaments* (Neukirchen, 1956); S. Loersch, *Deuteronomium und seine Deutungen* (Katholisches Bibelwerk, Stuttgart, 1967); R.J. Thompson, *Moses and the Law in a Century of Criticism since Graf* (*VTS* 19, Brill, Leiden, 1970).

[47]This view was popularized by J. Wellhausen in *Prolegomena to the History of Ancient Israel* (1878; Meridian, Cleveland, 1965), pp. 171 ff.

[48]W.E. Lemke, 'The Synoptic Problem in the Chronicler's History', *HThR* 58, 1965, pp. 349-63.

[49]A modern and positive evaluation of the Chronicler's historical sources is given by J.M. Myers, *Chronicles* (Anchor Bible, Doubleday, Garden City, 1965).

[50]R.A.F. MacKenzie, in W.S. McCullough (ed.), *The Seed of Wisdom: Essays in Honour of T.J. Meek* (University of Toronto, 1964), pp. 32 f. *Cf.* S.M. Paul, *Studies in the Book of the Covenant in the Light of Cuneiform and Biblical Law* (*VTS* 18, Brill, Leiden, 1970).

[51]W. Kaufmann, *Critique of Religion and Philosophy* (Faber, 1959), pp. 266 ff. Kaufmann, a non-Christian philosopher, claims that pentateuchal criticism rests on false premises and bad argument, and in particular fails to understand the processes of artistic creation. 'The gross materialism underlying the Higher Criticism has perhaps never been duly noted. Nowhere else do we find a comparable example of the mechanistic outlook which Bergson criticized: these men literally believed that artistic creation could be explained in terms of a purely spatial construction out of separate particles. We know of no major work of literature that originated in any such fashion, even if we waive the requirement that the artist who put the work together must have been an idiot. And Genesis, with its less than 100 pages, need not fear comparison in content and form, in its inexhaustibility and in its impact on human thought and art, with any other book of any length in any tongue' (p. 273).

[52]M. Greenberg, in M. Haran (ed.), *Y. Kaufmann Jubilee Volume* (Magnes Press, Jerusalem, 1960), pp. 5 ff.; K.A. Kitchen, *Ancient Orient and Old Testament* (Inter-Varsity Press, 1966), pp. 112 ff.; R.K. Harrison, *Introduction to the Old Testament* (Inter-Varsity Press, 1970), pp. 515 ff.; D.B. Redford, *A Study of the Biblical Story of Joseph* (*VTS* 20, Brill, Leiden, 1970).

[53]See, *e.g.*, S. Mowinckel, *The Psalms in Israel's Worship* (Blackwell, 1962), and modern commentaries on the Psalms. D.J.A. Clines surveys recent studies of the psalms in *TB* 18, 1967, pp. 103-26, and 20, 1969, pp. 105-25.

[54]*E.g.* W. Beyerlin, *Origins and History of the Oldest Sinaitic Traditions* (Blackwell, 1965); K. Baltzer, *The Covenant Formulary* (Blackwell, 1971); D.J.

McCarthy, *Old Testament Covenant: A Survey of Current Opinions* (Blackwell, 1972).

[55]It is commonly supposed that in the earliest form of the decalogue each commandment was quite short, and various attempts to recover the original form have been made on this basis. *Cf.* J.J. Stamm, *The Ten Commandments in Recent Research* (SCM Press, 1967), pp. 13 ff.; E. Nielsen, *The Ten Commandments in New Perspective* (SCM Press, 1968), pp. 78 ff.

[56]N. Lohfink, *Das Hauptgebot* (Pontifical Biblical Institute, 1963), and his various articles, contain many valuable insights. *Cf.* G.J. Wenham, 'The Deuteronomic Theology of the Book of Joshua', *JBL* 90, 1971, pp. 140-8.

[57]See F.M. Cross, 'The Development of the Jewish Scripts', in G.E. Wright (ed.), *The Bible and the Ancient Near East* (Doubleday Anchor, Garden City, 1965), pp. 170-264.

[58]F.M. Cross and D.N. Freedman, *Early Hebrew Orthography* (American Oriental Society, New Haven, 1952), and D.N. Freedman, 'The Massoretic Text and the Qumran Scrolls', *Textus* 2, 1962, pp. 87-102. *Cf.* K.A. Kitchen's comments on the modernization of style and spelling in Egyptian literature in J.D. Douglas *et al.* (eds.), *The New Bible Dictionary* (InterVarsity Press, 1962), pp. 349 ff.

[59]For a fuller exposition see G. von Rad, *Studies in Deuteronomy* (SCM Press, 1953), pp. 45 ff.

[60]S. Erlandsson (*The Burden of Babylon*, Gleerup, Lund, 1970, pp. 43 ff.) points out that many attempts to date the oracles in Isaiah suffer from the same fallacy.

[61]Jdg. 17:6; *cf.* 18:1; 19:1.

[62]Fuller presentations may be found in G.W. Anderson, *A Critical Introduction to the Old Testament* (Duckworth, 1959), pp. 19 ff.; O. Eissfeldt, *The Old Testament: An Introduction* (Blackwell, 1965), pp. 158 ff.; G. Fohrer, *Introduction to the Old Testament* (Abingdon, New York, 1968), pp. 103 ff.; G.J. Wenham, 'Trends in Pentateuchal Criticism since 1950', *TSFB* 70, 1974, pp. 1-6.

[63]Among those who disagree with the above scheme may be mentioned O. Eissfeldt and G. Fohrer (see n. 62), who identify a source in the Pentateuch earlier than J; F.I. Andersen (*The Sentence in Biblical Hebrew*, Mouton, The Hague, 1974, pp. 124 ff.), who maintains that the J-E-D-P source analysis splits up syntactical units without sufficient justification; Y. Kaufmann (*The Religion of Israel*, Allen & Unwin, 1961, pp. 175 ff.) and M. Weinfeld, (*Deuteronomy and the Deuteronomic School*, pp. 179 ff.), who think P antedates D; J.N.M. Wijngaards (*The Dramatization of Salvific History in the Deuteronomic Schools*, Brill, Leiden, 1969, pp. 109 ff.) and G.J. Wenham ('Deuteronomy and the Central Sanctuary', *TB* 22, 1961, pp. 103-18), who date Deuteronomy earlier than 622 BC.

[64]G.E. Wright (*JNES* 5, 1964, pp. 105-14), argues that archaeological discovery supported D's version of a military conquest, but see the present

essay, pp. 55 ff.

[65]M. Noth, *Überlieferungsgeschichte des Pentateuch* (1948), available in translation as *A History of Pentateuchal Traditions* (Prentice-Hall, Englewood Cliffs, 1972). References are to this translation.

[66]*Ibid.*, pp. 38 ff.

[67]Noth is cagey about dating his sources precisely, but this date for G would seem to be implied by his work. *Cf.* J. Bright, *Early Israel in Recent History Writing*, p. 42.

[68]*A History of Pentateuchal Traditions*, pp. 46 ff.

[69]*Ibid.*, pp. 156 ff.

[70]*Ibid.*, pp. 173 ff.

[71]*Ibid.*, pp. 42 ff.

[72]*Das Buch Josua*[2] (Mohr, Tübingen, 1953), pp. 43 ff., 60 f.

[73]*A History of Pentateuchal Traditions*, pp. 80 f.

[74]*The History of Israel*[2] (A. & C. Black, 1960).

[75]See above, pp. 24 ff.

[76]*Op. cit.*, pp. 53 f.

[77]*Ibid.*, pp. 41 f., 79 ff. S. Herrmann (*Israel in Egypt*, SCM Press, 1973) and E.W. Nicholson (*Exodus and Sinai in History and Tradition*, Blackwell, 1973), while broadly agreeing with Noth's methods, reach less pessimistic conclusions about the historical value of the traditions.

[78]*Early Israel in Recent History Writing*, pp. 105 f.

[79]*Ibid.*, pp. 91 ff.

[80]*Ibid.*, p. 91.

[81]*Ibid.*, pp. 84 ff.

[82]*Ibid.*, pp. 87 ff.

[83]*Ibid.*, p. 109.

[84]*TB* 20, 1969, pp. 76-94. Earlier studies include W.F. Albright, *JBL* 63, 1944, pp. 207-33; F.M. Cross and D.N. Freedman, *JBL* 67, 1948, pp. 191-210; and *idem*, *JNES* 14, 1955, pp. 237-50.

[85]'The Conquest and Early Hebrew Poetry', p. 94.

[86]'A Study of the Formula "Until This Day" ', *JBL* 82, 1963, pp. 279-92. See also B.O. Long, *The Problem of Etiological Narrative in the Old Testament* (*BZAW* 108, Töpelmann, Berlin, 1968); F. Golka, 'Zur Erforschung der Ätiologien im Alten Testament', *VT* 20, 1970, pp. 90-8.

[87]M. Noth, 'Der Beitrag der Archäologie zur Geschichte Israels', (*VTS* 7, Brill, Leiden, 1960), p. 279.

[88]R. de Vaux, in J.P. Hyatt (ed.), *The Bible in Modern Scholarship*, p. 22.

[89]Discussed by S. Yeivin, *The Israelite Conquest of Canaan* (Nederlands Historisch-Archaeologisch Instituut in het Nabije Oosten, Istanbul, 1971), pp. 26-31.

[90]R. de Vaux has not only preached this principle in various articles (see the bibliography), but has put it into practice in his *Histoire ancienne d'Israel*, I and II (J. Gabalda, Paris, 1971-3).

[91]S. Yeivin (*The Israelite Conquest of Canaan*, pp. 69 ff.) believes that the conquest began in the late fourteenth century and lasted for about 100 years.

[92]See W.F. Albright, *The Archaeology of Palestine* (Penguin, 1960), pp. 108 ff.; *idem, The Biblical Period from Abraham to Ezra* (Harper & Row, New York, 1963), pp. 24 ff.
[93]*The History of Israel*, pp. 80 ff.
[94]*The Settlement of the Israelite Tribes in Palestine* (SCM Press, 1971), pp. 24 ff.
[95]*Ibid.*, pp. 28 f.
[96]*Ibid.*, pp. 50, 53.
[97]*Ibid.*, pp. 128 f.
[98]*Ibid.*, p. 128.
[99]*Ibid.*, pp. 131 f.
[100]*Ibid.*, pp. 133 f.
[101]*Ibid.*, p. 135.
[102]*CThM* 38, 1967, pp. 283-300.
[103]*Ibid.*, pp. 299 f.
[104]*Ibid.*, pp. 287 ff.
[105]Y. Yadin, 'The Fourth Season of Excavation at Hazor', *BA* 22, 1959, pp. 13 f. Yadin gives a fuller description of his findings in *Hazor* (Oxford University Press, for the British Academy, 1972), pp. 129 ff.
[106]P.W. Lapp, 'The Conquest of Palestine in the Light of Archaeology', pp. 294-6.
[107]*Ibid.*, p. 296.
[108]*Ibid.*, pp. 297 f.
[109]*Ibid.*, p. 298.
[110]*Ibid.*, p. 298.
[111]*Ibid.*, p. 299.
[112]*Ibid.*, p. 291. This is also the view of W.F. Albright (*The Biblical Period from Abraham to Ezra*, pp. 28 f.) and R. de Vaux (*Histoire ancienne d'Israel*, I, pp. 562 ff.).
[113]P.W. Lapp, 'The Conquest of Palestine in the Light of Archaeology', p. 290, n. 53; W.F. Albright, *The Biblical Period from Abraham to Ezra*, pp. 29 f.; J. Bright, *A History of Israel²* (SCM Press, 1972), p. 128.
[114]P.W. Lapp, *op. cit.*, p. 290; J.A. Callaway, *BASOR* 178, 1965, pp. 27 f. More recently, in *JBL* 87, 1968, pp. 312-20, Callaway has argued that Et-Tell is the site of Ai and that the Early Iron deposits (from the twelfth century?) are the remains of the town captured by Joshua. This is disputed by R. de Vaux, *Histoire ancienne d'Israel*, I, p. 568.
[115]R. de Vaux, *op. cit.*, p. 568.
[116]R. de Vaux (*op. cit.*, pp. 568 ff.) compares the story of the defeat and ambush at Ai (Jos. 7, 8) with that at Gibeah in Jdg. 20. He thinks that both stories were preserved in the sanctuary at Bethel, and that there is no historical basis to the story of Ai except the distant memory of a general conquest. The details of the aetiology of Ai were borrowed from the story in Jdg. 20. Though this is the most plausible attempt yet put forward to explain the story of Ai as an aetiology, there are a number of differences between Jos. 7 and 8 and Jdg. 20 which make the explanation uncertain (notably the role of Achan in Jos. 7). A. Malamat (in B.

Mazar (ed.), *The World History of the Jewish People*, III, W.H. Allen, 1971, p. 323, n. 92) regards both the Ai and the Gibeah episodes as historical. The Ai episode certainly coheres well with the over-all theology of the book of Joshua (see G.J. Wenham, *JBL* 90, 1971, pp. 140-8).

[117]'Is it Possible to Write a "Theology of the Old Testament"?', pp. 57 ff.

[118]See above, pp. 37 ff. and nn. 45, 51.

[119]*Ep*. 82.1.2, quoted by P. Brown, *Augustine of Hippo* (Faber, 1967), p. 275.

BIBLIOGRAPHY

Historical and biblical theology
Barr, J., *Old and New in Interpretation* (SCM Press, 1966).
Bright, J., *The Authority of the Old Testament* (SCM Press, 1967). An invaluable work expounding the authority of the OT and showing how it should be interpreted and applied today.
Eichrodt, W., *Theology of the Old Testament*, I - II (SCM Press, 1961-7). One of the great OT theologies. Emphasizes the importance of the covenant. For a brief evaluation see the book by Hasel, below.
Hasel, G.F., *Old Testament Theology: Basic Issues in the Current Debate* (Eerdmans, 1972). Brief but useful.
Kraus, H.-J., *Die Biblische Theologie: Ihre Geschichte und Problematik* (Neukirchen, 1970).
von Rad, G., *Old Testament Theology*, I-II (Oliver & Boyd, 1962-5). Another great OT theology. Brings out the particular contributions of different parts of the OT. See Hasel's book (above) for an evaluation.
Idem, 'Offene Fragen im Umkreis einer Theologie des Alten Testaments', *ThL* 88, 1963, pp. 401-16.
de Vaux, R., 'Is it Possible to Write a "Theology of the Old Testament"?', in *The Bible and the Ancient Near East* (Darton, Longman & Todd, 1972), pp. 49-62. Argues that OT theology should combine historical understanding of the text with Christian theology.
Wright, G.E., *The Old Testament and Theology* (Harper & Row, New York, 1969).

Methods of criticism
Anderson, G.W., *A Critical Introduction to the Old Testament* (Duckworth, 1959). Outlines the most widely held theories of OT scholarship.
Bright, J., *Early Israel in Recent History Writing* (SCM Press, 1956). A critique of Noth's method of tradition criticism and a defence of Bright's more positive evaluation of the early history of Israel.
Harrison, R.K., *Introduction to the Old Testament* (Inter-Varsity Press, 1970). A new look at the problems of OT study through the eyes of an evangelical orientalist.
Hyatt, J.P. (ed.), *The Bible in Modern Scholarship* (Carey Kingsgate Press, 1966). Papers read at the 100th meeting of the Society of Biblical Literature, December 1964. Various approaches to OT study; mainly American contributors.
Kitchen, K.A., *Ancient Orient and Old Testament* (Inter-Varsity Press, 1966). An Egyptologist's critique of accepted OT critical methods and conclusions.
Koch, K., *The Growth of the Biblical Tradition* (A. & C. Black, 1969). Discusses the main methods of OT criticism.
Noth, M., *A History of Pentateuchal Traditions* (Prentice-Hall, Englewood

Cliffs, 1972). A difficult but important work, applying the principles of tradition criticism to the Pentateuch.

Redford, D.B., *A Study of the Biblical Story of Joseph* (Brill, Leiden, 1970). A valuable new look at the literary criticism of Genesis 37-50. Uses Egyptian comparisons to check the source criticism of Genesis.

Rowley, H.H. (ed.), *The Old Testament and Modern Study: A Generation of Discovery and Research* (Oxford University Press, 1951).

Wenham, G.J., 'Trends in Pentateuchal Criticism since 1950', *The Churchman* 84, 1970, pp. 210-20; updated in *TSFB* 70, 1974, pp. 1-6. Footnotes to the essay on pentateuchal criticism in Rowley's volume, above.

Archaeology and the conquest

Alt, A., 'The Settlement of the Israelites in Palestine', in *Essays on Old Testament History and Religion* (Doubleday Anchor, Garden City, 1968), pp. 173-221. Maintains that the conquest was a gradual infiltration and settlement.

Bright, J., *A History of Israel*[2] (SCM Press, 1972). The standard work in English.

Franken, H.J., *Palestine in the Time of the Nineteenth Dynasty: The Archaeological Evidence* (Cambridge University Press, 1968). A chapter from the new *Cambridge Ancient History*.

Lapp, P.W., 'The Conquest of Palestine in the Light of Archaeology', *CThM* 38, 1967, pp. 283-300. A positive evaluation of the evidence for a violent conquest.

Mazar, B. (ed.), *The World History of the Jewish People*, III (W.H. Allen, 1971). Essays by eminent Jewish scholars dealing with the history of Israel from the conquest to the monarchy. Adopts a positive attitude to biblical tradition and to archaeological discovery.

Noth, M., 'Der Beitrag der Archäologie zur Geschichte Israels', *VTS* 7, 1960, pp. 262-82.

Thomas, D.W. (ed.), *Archaeology and the Old Testament* (Oxford University Press, 1967). Summaries of the archaeological findings on different sites.

de Vaux, R., *Histoire ancienne d'Israel*, I - II (J. Gabalda, Paris, 1971-3). Unfortunately de Vaux died before his great history of Israel was completed, and these volumes cover only the period from the patriarchs to the judges. He endeavoured to combine Noth's attention to literary and tradition criticism with Bright's positive approach to the archaeological data.

Idem, 'Method in the Study of Early Hebrew History', in J.P. Hyatt (ed.), *The Bible and Modern Scholarship* (see above), pp. 15-29.

Idem, 'On Right and Wrong Uses of Archaeology', in J.A. Sanders (ed.), *Essays in Honor of Nelson Glueck: Near Eastern Archaeology in the Twentieth Century* (Doubleday, Garden City, 1970), pp. 64-80.

Weippert, M., *The Settlement of the Israelite Tribes in Palestine* (SCM Press, 1971). Follows Alt and Noth.

Yeivin, S., *The Israelite Conquest of Canaan* (Nederlands Historisch-Archaeologisch Instituut in het Nabije Oosten, Istanbul, 1971). An eclectic approach.

II
HISTORY &
THE NEW
TESTAMENT

2. MYTH & HISTORY

F. F. BRUCE

Since the publication of the first edition of David Friedrich Strauss's *The Life of Jesus Critically Examined*,[1] if not earlier, the question whether there is an element of myth in the New Testament presentation of the Gospel story (and if so, to what extent) has been a recurring subject of study and debate. This is no mere question of the use of originally mythical forms as a pictorial means of relating essentially historical facts, such as we find in Old Testament poetry;[2] it is a question of the mythical or mythological character of the central affirmation of the New Testament—that 'in Christ God was reconciling the world to himself' (2 Cor. 5:19).[3]

1. MYTH AND RITUAL

In any discussion of the term 'myth' it is necessary to begin with a definition; there are few words which can mean so many things. In popular parlance a myth is a sheer invention, a piece of falsehood lacking any foundation in fact. In theological parlance the word is used with a closer reference to its origin. The Greek *mythos* is originally an utterance or a story which may be true or false. In the earliest literature it is a synonym of *logos*; some later writers contrast the two words, *mythos* being a fictional narrative whereas *logos* is the prosaic fact. But in a religious context a *mythos* is a story about one or more of the gods, especially a story which was enacted in a sacred ritual. It comprises the *legomena* (the things spoken) which accompany and interpret the *drōmena* (the things done) or the *deiknymena* (the things shown). So the mysteries enacted at Eleusis were explained by the *hieros logos* (sacred story) recounted in the Homeric *Hymn to Demeter*.[4]

This is the sense of 'myth' which lies behind the use of the word by the 'myth and ritual' school.[5] In Greece an important development of early 'myth and ritual' is seen in tragedy and comedy, where *drama* (or 'action') is accompanied by *mythos* (or 'plot'). The *mythos* tells the story which is enacted in the *drama*. It is pointless to ask which came first—the myth or the ritual, the plot or the drama—for they were involved in each other from time out of mind.

Much of the ancient poetry of western Asia has been interpreted along these lines; for example, T.H. Gaster has explained the religious texts from Ugarit and elsewhere as the *mythoi* or *hieroi logoi* of seasonal rites of 'emptying' and 'filling' which he endeavours to reconstruct.[6] It is against this background that much discussion of myth in the Old Testament is carried on; and if we use the terms in these technical senses it would be proper to say, for example, that the first fifteen chapters of Exodus constitute the *mythos* or *hieros logos* of the annually repeated passover ritual in Israel. To this day, as the ancient *drama* is enacted at the paschal table, the head of the household is given the cue to repeat the story of that memorable night when the God of Israel came down to redeem his people from bondage in Egypt. But—and herein lies the whole *differentia* of Israel's faith as contrasted with the surrounding religions of Old Testament days—the *mythos* in this instance is not the casting of a recurring fertility pattern in the form of a story thrown back to primeval times, but the recital of something that really happened in history, interpreted as the mighty, self-revealing act of Israel's God.

So in the New Testament the sacramental action of the eucharist was accompanied by words in which its meaning was made plain—not only the record of its institution by Jesus 'on the night when he was betrayed', as Paul repeats it in 1 Corinthians 11:23-25, but the relating of the passion narrative itself. 'For as often as you eat this bread and drink the cup,' Paul goes on, 'you proclaim the Lord's death until he comes' (1 Cor. 11:26). This probably means, not that the partaking of the bread and cup is in itself a visible proclamation of the Lord's death (although that is certainly true), but that it was accompanied by a recital of the saving events which were symbolized in the sacramental action. Again, to use the terms in their technical sense, the *drama* was accompanied by the *mythos* or *hieros logos*; again, as in the case of the passover, the *mythos* was the recital of something that really happened in history—the Lord's death—interpreted as God's saving act on behalf of mankind. The emperor Julian might say that the details of the story set forth in the mysteries of Attis never happened and yet were eternally true;[7] but of the events set forth in the Christian eucharist, as of those set forth in the Jewish passover, it must be said, 'These things happened once for all, and therefore they are eternally true.'

But how was the story told?

There are several ways in which the death of Jesus and its attendant circumstances might be related. One could, for example, imagine a dispassionate historian, after some reference to the activity of John the Baptist, continuing his account somewhat as follows:

> Scarcely had John been imprisoned in Machaerus, when Galilee, the more important of the two regions of Antipas's tetrarchy, witnessed the emergence of another preacher. He was a former associate of John and proclaimed the advent of the kingdom of God, Daniel's fifth monarchy which was to supersede Gentile world power. His preaching, attended by an impressive healing ministry, caused great excitement throughout the region; and many thought that he was the man to lead a successful attack not only on the Herodian dynasty but on the Roman dominion, whose creatures the Herods were. He made it plain, however, that submission and conciliation, not violence and revolt, were the marks of the new kingdom as he envisaged it, and the majority of his original adherents lost interest in him.
>
> Shortly before the passover of (probably) AD 30 he went to Jerusalem to confront the capital with his message, and entered the city in a manner reminiscent of a messianic oracle (Zc. 9:9), acclaimed by a crowd of enthusiastic pilgrims. He alienated many of the common people there by his unsatisfactory answer to a test question about the payment of tribute to the Roman emperor, and incurred the hositility of the temple authorities

by a demonstration against various commercial practices inseparable from the sacrificial order. In their alarm lest his actions and words might excite a riot which would bring down the heavy hand of Roman ascendancy, they took steps to arrest him. One of his own close followers aided them in achieving this aim. They then handed him over to the Roman prefect of Judea, Pontius Pilate, who sentenced him to death on a charge of sedition: the death sentence was carried out by crucifixion.

That this was not the end of the matter was due to the conviction of his Galilaean disciples that he had risen from the dead and had appeared to them alive again, charging them to carry on his programme.

Few Christians would disagree with any of the statements made in this imaginary extract from a history of Palestine under the Romans, but most Christians would regard it as a very inadequate representation of the Gospel story and as a quite unsuitable recital to be incorporated in a liturgical service. If we look for an acceptable recital in a liturgical context, we shall find one in the second division of the Nicene Creed:

... one Lord Jesus Christ, the only-begotten Son of God, Begotten of his Father before all worlds, God of God, Light of Light, Very God of very God, Begotten, not made, Being of one substance with the Father, By whom all things were made: Who for us men and for our salvation came down from heaven, And was incarnate by the Holy Ghost of the Virgin Mary, And was made man, And was crucified also for us under Pontius Pilate. He suffered and was buried, And the third day he rose again according to the Scriptures, And ascended into heaven, And sitteth on the right hand of the Father. And he shall come again with glory to judge both the quick and the dead: Whose kingdom shall have no end.

Or we might go back beyond Nicaea to the Pauline Letters and quote passages in them which have sometimes been identified as pre-Pauline hymns or confessions. Here is one:

Though he existed in the form of God,
He did not exploit equality with God for his own advantage,
But emptied himself and took a servile form,

Appearing in the likeness of men.

And thus appearing in human shape,
He humbled himself and became obedient—
Obedient up to the hour of death,
Even death on a cross.

Therefore God exalted him on high,
And gave him the name above all names,
That in Jesus' name each knee should bend,
In heaven and earth and underworld;

And each tongue confess Jesus Christ as Lord,
To the glory of God the Father.[8] (Phil. 2:6-11)

And here is another:

[He is] the very image of the God whom none can see;
He is the Firstborn, prior to all creation,
Because it was through him that the universe was created.
Yes, all things in heaven and on earth, visible
    things and things invisible—
Thrones, dominions, principalities or powers —
They have all been created through him and for him.
He himself exists before them all;
It is through him that everything holds together.
He is, moreover, the head of his body, the church;
He is the beginning, the Firstborn from the dead:
Thus over old and new creation his pre-eminence is universal.
It is God's good pleasure, in short, that the
    totality of divine fullness should reside in him
And that through him the universe should be reconciled to
    God,
Through the shedding of his blood on the cross.[9] (Col. 1:15-20)

Coming forward many centuries, we find a presentation in a
different idiom in Isaac Watts' poem which begins with the stanzas:

Nature with open volume stands
    To spread her Maker's praise abroad,

And every labour of his hands
Shows something worthy of a God.

But in the grace that rescued man
His brightest form of glory shines;
Here on the cross 'tis fairest drawn
In precious blood, and crimson lines.[10]

And so we might go on. But sufficient examples have been adduced to show that, in whatever form the Christian story is told, the cross is a constant feature. In the cross the creeds are 'earthed'.

2. HISTORICAL EVENT AND THEOLOGICAL INTERPRETATION

But how are we to describe the four quotations which follow our bald 'historical' summary of Christian beginnings? They would be described by many as a 'mythologization' of history—which at least is a less unsatisfactory procedure than to call the Christian story the historicization of myth.[11] It would be better, however, to say that they convey a theological interpretation of historical events—an interpretation which, as Christians believe, brings out their true meaning.

But is the interpretation part of the history? If we are to operate with that form of the historical-critical method which stems from the Enlightenment and cannot accommodate salvation-history;[12] if the 'historical Jesus' means 'what can be known of Jesus of Nazareth by means of the scientific methods of the historian',[13] then God, whose gracious initiative is emphasized in our four interpretative quotations, can have no place in the 'history'. To a Christian, let it be said plainly, this conclusion is the *reductio ad absurdum* of the premises on which it is based.

How, for example, should a historian who wishes to establish the course of events *wie es eigentlich gewesen*[14] (as it actually was) deal with the resurrection of Jesus? He will recognize the resurrection faith, but what of the resurrection fact, apart from which, as Paul affirms, the resurrection 'faith is in vain' (1 Cor. 15: 14)? He may say (1) 'Jesus was believed to have risen from the dead', but if he wishes to penetrate behind that belief he may go so far as to say (2) 'Jesus "rose" from the dead, whatever may be meant by that statement'. But can the historian go farther, and say (3) 'God raised him from the dead'? It depends partly on his *Weltanschauung* and partly on our definition of 'historian'.[15] But for the Christian nothing less will adequately express the event 'as it actually was'.

The application of 'myth' to the contents of the New Testament, which involves a different sense of the word from that of the 'myth and ritual' pattern noticed above, has come prominently to the fore during the past thirty years as a result of Professor Rudolf Bultmann's demythologizing programme. Bultmann's thesis, in brief, is that, if the gospel is to make its impact on men and women today, it must be freed from its 'mythological' formulation and presented in such terms as will expose the hearers immediately to its challenge and its 'offence'. It is no part of his programme to remove the 'offence of the cross'; rather he believes that that 'offence' is obscured by the mythological language in which it has been traditionally wrapped up. When that language has been reinterpreted and the gospel restated, the restatement turns out to resemble a Christianized version of Heidegger's existential analysis:[16] the moment of revelation is not in the person or work of Jesus but in the existence of the man of today.

Whatever be thought of the validity or success of this restatement, it is clear that Bultmann's motive is different from that of the typical nineteenth-century rewriters of the life of Jesus, who hoped by stripping away the miraculous incrustation from the story to recover the picture of the inoffensive teacher of the Fatherhood of God and the brotherhood of man; and more different still from that of the proponents of the Christ-myth theory. Bultmann's motive is evangelistic; it is to prevent the essential *skandalon* of the gospel from being so entangled with the dispensable *skandala* of its 'mythological' concomitants that people who cannot accept the latter reject the former along with them.

When we ask what these mythological concomitants are, we are given more than one answer. One of them is the conception of the three-decker universe: earth is the floor on which we live, heaven is the floor above, Hades is the basement beneath.[17] In the traditional formulation of the Gospel story, Christ came down from heaven to earth, descended farther from earth to Hades, and came up again from Hades to this earth, from which he 'ascended into heaven, and sitteth on the right hand of God the Father Almighty; from thence he shall come [back to earth] to judge the quick and dead'. But this is not really mythological; it is a pictorial framework, going back, admittedly, to pre-Copernican and even pre-Ptolemaic times. A Christian astronomer, when he recites the creed, is no more bothered by language of this kind than he is in ordinary conversation when he speaks of the sun rising and setting. Bishop John Robinson agrees that for thinking people the conception of God as 'up there' has long since been given up as having any 'geographical' precision (if it was ever thought to have any)—although we may question whether they have replaced it in any comparable sense by the conception of God as 'out there'.[18] Such phrases are but spatial metaphors for God's transcendence, just as the Bishop's preferred conception of him as 'in the depths of being' is an equally spatial metaphor for his immanence. 'To all life thou givest' is as true as the companion confession, 'In all life thou livest.' From beyond our own existence and resources God comes into our human life to impart grace in time of need; the language of personal relationship (even though it too would be regarded as mythological by some) best expresses the Gospel witness about God and man, and if that witness is sometimes conveyed in spatial metaphors, they are metaphors for the divine-human encounter embodied in the person and work of Christ, for what Bultmann himself calls the 'act of God' in Christ, the 'decisive, eschatological event'.[19]

We need not trouble ourselves, then, about the necessity to demythologize that form of thought and speech in which 'divine transcendence is expressed as spatial distance';[20] that is a natural use of language, and if 'demythologization' is the right word for the translation of metaphorical into non-metaphorical terms (I am sure it is not), we can do our own demythologizing in this respect as we go along.

3. THE DEMYTHOLOGIZING PROGRAMME
There is another sense in which Bultmann uses 'myth'. Myth, in this sense, 'is the account of an event or happening in which super-

natural and superhuman powers are operative. . . . Mythical thinking regards the world and world-events as "open"—open to invasion
by transcendent powers, and so not watertight from the point of
view of scientific thought."[21] Getting rid of myth in this sense means
the rigorous exclusion from the gospel of everything that savours of
miracle, but—more drastic still—it means the exclusion from the
gospel even of that account of the coming of God's grace which
might be given when the metaphorical terminology of the 'three-
decker universe' has been replaced by non-metaphorical language.
The transcendence of God, the pre-existence of Christ, his being
sent by his Father in the fullness of time, his rising from the dead as a
historic event, the personal activity of the Holy Spirit—in fact, many
(perhaps most) of the central affirmations of Christian doctrine—
are given up. Bultmann is no doubt anxious that Christians should
not rest their faith on history or natural science, but one may
question whether the best way to teach them where they ought to
rest their faith is to assure them that much of what they have been
accustomed to accept as divine revelation is to be rejected as either
unscientific or unhistorical or both.

> God withholds Himself from view and observation. We can
> believe in God only in spite of experience, just as we can accept
> justification only in spite of conscience. Indeed, de-mythologiz-
> ing is a task parallel to that performed by Paul and Luther in
> their doctrine of justification by faith alone without the works
> of law. More precisely, de-mythologizing is the radical
> application of the doctrine of justification by faith to the sphere
> of knowledge and thought. Like the doctrine of justification,
> de-mythologizing destroys every longing for security. There is
> no difference between security based on good works and
> security built on objectifying knowledge.[22]

There is much truth is all this, but Bultmann overdoes it. One gets
the idea that he thinks it better that the resurrection of Christ should
be demythologized than that its claims to be regarded as a historical
event should be objectively examined, because in the latter case we
are in danger of placing our faith in history—*i.e.* in the historical
event called the resurrection rather than in the risen Christ who is
knowable by faith alone. Similarly, it is not so much because certain

other affirmations of the historic faith are really incompatible with
the scientific world-view that he insists on their rejection, but because they may come between the believer and the one who should
be the sole resting-place for his faith. We would not gather from
Bultmann's writings that he has ever heard of the principle of com-
plementarity; probably indeed he has heard of it, but clearly he has
no use for it. It is not the scientific world-view that compels him to
abandon belief in the Holy Spirit, save as 'the possibility of a new life
which is opened up by faith'.[23] What is it then? Bultmann's aim is certainly not to make Christianity palatable to modern man or to reduce
it to as much as Jones will swallow; but repeatedly it appears that the
features of historic Christianity which are dismissed as 'mythological' are those which are unacceptable in the climate of contemporary opinion, apart from the irreducible existential challenge. (It
must be added, in fairness to a great man, that such an outline of
Bultmann's demythologizing programme may do him an injustice
and give a distorted impression of his thought unless it is set in the
context of his theology as a whole.[24])

4. DEMYTHOLOGIZING IN THE NEW TESTAMENT
One area in the New Testament where mythological elements might
indeed be recognized is the book of the Revelation and other apocalyptic sections. But Bultmann does not insist so much on these,
probably because the symbolical character of apocalyptic imagery
has been generally recognized. Whatever be the origin of the drama
of the dragon, the woman and the child in Revelation 12, that origin
had been thoroughly 'demythologized' long before John's time. The
dragon is recognizably the dragon of chaos, the seven-headed
Leviathan;[25] but already in the Old Testament, psalmists and
prophets had 'demythologized' Leviathan to make him serve as a
picture of the powers opposed to God and overcome by him at the
exodus.[26]

Such demythologizing of apocalyptic figures Bultmann finds in
one specific instance—in the figure of Antichrist. In Jewish eschatological expectation, he points out, Antichrist is 'a thoroughly mythological figure', as also in a New Testament passage such as 2 Thessa-
lonians 2: 7-12. But in 1 John 2: 18; 4: 3 and 2 John 7 'false teachers

play the role of this mythological figure. Mythology has been transposed into history. These examples show, it seems to me, that demythologizing has its beginning in the New Testament itself, and therefore our task of demythologizing today is justified.'[27] One might ask, however, whether John's view was not that the emergence of these 'many antichrists' prefigured the early appearance of the last Antichrist.

Or, if we think of the principalities and powers of the Pauline Epistles, we may ask whether in Paul's own mind these may not have been 'demythologized' to stand for all the forces in the universe opposed to Christ and his people. Bultmann points out that

> in our day and generation, although we no longer think mythologically, we often speak of demonic powers which rule history, corrupting political and social life. Such language is metaphorical, a figure of speech, but in it is expressed the knowledge, the insight, that the evil for which every man is responsible individually has nevertheless become a power which mysteriously enslaves every member of the human race.[28]

This is reminiscent of H.H. Rowley's striking treatment of the apocalyptic figure of 'Beliar'.[29] But may not Paul have had a very similar understanding of the principalities and powers, which, he affirmed, for all their malignity were unable to separate believers from the love of Christ? They might indeed continue to have a potent existence in the minds of those who believed in them and were enslaved by them, but for those who shared the fruits of Christ's conquest of them they were demoted to the status, at best, of 'weak and beggarly elemental spirits' (Gal. 4:9).

5. 'MYTH' IN FORM CRITICISM

Thus far we have concentrated on Bultmann because he more than anyone else has compelled attention to these subjects, but he is not alone in seeing myth of one kind and another in the New Testament. Martin Dibelius used the term 'myths' for such stories about Jesus as the baptism, the transfiguration and the resurrection[30]—stories which Bultmann in his form-critical analysis prefers to call 'legends'. Dibelius called them myths because in his judgment they belonged to the category of stories usually so designated—stories explaining the origin of religious rites or of cosmic phenomena. In so far as the use of this designation is a purely form-critical judgment, no objection need be taken—in T. W. Manson's words, 'a paragraph of Mark is not a penny the better or the worse as historical evidence for being labelled "Apothegm" or "Pronouncement Story" or "Paradigm" '[31] —nor yet, we may add, for being labelled 'myth' or 'legend' in the technical form-critical sense. But too often there is an unobtrusive passage from a form-critical judgment to a historical judgment, a passage which is all the easier because in ordinary usage the historicity of a narrative is doubted or denied when it is called a myth or a legend.

6. THE GNOSTIC MYTH

The designation of elements in the New Testament or in the traditional formulations of Christian doctrine as 'mythological' has been related by some scholars to a mythical pattern which they believe to have been current in the Near East around the time when Christianity first appeared. Unlike the dying-and-rising-god pattern of earlier times, this was a redeemer-myth, originating in Iranian religion and passing thence to Gnosticism. An outstanding proponent of this theory was R. Reitzenstein, whose *magnum opus* on the 'Iranian redemption mystery' was published over fifty years ago.[32] In its Iranian form the myth relates to Gayōmart, the first man (whose name means 'mortal life').[33] In the Avesta, Gayōmart appears occasionally as the ancestor of the Aryan peoples and the first believer in the teaching of Ahura Mazda.[34] In the *Bundahišn* and other Zoroastrian texts of the seventh century AD and later, however, Gayōmart appears as an important figure in the cosmic drama: he is a heavenly being, the primal man, son of Ohrmazd (Avestan *Ahura-Mazda*); he battled with Ahriman (Avestan *Angra-Mainyu*), the evil power, for a cycle of 3,000 years, at the end of which he was overcome and killed by Ahriman. From him, after his death, the human race sprang up; and when, at the end of time, Saošyant ('the Saviour') appears to raise the dead, Gayōmart will rise first and be exalted to archangelic rank. This myth certainly had a long career in oral tradition before it received literary form, but it can scarcely be dated earlier than the Sassanian era (AD 226). Quite apart from its relatively late date, there is little enough in the Gayōmart myth that could give rise to the New Testament concepts of the Son of man or the man from heaven.[35] It is possible, however, that it is related to some of the Gnostic myths—more particularly, that its influence may be traced in the Mandaean[36] and Manichaean[37] texts.

The general pattern of the Gnostic myth (if it is not too bold to speak of a 'general pattern' amid such a bewildering proliferation of mythology) portrays a heavenly essence which falls from the upper world of light into the lower world of material darkness and is imprisoned in a multitude of earthly bodies. To liberate this pure essence from its imprisonment a saviour comes from the world of light to impart the true knowledge: he is at once revealer and redeemer. By acceptance of the revealed knowledge the pure essence attains release from the thraldom of matter and reascends to its true abode.

In Mandaean literature it is Manda d'Hayye ('Knowledge of Life'), or his son Hibil Ziwa ('Abel the radiant'), who comes to instruct and redeem the soul of man, imprisoned in material darkness; in passing through the successive spheres lying between the upper world of light and this world he has conquered their demonic warders, so that they can present no barrier to the liberated soul on its way back to the world above. The victory of the redeemer over the demonic powers is re-enacted in Mandaean baptism, which is further—and later—associated with the baptism of John.[38]

The form in which the Mandaean myth appears is not earlier than the seventh or eighth century AD; its detailed indebtedness both to Manichaeism and to the Peshitta has been established.[39] There is no evidence to support the view that here we have in essence the Gnostic myth on which a number of New Testament writers draw.[40] A Palestinian origin for the Mandaeans is quite probable; they may have migrated to Mesopotamia in the first century AD.[41] A careful comparative study might indicate an affinity between them and one or more of the baptist sects operating in the Jordan valley at the beginning of the Christian era. But it is illegitimate to date the Mandaean myth so early as that. The model of Bultmann's Gnostic myth was constructed by him on the basis of the later Mandaean literature; the model was then used for the interpretation of the *Acts of Thomas* and other Gnostic writings.[42] But in fact, there is much more reason to think that certain aspects of the Mandaean myth are due to the New Testament than to trace the influence the other way round. It can even be claimed that primal man and the redeemer-revealer are nowhere brought together in Gnosticism except under the influence of the gospel.

It is indeed extremely difficult to find convincing evidence of the typical Gnostic myth in a pre-Christian form. It is suspected by certain students of Gnosticism that some of the documents in the Nag Hammadi collection, Christian though they are in their present form, may in fact be christianized recensions of pre-Christian Gnostic documents; but the arguments for regarding them as such are precarious.[43] Perhaps when the whole collection is published we shall be in a better position to speak confidently on this point. As it is, one of the documents thus far published which shows unusually little Christian colouring, the *Apocalypse of Adam*,[44] speaks of the 'incorruptible *phosteres* which have come forth from the holy seed, Jesseus, Mazaraeus, Jessedekeus'. It is difficult to avoid seeing in 'Jesseus, Mazareus' a corruption of 'Jesus the Nazarene' (Gk. *Iesous Nazōraios*), while 'Jessedekeus' could be a still more corrupt form combining the name 'Jesus' with Hebrew *ṣaddiq* ('righteous') or even bearing some relation to 'Melchizedek'.[45]

7. COSMIC VICTORY

In the hymn which (as has been mentioned above) Paul incorporates into Philippians 2: 6-11, 'Christ Jesus' is the one who, pre-existing in the form of God, refuses to exploit his equality with God for self-aggrandizement, but humbles himself to man's estate and submits obediently to death; in consequence, he is exalted by God to the place of supremacy and endowed with the ineffable name so that all intelligent beings in the universe may render him homage and glorify God by doing so. In Colossians 1:15 ff. Jesus is presented as Lord of the old creation and of the new, the one in whom the present universe has its being and in whom, by his rising from the dead, his people enjoy new and endless life as members of the body of which he is head. The principalities and powers of the old creation, unwilling to have their captives released from their custody, tried to prevent him from accomplishing his redeeming work and thought they had succeeded when they found him, as they imagined, at their mercy on the cross. There they flung themselves on him with hostile intent, but he grappled with them, disarmed them, liberated their captives, and transformed the cross into his triumphal car before which the hostile powers were driven in mute acknowledgment of his supremacy. He then ascended to the throne of God—a place to which he was antecedently entitled as 'the image of the invisible God' —but thanks to his victory and liberation of his people he has now established their title to join him there (Col. 2:13-3:4).

To this it could be added that, according to Ephesians 2:14, part of the victorious accomplishment of Christ is his breaking down of the 'middle wall of partition'—a concept which H. Schlier has explained in terms of the wall which, in one form of Gnostic mythology, separates the heavenly realm from the world below.[46] That this latter concept underlies the expression in Ephesians is supported by the consideration that other elements from the same conceptual complex are found in the context—the ascension of the redeemer, the heavenly man, the church as the body of Christ, the body of Christ as a heavenly building, and the heavenly marriage. The identification of some of these elements as of Gnostic origin should be contested, but one point calls for attention here. The wall which Christ demolishes in Ephesians 2:14 is not a horizontal wall, dividing the world above from the world below, but a vertical wall, which has hitherto divided two communities on earth, the Jews and the Gentiles. The resemblance between this wall and the Gnostic wall is purely superficial. Yet Schlier's account has profoundly influenced many exegetes, especially among his fellow countrymen. It has been pointed out that while British commentators tend to illustrate the 'middle wall of partition' by the barrier which excluded Gentiles from the inner courts of the temple in Jerusalem,[47] German commentators tend to reproduce Schlier's illustration. There is no doubt which of the two is more apt to the argument in Ephesians 2.

Again, in John's Gospel, the Logos who was with God in the beginning, and through whom all things came into being, the Logos of God who is at the same time the Son of the Father, came down from heaven to earth to become flesh and give his life for man's salvation, so that all who receive him by faith may have eternal life in him and be enrolled as children of God. Having accomplished the work which the Father gave him to do, he returns to the Father to resume the glory which he had with the Father before the world existed, but now he has won for his people the privilege of being with him where he is.

8. INCARNATE WISDOM

When the historic mission of Jesus is described in language of this kind, there is naturally a tendency to think that it is couched in terms of a current myth of a heavenly being who humbles himself for the sake of men on earth, and thus succeeds in his task of bringing them with him back to the heavenly realm. The trouble about this is that no such myth is ascertainable at this period. When the myth does appear, it is much more probable that it is based on the Christian message of one who was sent by God for man's salvation, and as man on earth endured humiliation, suffering and death—who did, moreover, as a matter of widespread experience, procure salvation for those who received him by faith, and assure them of eternal life with him in fellowship with God. If the language in which the Christian message itself is sometimes told presents features which suggest mythological affinity, these features are derived most probably from the terms in which Divine Wisdom is personified in Jewish literature of the immediate pre-Christian period.[48] Divine Wisdom both fills a cosmic role and dwells with men on earth. That such portrayals of Wisdom underlie the Johannine Prologue[49] and such a passage as Colossians 1: 15 ff.[50] has long been recognized. Further speculative elaborations of this Wisdom figure are familiar in Gnostic literature from the *Odes of Solomon* onwards—not least in those documents which feature *Sophia* in their titles.[51]

But when the Christian story was gnosticized, the varieties of Gnostic myth into which it was transmuted tended to embody the Gnostic antipathy to matter (so that the real incarnation of the Son of God was denied) and to replace the gospel emphasis on *agapē* by the Gnostic emphasis on *gnōsis*. I would hazard the guess that one of the earliest attempts at transmuting the gospel message into a Gnostic type of myth can be detected in the heresy to which Paul replies in the Epistle to the Colossians.[52] When Paul replies to it, he does so in some degree by taking some of the concepts of the Colossian heresy and using them in what has been called a 'disinfected' sense[53] to set forth the gospel truth which that heresy had subverted. But this is a far different matter from re-presenting the gospel in terms of Gnostic myth. Any demythologizing which is called for had been done by Paul before he pressed those terms into the service of the truth as it is in Jesus.

Let us repeat: it is the person and work of Christ that are at issue. How much mythology has entered into the traditional concept of the combining of the divine and human natures in his person? None, we may say, in the sense that the long-accepted formulations are cast in metaphysical and not mythical language. But if the term 'mythical' or 'mythological' is used with a wider range of meaning, it can properly be applied to any statement about Christ which gives the impression, however faintly, that there was something vaguely 'unreal' about his manhood—that his temptations, his sufferings and his death were not as 'real' as ours are. Since God created man in his image, humanity provided a congenial medium for the revelation of God to this world. The 'human face of God'[54] is a real face, not a mask assumed for a dramatic purpose. It is *in* the manhood of Jesus, not merely *through* it, that the divine glory shines for those who have eyes to see it. It was in 'the form of a servant' that the 'form of God' was most adequately displayed on earth (Phil. 2:6 f.). John the Evangelist knows what he is doing when he speaks of Jesus' being 'lifted up' on the cross as the means of his being 'lifted up' in glory: the royalty of the God whom we adore is fully seen in the crucified one. To the same effect Mark the evangelist associates the moment of Jesus' death with the rending of the temple veil and the centurion's confession: 'Truly this man was the Son of God' (Mk. 15:38 f.). It is not on the dying and rising god of a ritual drama but on the once-for-all event of the passion and triumph of Jesus of Nazareth that the gospel of our salvation is firmly based.

NOTES

[1]*Das Leben Jesu kritisch untersucht* (1835-6); Eng. trans. of fourth German edition (1840), *The Life of Jesus Critically Examined* (1846), reissued with an introduction by P.C. Hodgson (SCM Press, 1973). Since Strauss found it impossible to believe in a transcendent God intervening in the life of the world, he was unable to accept the Gospel witness to Christ, and replaced it by a careful reconstruction based on a thorough-going typology of miracle and myth.

[2]*Cf.* A.S. Peake, *Faded Myths* (Hodder & Stoughton, 1908).

[3]W. Pannenberg's essay, 'The Later Dimensions of Myth in Biblical and Christian Tradition', in *Basic Questions in Theology*, III (SCM Press, 1973), pp. 1-79, is now indispensable reading for all who are concerned about this subject.

[4]*Cf.* G.E. Mylonas, *Eleusis and the Eleusinian Mysteries* (Routledge & Kegan Paul, 1962).

[5]*Cf.* S.H. Hooke (ed:), *Myth and Ritual* (Oxford University Press, 1933); *The Labyrinth* (SPCK, 1935); *Myth, Ritual and Kingship* (Oxford University Press, 1958).

[6]*Thespis* (Schuman, New York, 1950).

[7]Julian, *Hymn to the Mother of the Gods*, 169d-170c (perhaps with an implied criticism of the 'Galilaeans', who believed that their *hieroi logoi* really had happened); *cf. To Heraclius the Cynic*, 216c. See also Sallustius, *Concerning the Gods*, iv, 9.

[8]*Cf.* R.P. Martin, *Carmen Christi* (Cambridge University Press, 1967); C.F.D. Moule, 'Further Reflexions on Philippians 2:5-11', in W.W. Gasque and R.P. Martin (eds.), *Apostolic History and the Gospel* (Paternoster Press, 1970), pp. 264 ff.

[9]*Cf.* E. Norden, *Agnostos Theos* (Teubner, Leipzig, 1913), pp. 250 ff.; E. Käsemann, 'A Primitive Christian Baptismal Liturgy', in *Essays on New Testament Themes* (SCM Press, 1964), pp. 149 ff.; J.M. Robinson, 'A Formal Analysis of Colossians 1: 15-20', *JBL* 76, 1957, pp. 270 ff.; R.P. Martin, 'An Early Christian Hymn', *EQ* 36, 1964, pp. 195 ff.; *idem, Colossians: The Church's Lord and the Christian's Liberty* (Paternoster Press, 1972), pp. 40 ff.

[10]Described by Erik Routley as 'the greatest of all hymns on the atonement written since the reformation' (*Hymns Today and Tomorrow*, Darton, Longman & Todd, 1966, p. 68).

[11]*Cf.* G.A. Wells, *The Jesus of the Early Christians* (Pemberton, 1971), where arguments are presented for the possibility that the story of Jesus results from the historicization of a mythical or mystery figure. For the commoner mythologizing of a historical figure we have present-day evidence in the Che Guevara cult.

[12]G.E. Ladd, 'The Search for Perspective', *Interpretation* 25, 1971, p. 49.

[13]J.M. Robinson, *A New Quest of the Historical Jesus* (SCM Press, 1959), p. 26. He adds that this 'historical Jesus' need not be identical with 'Jesus of

Nazareth as he actually was' (pp. 28 f.). *Cf.* the report on *The Nature and Extent of Biblical Authority* presented to the Christian Reformed Church (Christian Reformed Church, Grand Rapids, 1971), pp. 478 ff.

[14]L. von Ranke, *Geschichten der romanischen und germanischen Völker, 1494-1535* (Reimer, Berlin, 1824), preface. A translation of the preface is given in F. Stern (ed.), *The Varieties of History: From Voltaire to the Present* (Macmillan, 1970), pp. 55-8. *Cf.* also C. Brown's essay, p. 177.

[15]*Cf.* C. Brown's discussion on p. 177 ff.

[16]Bultmann's reply to this representation is: 'Some critics have objected that I am borrowing Heidegger's categories and forcing them upon the New Testament. I am afraid this only shows that they are blinding their eyes to the real problem, which is that philosophers are saying the same thing as the New Testament and saying it quite independently' ('New Testament and Mythology', in H.-W. Bartsch (ed.), *Kerygma and Myth*, I (SPCK, 1953; combined edn. with vol. II, 1972), p. 25).

[17]*Cf.* R. Bultmann, *op. cit.*, p. 4.

[18]J.A.T. Robinson, *Honest to God* (SCM Press, 1963), pp. 11 ff.

[19]*Kerygma and Myth*, I, p. 43.

[20]*Ibid.*, p. 10, n. 2; *cf.* Bultmann's *Jesus Christ and Mythology* (SCM Press, 1960), p. 20.

[21]'Zur Frage der Entmythologisierung,' in H.-W. Bartsch (ed.), *Kerygma und Mythos*, II (Herbert Reich, Evangelischer Verlag, Hamburg-Volksdorf, 1952), pp. 180 ff.

[22]*Jesus Christ and Mythology*, p. 84.

[23]*Kerygma and Myth*, I, p. 22.

[24]See G. Miegge, *Gospel and Myth in the Thought of Rudolf Bultmann* (Lutterworth, 1960).

[25]*Cf.* C.H. Gordon, *Ugaritic Textbook* (Pontifical Biblical Institute, Rome, 1965), 67: I: 1-3.

[26]*Cf.* Is. 27: 1; Ps. 74: 14.

[27]*Jesus Christ and Mythology*, p. 34.

[28]*Ibid.*, p. 21.

[29]H.H. Rowley, *The Relevance of Apocalyptic*[3] (Lutterworth, 1963), pp. 177 ff.

[30]M. Dibelius, *From Tradition to Gospel* (Nicholson & Watson, 1934), pp. 266 ff.

[31]T.W. Manson, *Studies in the Gospels and Epistles* (Manchester University Press, 1962), p. 5.

[32]R. Reitzenstein, *Das iranische Erlösungsmysterium* (Marcus & Weber, Bonn, 1921).

[33]Avestan *Gaya-maretan*.

[34]In the Avesta the primal man is *Yima* (*cf.* Vedic *Yama*).

[35]*Cf.* J.M. Creed, 'The Heavenly Man', *JTS* 26, 1924-25, pp. 113 ff.

[36]*Cf.* E.S. Drower, *The Mandaeans of Iraq and Iran*[2] (Brill, Leiden, 1962); K. Rudolph, *Die Mandäer* (Mohr, Tübingen, 1966); E. Yamauchi, 'The Present State of Mandaean Studies', *JNES* 26, 1966, pp. 88 ff.; *idem, Gnostic Ethics and Mandaean Origins* (Harvard University Press, 1970).

[37]*Cf.* F.C. Burkitt, *The Religion of the Manichees* (Cambridge University Press, 1925).

[38]In its literary presentation Mandaean baptism presupposes the baptismal ritual of Syriac Christianity, and the figure of John belongs to the latest stratum of Mandaean tradition; cf. H. Lietzmann, 'Ein Beitrag zur Mandäerfrage', Sitzungsberichte der preussischen Akademie der Wissenschaften zu Berlin, phil.-hist Kl. (1930), pp. 596 ff. (TU 76, 1958, pp. 124 ff.).

[39]Cf. S.A. Pallis, Mandaean Studies (Oxford University Press, 1926), pp. 115 ff.; F.C. Burkitt, 'The Mandaeans', JTS 29, 1927-8, pp. 225 ff.; idem, Church and Gnosis (Cambridge University Press, 1932), pp. 100 ff.

[40]Cf., e.g., R. Bultmann, 'Die Bedeutung der neuerschlossenen mandäischen und manichäischen Quellen für das Verständnis des Johannesevangeliums', ZNW 24, 1925, pp. 100 ff.

[41]Cf. R. Macuch, 'Alter und Heimat des Mandäismus nach neuerschlossenen Quellen', TLZ 82, 1957, cols. 401 ff., where he infers this from a passage in the Haran Gawaitha which mentions a migration of 60,000 Naṣôrayya from Palestine to the Median highlands under King Artabanus—identified by him with Artabanus III of Parthia (AD 12-38). See also idem, 'Zur Frühgeschichte der Mandäer', TLZ 90, 1961, cols. 650 ff.; E.S. Drower, The Mandaeans of Iraq and Iran, pp. 5 ff.

[42]Cf. G. Bornkamm, Mythus und Legende in den apokryphen Thomasakten (Vandenhoek & Ruprecht, Göttingen, 1933).

[43]Cf. E.M. Yamauchi, Pre-Christian Gnosticism (Inter-Varsity Press, 1973).

[44]Cf. A. Böhlig, 'Die Adamsapokalypse aus Codex V von Nag Hammadi als Zeugnis jüdisch-iranischer Gnosis', Oriens Christianus 48, 1964, pp. 44 ff., for the view that this work provides evidence of pre-Christian Gnosticism.

[45]Cf. R. McL. Wilson, Gnosis and the New Testament (Blackwell, 1968), pp. 135 ff.

[46]H. Schlier, Christus und die Kirche im Epheserbrief (Mohr, Tübingen, 1930), pp. 18 ff.; idem, Der Brief an die Epheser (Patmos Verlag, Düsseldorf, 1965), pp. 126 ff. With the mesotoichon tou phragmou cf. Acts of Thaddaeus, quoted in Eusebius, EH i, 13, 20: 'He divided asunder the partition (ton phragmon) which had not been divided from eternity' (this partition being that which separated earth from Hades; cf. Acts of Thomas, 156).

[47]Cf. J.A. Robinson, St Paul's Epistle to the Ephesians (Macmillan, 1904), pp. 18 ff. (The temple barrier is described by Josephus, War v. 193 f.; Ant. xv. 417.)

[48]Cf. J.T. Sanders, The New Testament Christological Hymns (Cambridge University Press, 1971), pp. 29 ff. et passim.

[49]Cf. J.R. Harris, The Origin of the Prologue to St John's Gospel (Cambridge University Press, 1917); for a 'Gnostic' interpretation, cf. R. Bultmann, 'Der religionsgeschichtliche Hintergrund des Prologs zum Johannes-Evangelium', Eucharisterion, Festschrift für H. Gunkel (Vandenhoeck & Ruprecht, Göttingen, 1923), pp. 1 ff.; idem, The Gospel of John (Blackwell, 1971), pp. 13 ff.

[50]Cf. C.F. Burney, 'Christ as the APXH of Creation', JTS 27, 1925-6, pp. 160 ff.; for a 'Gnostic' interpretation cf. E. Käsemann, 'A Primitive Christian Baptismal Liturgy' (see n. 9 above).

[51]Such as *Pistis Sophia* and in the Nag Hammadi collection, *Sophia Jesu Christi*. In one as yet unpublished 'Wisdom' myth in the Jung Codex the being that fell is called not Sophia but Logos.

[52]The Simon Magus myth, in a more primitive form than that described by church fathers, might be even earlier: it was perhaps 'an assimilation of imperfectly understood Christian doctrines to a fundamentally pagan scheme' (R.McL. Wilson, *The Gnostic Problem*, Mowbray, 1958, p. 100). *Cf.* K. Beyschlag, 'Zur Simon-Magus Frage', *ZThK*, 68, 1971, pp. 395 ff.

[53]*Cf.* H. Chadwick, 'All Things to All Men', *NTS* 1, 1954-5, p. 272.

[54]*Cf.* the title of J.A.T. Robinson's Hulsean Lectures on Christology, *The Human Face of God* (SCM Press, 1973). This work contains several observations on the 'mythological' quality of certain kinds of language about the person and work of Christ (pp. 20 ff., 116 ff., *et passim*).

BIBLIOGRAPHY

Bartsch, H.-W. (ed.), *Kerygma und Mythos*, I - V (Herbert Reich, Evangelischer Verlag, Hamburg-Volksdorf, 1948-55); *Kerygma and Myth*, I (selections from the German vols. I and II; SPCK, 1953) and II (selections from the German vols. III-V; 1962); vols. I and II combined with enlarged bibliography (SPCK, 1972).

Bultmann, R., 'The New Testament and Mythology' (1941), in *Kerygma and Myth*, I, pp. 1-44.

Idem, Jesus Christ and Mythology (SCM Press, 1960).

Cairns, D., *A Gospel without Myth?* (SCM Press, 1960).

Colpe, C., *Die religionsgeschichtliche Schule* (Vandenhoeck & Ruprecht, Göttingen, 1961).

Cunningham, A., *The Theory of Myth* (Sheed & Ward, 1974).

Gogarten, F., *Demythologizing and History* (SCM Press, 1955).

Hartlich, C., and Sachs, W., *Der Ursprung des Mythosbegriffes in der modernen Bibelwissenschaft* (Mohr, Tübingen, 1952).

Henderson, I., *Myth in the New Testament* (SCM Press, 1952).

Johnson, R.A., *The Origins of Demythologizing: Philosophy and Historiography in the Theology of Rudolf Bultmann* (Brill, Leiden, 1974).

Jones, G.V., *Christology and Myth in the New Testament* (Allen & Unwin, 1956).

Macquarrie, J., *The Scope of Demythologizing* (SCM Press, 1960).

Malevez, L., *The Christian Message and Myth* (SCM Press, 1958).

Miegge, G., *Gospel and Myth in the Thought of Rudolf Bultmann* (Lutterworth, 1960).

Ogden, S.M., *Christ without Myth* (Collins, 1962).

Pannenberg, W., 'The Later Dimensions of Myth in Biblical and Christian Tradition', in *Basic Questions in Theology*, III (SCM Press, 1973), pp. 1-79.

Reitzenstein, R., *Das iranische Erlösungsmysterium* (Marcus & Weber, Bonn, 1921).

Sanders, J.T., *The New Testament Christological Hymns* (Cambridge University Press, 1971).

Throckmorton, B.H., *The New Testament and Mythology* (Westminster Press, Philadelphia, 1960).

Wilson, R.McL., *The Gnostic Problem* (Mowbray, 1958).

Idem, Gnosis and the New Testament (Blackwell, 1968).

Yamauchi, E.M., *Pre-Christian Gnosticism* (Inter-Varsity Press, 1973).

3. THE AUTHENTICITY OF THE SAYINGS OF JESUS

R. T. FRANCE

Professor Bruce's essay on 'Myth and History' has opened up that aspect of criticism which is probably of most pressing concern to the New Testament student today. It would not be too much to describe the sceptical approach to the historicity of the Gospels, as formulated by Rudolf Bultmann, as a new orthodoxy. It has spread far beyond its native Germany, and wherever New Testament scholarship flourishes it meets the student at every turn of the library shelves. The present chapter therefore aims, without apology, to explore further into the hinterland of Bultmann's domain by discussing how the critical approach associated with his name deals in particular with the *sayings* of Jesus.[1]*

The question before us, then, is: How far are the sayings of Jesus in the Gospels authentic? And by this I mean simply: Did Jesus say the words which the Gospel writers put in his mouth, or did he not?†

It is on this point that the conservative student of the New Testament finds himself confronted by what seems to him a quite unrea-

---

*Among recent treatments of the sayings of Jesus from a Bultmannian standpoint, we shall have to pay particular attention to N. Perrin, *Rediscovering the Teaching of Jesus* (SCM Press, 1967), which combines a forceful, if rather extreme, statement of Bultmannian principles with a detailed study of some selected parts of the sayings tradition.

†'Authentic' is an ambiguous word. Applied to the sayings attributed to Jesus in the Gospels, it can convey at least three distinct meanings. (i) 'Authoritative'. Are these sayings to be accorded a special authority? (This use of 'authentic' seems to be particularly prevalent in North America.) (ii) 'Credible'. Are these sayings consonant

sonable scepticism on the part of the school of Bultmann. This essay will examine the foundations on which this scepticism is based, and the criteria which are used to distinguish between authentic words of Jesus and later Christian elaboration of and addition to his teaching. We shall then be able to see whether the basic assumptions are as indisputable as scholars of this persuasion would have us believe, or whether there is any alternative approach open to a reputable scholar. I shall then attempt to suggest guidelines, arising from this discussion, for those who wish to tackle the question of authenticity without necessarily subscribing to a Bultmannian scepticism.

It should be clearly stated before we go further that, while I shall have to register disagreement with Bultmannian criticism at many points, there is no intention to repudiate critical study of the Gospels as such. Basic disciplines such as textual criticism, source criticism, form criticism and redaction criticism are essential to a responsible study of the Gospels, whatever label the scholar may bear. All of them have provided materials of inestimable value to conservative scholarship, however slow some conservatives may have been in recognizing their importance. What is being questioned here is not these disciplines as such, but the sceptical presuppositions which underlie their use by many modern New Testament scholars.[2]

It has been necessary to limit this discussion to the synoptic Gospels. The Johannine literature raises different problems, and to discuss these adequately would have taken as much space again. It is with reference to the synoptic Gospels, however, that the debate on authenticity is being most actively pursued at present. It is here that the New Testament student is likely to meet the question first, and in its most acute form.

---

with what we know of the life and teaching of Jesus? Are they the sort of thing Jesus would have said? (iii) 'Genuine'. Did Jesus actually say this? These three uses are quite different from one another, and give three totally distinct meanings to the question, 'Are these sayings authentic?' It would be possible (in fact it is quite common) to answer this question affirmatively with regard to senses (i) and (ii), but negatively (or at least in a non-committal manner) with reference to (iii). Debate on this question is bedevilled by this ambiguity. In this essay I shall aim to use 'authentic' only in the third sense. The question under discussion is not whether the sayings in the Gospels are authoritative, nor whether they are Christlike, but whether Jesus actually said them (and by 'Jesus' in this context I mean the earthly Jesus, not the ascended Christ speaking through his prophets, etc. See pp. 103 f. below).

1. SOME PRESUPPOSITIONS OF THE SCEPTICAL APPROACH

I cannot, of course, attempt here a complete account of the rationale of Bultmann's critical method. All I hope to do is to indicate some of the presuppositions which give rise to what often seems a quite arbitrary presumption against the authenticity of the sayings attributed to Jesus.

The fundamental point in this sceptical approach is focused in the distinction between *Historie* and *Geschichte* (which may be crudely paraphrased as, respectively, 'a bare account of what actually happened' and 'an account of past events in terms of their contemporary significance') and in the assertion that the early church's* overriding concern with the latter left the former a matter of almost complete indifference to them.[3] Or, as it is frequently stated, the church was concerned with the Christ of faith, not with the Jesus of history. To be a little more accurate, the church assumed that the Jesus of history was the same as the Christ of faith, and they were not interested in finding out if this were really so. Their concern was to preach and live Christ, not to conduct antiquarian research into what Jesus of Nazareth actually said and did before his crucifixion. For Jesus had risen, and was alive in their midst. The inspired teaching of Christian prophets and other leaders was the teaching of the risen Christ through them. Whether a saying originated from Jesus before his death or from the risen Christ through his church was irrelevant to them, since both were equally authoritative; both were the teaching of Christ.† As Norman Perrin frequently puts it, 'The

---

*There will be frequent references in this essay to 'the early church'. It is not intended to suggest that there was a completely homogenous Christian movement in the first century. We may assume that different emphases were current in different local situations, and that individual Christian leaders and teachers had distinctive contributions to make. The four Gospels may well give expression in their peculiar concerns to such differences. But to spell out this point on each occasion would be extremely tedious. I must ask the reader to accept 'the early church' as a convenient shorthand term.

†A recent article by David Hill ('On the Evidence for the Creative Role of Christian Prophets', *NTS* 20, 1973-4, pp. 262-74) exposes the total lack of evidence on which this commonly repeated idea of Christian prophets as originators of 'sayings of Jesus' is built. F. Neugebauer ('Geistsprüche und Jesuslogien', *ZNTW* 53, 1962, pp. 218-28) points out that visions and prophecies in both Jewish and early Christian literature are always ascribed to a named person as recipient of the revelation,

Lord who spoke is the Lord who speaks.[4]*

So, it is argued, the question of the authenticity of the sayings attributed to Jesus would have had no meaning for them. *All* the sayings came from Jesus, whether on earth or in heaven, so *all* were authentic. It is only we moderns, with our academic concern for *Historie*, who have raised the question. It is only we who can see any difference between a saying faithfully transmitted as Jesus said it and a saying 'put into his mouth' by a Christian preacher. They would not so describe it: it was a saying inspired by the risen Christ, and therefore it *was* a saying of Jesus. To say that Jesus said it, even though it was first formulated by one of his followers long after his death, was not deception; to them, it was true.

More generally, it is frequently stated that the biography of Jesus (what he *did* as well as what he said) was of no interest to the primitive church.[5] They had a true existentialist concern for the present moment of their own experience. If something which Jesus actually said or did happened to be relevant to that situation, well and good; if not, it was of no concern—and it is remarkable how freely the assumption is made that most of what Jesus said was in fact irrelevant to the concerns of his followers thirty or forty years later![6] Conversely, if certain teaching did prove relevant, whether Jesus actually said it mattered little, provided it enshrined what Christ was teaching his church now; it was what the Christ of their faith would have said—indeed, was saying. It was the teaching of Jesus. Thus Perrin can summarize: 'So far as we can tell today, there is no single pericope anywhere in the gospels, the present purpose of which is to preserve a historical reminiscence of the earthly Jesus, although there may be some which do in fact come near to doing so because a reminiscence, especially of an aspect of teaching such as a parable, could be used to serve the purpose of the Church or the evangelist.'[7]

A further significant step is made when scholars assume that a theological motivation in the writing of the Gospels *excludes* a con-

---

whereas the Gospels were published anonymously. He thus argues that there was a clear distinction between prophecy and Gospel-writing, between revelations of the exalted Christ and recorded words of the earthly Jesus. *Cf.* also I.H. Marshall, 'Questions about the Gospels—II. History or Fiction', *TSFB* 53, 1969, pp. 5-7.
*The frequent references to Perrin's work in the following pages should not be taken as implying that he alone holds the views discussed; for convenience, I am concentrating on one exponent of a widespread current of thought.

cern for historical authenticity. Notice this assumption in the following words of Perrin, which could be paralleled many times: he speaks of 'an assumption about early Christian preaching, that it was interested in historical reminiscence, for which we have absolutely no evidence. The opposite view, that it was theologically motivated, is the one for which we have evidence.'[8] That word 'opposite' reveals a lot. What is the logical incompatibility between theological motivation and an interest in historical reminiscence? As Gerhardsson complains, 'It seems to be an extremely tenaciously-held misapprehension among exegetes that an early Christian author must *either* be a purposeful theologian and writer *or* a fairly reliable historian.'[9]

Perrin's provocative little book on redaction criticism provides us with an admirably clear summary of the sceptical stance at this point: 'We must take as our starting-point the assumption that the Gospels offer us directly information about the theology of the early church and not about the teaching of the historical Jesus, and that any information we may derive from them about Jesus can only come as a result of the stringent application of very carefully contrived criteria for authenticity.'[10] Note in this statement first the same unquestioned assumption that documents relevant to the church's theology cannot also convey what Jesus himself taught; and secondly that the 'very carefully contrived criteria for authenticity' to which we shall shortly turn our attention are explicitly based on this admitted 'assumption'. They derive their validity from the assumed incompatibility between concern for contemporary theological relevance and interest in preserving the authentic teaching of Jesus. Without this prior assumption, they have no force, nor is there any need for them.*

Another presupposition, more fundamental than the above and therefore less often brought to light, must be touched on briefly even though a full discussion is not possible. This is the assumption that the supernatural element in the Gospel tradition cannot be treated as historical. History is, according to Bultmann, a 'closed

---

*The word 'assumption' in Perrin's statement is perhaps unfortunate, as it might be taken to imply a quite arbitrary supposition, whereas Perrin would certainly maintain that the 'assumption' is made on good grounds. We shall be examining those grounds in what follows. Meanwhile, the use of a rather more neutral word, such as 'premise', would have made his case sound less tendentious.

continuum of effects', limited to the categories of normal human experience. Or, to quote D.E. Nineham, 'Since the historian's essential criteria presuppose the absence of radical abnormality or discontinuity, only those events can be described as "historical" which are fully and exclusively human and entirely confined within the limits of this world.'[11] So the miraculous, and indeed all that transcends our normal materialistic categories of thought, falls outside the historian's proper sphere of reference and therefore cannot be called 'historical'. It is thus decreed in advance that the 'historical' Jesus, both in his deeds and in his words, will be compatible with the anti-supernaturalistic world-view (the closed mind) of modern scientific man. This is, of course, the aim of Bultmann's programme of demythologization, to eliminate the categories alien to a materialistic world-view. So it happens that whatever in the life or teaching of Jesus is incompatible with such a world-view *must* be pronounced unhistorical, or unauthentic, in the sense that it is the product of pious reflection and imagination, not of sober fact.

To state this point so baldly is, of course, to invite indignant denials from those who return a sceptical verdict on the sayings of Jesus. They will appeal to objective criteria, not to such an arbitrary presumption. But the fact remains that if underlying these criteria there is a definition of 'historical' which excludes the supernatural, then one is committed in advance to finding means of disqualifying a large part of the Gospel tradition as authentic history. It must be the product of early Christian theology, or rather mythology, because supernatural things simply do not happen.*

Until this presupposition is brought into the open, it is liable to cloud the issue. I have mentioned it here, however crudely, in order to open the way for a different approach by those who find that they *can* accept the supernatural into their world-view, who are capable

---

*What has happened here is a concealed semantic leap which should never have been allowed. To most English speakers (and to English dictionaries!) 'historical' means 'what actually happened', and 'the historical Jesus' means 'Jesus as he actually was'. If a scholar sees fit to redefine 'historical' as meaning 'confined to the dimensions of the natural world', he has, of course, a right to do so, provided that he makes his new definition clear. But he has no right to bring together the two quite different senses of the word, and conclude by a simple equation that 'Jesus as he actually was' must be shorn of all supernatural characteristics.

of imagining 'history' which transcends the categories of scientific analysis—in other words, those who believe in a God who acts. For them this anti-supernaturalistic presupposition which lies unquestioned beneath most of the sceptical estimates of the Gospel tradition has no validity, nor is there any need to redefine the word 'historical' to mean not 'what actually happened' but 'what modern "scientific" man can conceive to have happened'. To allow such a presupposition to lurk unchallenged is to invite confusion. If for me 'historical' and 'authentic' mean what actually happened or was said, whether it is explicable in terms of empirical analysis or not, I must not submit to critical criteria which reject *a priori* as unhistorical all that is abnormal.

Returning now to the more overt assumptions of the sceptical approach, the crucial issue for our purposes is that of the burden of proof. It is no longer permissible, we are told, to presume that the Gospel tradition is authentic where there is no evidence against it. 'The obligation now laid upon us is to investigate and make credible not the possible unauthenticity of the individual unit of material but, on the contrary, its genuineness.'[12] 'The nature of the synoptic tradition is such that the burden of proof will be upon the claim to authenticity.'[13] The whole tradition of narratives and sayings must be presumed to owe its origin to the early church, not to the life and teachings of Jesus, unless clear reasons can be produced for regarding it as authentic. Earlier generations of scholars assumed in their simplicity that the tradition is innocent until proved guilty, but now we are assured on every hand that it must be reckoned guilty until proved innocent.* The burden of proof lies squarely on those who would regard a saying as authentic.

It is on the basis of this assumption that scholars have recently expended much energy on the search for criteria of authenticity, and on the application of these criteria to the synoptic tradition to determine where in it, if anywhere, we may find the authentic teaching of the Jesus of history. These criteria must now be briefly examined.

---

*In using this convenient legal analogy, here and in later pages, there is, of course, no intention of suggesting that scholars of any persuasion would impute guilt or dishonesty to the evangelists.

2. CRITERIA OF AUTHENTICITY[14]

The chief criterion accepted by the school of Bultmann is now too well known to need much introduction. It is that which Perrin labels the 'criterion of dissimilarity'.[15] If a saying displays the thought or concerns of the primitive church, it must be presumed to owe its origin to that source, not to Jesus; if it is such that any Jew of the period could have said it, then it must be presumed to be a piece of popular teaching put into the mouth of Jesus; but if it shows neither of these characteristics, the presumption is that it is a genuine saying of Jesus. A saying must be such that no one else, Jew or Christian, in the first century could have said it, before it is accepted as the teaching of Jesus. This criterion, clearly set out and constantly used in Bultmann's *History of the Synoptic Tradition*,[16] and taken for granted by all his followers, is in essence the same as that used by P.W. Schmiedel in his selection of nine 'foundation-pillars for a truly scientific life of Jesus' at the turn of the century:[17] the sayings must be so striking or so embarrassing that no follower of Jesus would have dared to invent them.

This is the essential criterion, around which all others revolve. Thus Perrin's second main criterion, that of 'coherence', is stated as follows: 'Material from the earliest strata of the tradition may be accepted as authentic if it can be shown to cohere with material established as authentic by means of the criterion of dissimilarity.'[18] This criterion, though not explicitly formulated, has also been freely used by Bultmann. Thus he finds that Matthew 12:28 'can, in my view, claim the highest degree of authenticity which we can make for any saying of Jesus: it is full of that feeling of eschatological power which must have characterized the activity of Jesus.'[19] It is by the criterion of dissimilarity that the 'feeling of eschatological power' has been established as authentic; any saying which contains this feeling is therefore likely to be genuine.

Thirdly, Perrin rather cautiously advances the 'criterion of multiple attestation', *i.e.*, that a saying which occurs in several or all of the strata of tradition underlying the Gospels has more claim to authenticity than one which appears in only one stratum. With regard to individual sayings, this criterion can find only a limited application, since there are not many examples of sayings which occur in the same form in different strata: it is seldom that an evangelist, having recorded a saying from one source, finds it necessary to repeat it from a different source in almost the same words. It is *themes* of teaching, not individual sayings, which can usually be traced in the different strata, and it is to themes rather than to specific sayings that Perrin proposes to apply the criterion of multiple attestation. Even so, he uses it only to confirm what has already been isolated by other criteria, and then with hesitation.[20] This hesitation is natural, since at some points this criterion is in conflict with the basic criterion of dissimilarity (*i.e.*, there are some sayings which reflect early Christian concerns, and yet are attested in more than one of the strata).[21]

Further subsidiary criteria are sometimes adduced, particularly those based on linguistic or cultural background. Thus a saying which shows the idiom of Aramaic, particularly Aramaic poetry, is regarded as more likely to be authentic.[22] Similarly, a saying which reflects the environment of Palestine, particularly the features of life in the Galilean countryside, has a higher claim to be accepted as a saying of Jesus. But these criteria must be used with caution. Jesus had no monopoly of the Aramaic language; Aramaic continued in use in the church throughout the period of the synoptic tradition and well beyond; not to mention the early growth of the Syriac church.[23] Many people besides Jesus could have originated Christian sayings with an Aramaic flavour and a Palestinian background. These features by themselves may indicate that a saying is Palestinian in origin, but not necessarily that it comes from Jesus. Thus in practice these criteria tend to be used only negatively, to exclude any saying which betrays a *Greek* background. One specific application of this negative use is to treat as unauthentic sayings which quote or allude to the LXX form of an Old Testament text; such sayings are presumed to originate in a Hellenistic milieu.[24]

Thus the essential criterion is that of dissimilarity. All others are extensions of it, or are used only to check and confirm its findings. If anyone else in the world of the New Testament could have said the saying in question, it cannot be taken as a saying of Jesus.

3. SOME CRITICISMS OF THE CRITERIA[25]

The first criticism is simply to repeat the point already made, that these criteria depend for their validity entirely on the sceptical assumptions outlined above. If you believe, however, that the tradition is authentic unless there is evidence to the contrary, then these criteria lose their point. Their aim is to salvage from a mass of suspect material a few genuine sayings. If you do not suspect the material, no salvage operation is necessary, or even possible. The criterion of dissimilarity is a counsel of despair, as Perrin's assessment of its validity makes clear: 'Of course, it is limited in scope—by definition it will exclude all teaching in which Jesus may have been at one with Judaism or the early Church at one with him. But the brutal fact of the matter is that we have no choice. There simply is no other starting-point that takes seriously enough the radical view of the nature of the sources which the results of contemporary research are forcing upon us.'[26] All well and good, if you find these 'results of contemporary research' convincing. If you do not, you have no need of such a last-ditch defence.

Perrin's words just quoted lead to the second criticism, that this criterion will by definition exclude any saying in which Jesus agreed with his contemporaries, and, still more improbably, any teaching of Jesus which the Christian church may have found valuable and preserved! R.H. Fuller grudgingly admits what to many would seem self-evident: 'On some points Jesus *could* have agreed with the post-Easter church. . . . Jesus might also have quoted or used with approval Rabbinic teaching.'[27] Yet this criterion excludes any such teaching. It presupposes a completely eccentric Jesus who took nothing from his Jewish environment, and a church which in a single generation had completely cut loose from its Master's teaching.

The immediate answer to this criticism, of course, is that the aim of the criterion of dissimilarity is to isolate those sayings which are pretty certainly authentic, to produce a reliable corpus of sayings, however minimal, which really are the teaching of Jesus himself. In so doing, we may dismiss much that was in fact Jesus' teaching, but which we cannot now prove to be so. This is a pity, but 'the brutal fact of the matter is that we have no choice'. This criterion will lead us to *some* authentic teaching of Jesus, however much may be sacrificed by the way.

But it will be only *some* authentic teaching of Jesus. And, by definition, it will be that part of Jesus' authentic teaching which his followers felt able to ignore. It will certainly not be the essential teaching of Jesus, the message on which his church was founded. It will consist of a few extraordinary sayings and ideas which failed to take root among his followers. To say that in this small corpus of teaching we have the *characteristic* emphases of Jesus' ministry is surely absurd, unless we have reason to believe that there was no continuity between the teaching of Jesus and early Christian theology, and not even the most radical sceptic would dare to assert that.[28]

If the criterion of dissimilarity were used only to confirm the authenticity of these few unusual sayings, we could have no quarrel with it. But it is not so innocuously used, for the presumption is that sayings which do not pass this test are not authentic. They do not enshrine the characteristic emphases of Jesus. In other words, *the criterion is used not only as a principle of validation, but also as a principle of exclusion.* Sayings which enshrine later Christian emphases are pronounced secondary in origin. If the church believed it, Jesus did not say it; it does not correspond to Jesus' characteristic teaching, which is, by definition, different from that of the church.

But *the criterion of dissimilarity has no right to pronounce any saying unauthentic.* It can point out that a saying *could* have come from the early church, but it can never prove that it *did*, unless it is agreed that the church never accepted and repeated what Jesus taught.

So the criterion of dissimilarity, and its companion the criterion of coherence, run the grave risk of exceeding their authority, and setting up as the characteristic emphases of Jesus' ministry a few eccentric themes. The result is, of course, a truncated and unbalanced portrait of Jesus, at best a half-truth. If this half-truth is taken to be the whole truth about Jesus, and sayings which do not tally with it are rejected, there is little hope of coming anywhere near to the historical Jesus.[29]

In fact the whole argument is circular. To discover what the Jesus of history really taught, criteria are adopted which *assume* that the theology of the early church cannot be the authentic teaching of Jesus. Not surprisingly, it is concluded that the early church has completely reinterpreted what Jesus said, and we can now have only the most shadowy idea of his teaching. But just suppose for a moment that the Christian church accepted, preserved, and repeated their Master's teaching (surely not the most improbably supposition); in that case the criterion of dissimilarity, as a principle of *exclusion*, breaks down, our knowledge of the teaching of Jesus is vastly enlarged, and a sceptical verdict on its authenticity is no longer necessary. Your conclusion depends on your starting-point. If you start as a sceptic, you end as a sceptic. But that is no reason for us all to become sceptics.

To see these criteria in operation is to realize that for all the vaunted objectivity of this approach, a rigid observance of the criteria gives way in practice to more subjective factors. For instance, Perrin declares Mark 2:21, 22 authentic because of a 'quality of freshness and of acute and sympathetic observation of Palestinian peasant life which we may claim is characteristic of Jesus'.[30] Surely a strict application of the criterion of dissimilarity would have condemned this very feature as clearly marking the saying as Jewish popular teaching: what is there here that any first-century Jew could not have said? Similarly, Käsemann pronounces the first, second, and fourth antitheses of Matthew 5 certainly authentic because of the 'unheard-of implication of the saying'[31] ('but *I* say to you'). But surely the early church (and Matthew in particular) was very anxious to establish the originality and authority of Jesus over against the scribes, so this formula could also be ascribed to early Christian polemic! By thus playing off one half of the criterion of dissimilarity against the other, it would be possible to exclude practically every saying of Jesus. Which ones are in fact excluded depends much more on the preference of the individual scholar than on any objective use of the criteria.

Thus Perrin argues for the authenticity of Jesus' teaching on the kingdom of God on the ground of differences in terminology between the synoptic Gospels and the rest of the New Testament, including 'the obvious point that the term itself is very frequently to be found in the synoptic tradition and comparatively infrequently outside it'. He concludes, very properly, that 'usages of Kingdom of God characteristic of the teaching of Jesus and not of the early

Church live on in the synoptic tradition'.[32] Quite so, but if the same arguments are applied to the use of the term 'Son of man', we shall have an even stronger case for concluding that the synoptic Gospels preserve usages characteristic of Jesus; in other words, that Jesus spoke of himself as the Son of man, destined to suffer and to reign in eschatological glory. But that is a conclusion which no respectable Bultmannian, certainly not Perrin himself, would wish to arrive at. We look in vain for a parallel use of the criterion of dissimilarity at that point.*

Conversely, Perrin concludes that Jesus could not have spoken of the coming of the Son of man, because no such concept existed in Jewish thought to be referred to.[33] But surely by the criterion of dissimilarity the absence of the idea from Judaism should mark it as authentic rather than otherwise. At this point Jesus is denied an original development of thought which is freely granted to the early church, while at other more congenial points such originality is taken as a mark of genuineness. This is hardly an objective use of the criteria. Its rationale is 'Heads I win, tails you lose'.[34]

It is truly astonishing to see the sovereign certainty with which Bultmann, for all his scepticism about our knowing much about the historical Jesus, is able to pronounce on what Jesus could or could not have said, what is characteristic of Jesus, and what is clearly secondary. He has drawn up a mental picture of 'the distinctive eschatological temper which characterized the preaching of Jesus', and tailors the tradition accordingly.[35] Perrin's account of Bultmann's use of the criterion of coherence contains the very revealing remark that in his book *Jesus* Bultmann utilizes not only the sayings isolated as authentic in his *History of the Synoptic Tradition*, but also 'any saying from the earliest stratum of the tradition which expresses something he has previously determined to be characteristic of the teaching of Jesus'.[36] The same comment could be made on many of Bultmann's followers: when they have worked out and applied their criteria, in the last analysis what determines whether a saying is genuine is whether it fits what 'he has previously deter-

---

*Incidentally, the criterion of multiple attestation would yield similar results, as 'Son of man' sayings are scattered indiscriminately through the various strata of the synoptic (and Johannine) tradition.

mined to be characteristic of the teaching of Jesus'. R.P.C. Hanson notices the different estimates of what is original given by different scholars, and concludes: 'There is, one suspects, no particular reason for choosing one estimate in preference to another, for it is crystal clear that what determines each scholar's choice is the presupposition about the *Sitz-im-leben*, the Church, and about the person of Jesus himself which each brings to the material.'[37]

We have wandered a little from the criteria of authenticity, but the essential criticism may be summarized as follows. These criteria may quite properly be used *positively*, to establish for the benefit of those inclined to be sceptical that certain sayings, motifs, and stylistic traits are derived from Jesus.[38] But that is the limit. It does not follow that other teaching is not characteristic of Jesus, nor does it follow that the aspects so isolated are central to what Jesus actually taught. It is not legitimate to use these criteria to isolate a supposed characteristic emphasis in Jesus' teaching to which all authentic sayings must conform; they should not be used *negatively* to exclude any saying.

4. THE HISTORICIST REACTION

H.E.W. Turner, declaring himself a 'historicist'* as opposed to the 'interpretative' school of Bultmann (the conflict between these two basic presuppositions being the main theme of his book, *Historicity and the Gospels*[39]), addresses himself to the criterion of dissimilarity, and attempts to disarm it by extending its scope to make it much more generously inclusive. Thus 'where there is an overlap of interest between the Gospels and the early Church' the sayings may still be treated as authentic if there is 'a marked difference in the scale of treatment', *i.e.*, if what bulks large in later Christian concern appears only incidentally in the teaching of Jesus, or vice

---

*I shall use Turner's word in this essay, for want of a better label, to denote those who start from the presumption that the Gospel writers intended to preserve the actual facts and the authentic teaching of Jesus, and that the Gospels may therefore be taken as a reliable guide to what Jesus said and did except where there is clear evidence to the contrary. The word 'conservative' is too narrow, and triggers off unnecessary emotional reactions; 'moderate' seems too wide and rather pompous. 'Historicist', for all its old-fashioned ring, seems the most objective word available. It should not, of course, be taken to imply that historical reporting was the *only* purpose of the evangelists, *i.e.*, that they wrote 'neutral' history.

versa. Then Turner lists various characteristics of Jesus' 'style of life and teaching' as 'an authoritative Person . . . teacher, healer, controversialist, and sufferer', and various formal characteristics, such as the use of parables, arguments *a fortiori*, 'Abba', 'Amen, I say to you', *etc.* This is really just a form of the criterion of coherence. In fact, all Turner's modifications of the criteria could be paralleled in the writings of convinced Bultmannians. So also when Turner asserts in conclusion that 'the closer the approximation of a passage in the Gospels to the style and idiom of contemporary Aramaic, the greater the presumption of authenticity', he is in good Bultmannian company. Thus while Turner tries to apply the Bultmannian criteria as generously as possible, the essential criteria remain unaltered, and, more important, so also does the assumption that the burden of proof rests upon the claim to authenticity. Turner, for all his avowed 'historicism', still operates on the presuppositions of the 'interpretative', sceptical school. He has not broken out of the charmed circle.

An attempt to shift the burden of proof with regard to at least some sayings attributed to Jesus is made in a recent short article by H.K. McArthur.[40] He proposes to take the criterion of multiple attestation as the starting-point. Assuming (rather boldly, one may well think) a four-source theory of synoptic origins, he proposes to treat as probably authentic any saying or theme which is found in three or four of the sources, but as probably unauthentic any saying or theme which occurs in only one or two of them. Thus for material in several sources the burden of proof is on the sceptic, but for material in only one or two it is on those who claim authenticity, and here the criteria of dissimilarity and coherence will come into play. This compromise solution is not likely to please many. It is incredibly mechanical in its view of synoptic origins: even if one believes in four watertight sources, by what logic must authentic sayings be preserved in all or most of them, while a saying omitted from two or three must be a secondary creation? It is good to see the sceptical assumption concerning the burden of proof challenged at all, but one could wish for a more realistic assessment of the synoptic tradition to replace it.

A more consistently historicist reaction to the sceptical challenge is not to tinker with the criteria to make them more elastic, nor to play off one criterion against the others, but to reject outright the burden of proof, and to say boldly that you propose to treat the sayings attributed to Jesus as authentic unless there is clear reason to do otherwise.[41] Thus J. Jeremias concludes that the linguistic and stylistic evidence in the synoptic Gospels 'shows so much faithfulness and such respect towards the tradition of the sayings of Jesus that we are justified in drawing up the following principle of method: In the Synoptic tradition it is the inauthenticity, and not the authenticity, of the sayings of Jesus that must be demonstrated'.[42] Similarly G.E. Ladd, in the name of what he calls 'Biblical Realism', proposes 'to interpret the Gospels as they stand as credible reports of Jesus and his preaching'.[43]

This of course is what orthodox Christians have always done, and what conservative scholars regularly do. They seldom bother to argue the case. If Luke says that Jesus said it, then they do not question that it was Jesus, not Luke or some intermediate agent who said it. But the question we must face is whether this simple historicism is critically defensible. Is it not just another example of the notorious prowess of conservative Christians at burying their heads in the sand?

It must first be made quite clear that this approach rests on an *assumption*, the assumption that the Gospel tradition was a reliable medium for preserving what Jesus actually said, that the early church did see some difference between what Jesus said on earth and what they themselves might like to add to his teaching, and that they were concerned to preserve the former as the uniquely authoritative *verba Christi*. It *is* an assumption. But so also is the sceptical axiom that historicity and authenticity were no concern of the early Christians, and that there was no distinction between Jesus teaching on earth and the risen Christ speaking through his church. Both these views are assumptions, and our task is not to beat the drum of our own assumption so loudly that the opposition cannot be heard, but to examine the assumptions to see which accords most closely with what may be discovered of the historical reality.

We all operate within our own set of assumptions, and we are not easily shaken out of them. This applies to the sceptic as much as to the historicist, and it is nothing to be ashamed of. We must all start somewhere. If someone else comes to the subject with a different set of assumptions, I am not being irresponsible if I refuse to operate on his assumptions; nor is he entitled to abuse me (or I him) because our starting-points differ. What we must both do is to examine our assumptions in the light of the available evidence. And it must be admitted that here conservative scholarship has not been conspicuously active. The Bultmannian school has expended a great deal of energy on the study of tradition in order to justify its basic assumption of a freely inventive sayings-tradition, while conservatives have, with some honourable exceptions, been content to cry 'Sceptic!' and to press on regardless with the more congenial tasks of exegesis and application. If we can fairly be called obscurantists, it is not because we make assumptions, but because we have been slow to examine and justify them.

If, then, I am to be able with a good critical conscience to reject the burden of proof, I must be able to show that my case rests on a historically defensible and realistic assessment of the nature of the synoptic tradition. To this we now turn, though of course only in the barest outline.

5. THE NATURE OF THE CHRISTIAN SAYINGS-TRADITION
In a full attempt to justify an optimistic estimate of the reliability of the tradition, we would need to set out and evaluate all the many debating-points which have been made against a radical, Bultmannian form criticism. Valuable as this exercise would surely be, space forbids it here. We must content ourselves with listing some of the main arguments, if only to show that the conservative position has not entirely gone by default. The following arguments occur in many critiques of Bultmannism:[44]

(i) The very short period (only one generation) between Jesus and the writing of the Gospels does not give time for an elaborate modification of the tradition.

(ii) Analogies drawn from folk-literature, epics, sagas, and fairy-tales are irrelevant to the milieu of Palestinian Judaism within which the synoptic tradition evolved.

(iii) It is individuals, not communities, who produce creative ideas.[45]

(iv) The 'laws of tradition' assumed by form critics, which specify how sayings will be altered in transmission, are not borne out by the evidence.[46]

(v) The presence in the church of those who actually saw and heard Jesus would exercise a restraining influence on modifications of the tradition.[47]

(vi) Where the synoptic writers can be checked against independent records (particularly Luke in Acts), they generally emerge as careful and accurate in their historical references.

(vii) It is wrong to assume that the tradition was purely oral.[48]

(viii) Radical form criticism will allow as genuine sayings of Jesus only basic simple sentences—he was apparently incapable of any complexity of thought or care in composition, any word of explanation or development of a theme, all of which are freely credited to his followers.

(ix) The unity of the teaching of Jesus as the Synoptics present it suggests that it is the product of one mind, not of a variegated creative tradition.[49]

(x) The whole method is circular: it uses the Gospel materials to reconstruct the situation and concerns of the early church, and then uses this reconstruction to explain the origin of the Gospel materials.[50]

(xi) It is not immediately apparent why a saying which is relevant to the concerns of, say, AD 60 should necessarily have been *coined* then.

(xii) In fact, Bultmann and his followers seldom justify their pronouncements on authenticity, but decree with sublime assurance what Jesus could and could not have said, what was and was not of concern to the apostolic church.[51]

These points, which are frequently made, are not all of equal force; but a bare recitation of them at least indicates that it is not pure obscurantism which leads some scholars to question the whole radical approach to the synoptic tradition.

Valuable as it would be to indulge in a fuller exploration of these points, we must confine ourselves now to the more basic assumptions of the sceptical approach which we outlined in section 1. It is these assumptions which determine the placing of the burden of proof. If they are valid, the arguments just listed cannot alter the point of departure—that the tradition is guilty until proved innocent—even though these arguments may modify the methods used and the results obtained.

First, we shall deal with the distinction between *Historie* and *Geschichte*, and with the often repeated assertions that the church's concern for the latter involves an almost complete lack of interest in the former, that the Gospels give us no biography of Jesus, and that what Jesus actually said and did on earth was not the concern of their writers.

We may note first that the assumption that an ideological purpose in writing rules out a concern for factual accuracy is not consistent with the recognized canons of historiography, either ancient or modern. Not only does it lack any logical force (why *should* a writer of kerygmatic history be unconcerned whether his history is factual of not?); it does not tally with what may be discovered of the way responsible historians operated in the ancient world[52] and the way they operate today. If a Gibbon or a Churchill is capable of writing 'good history' with an axe to grind, why should not a Mark or a Luke? When J.M. Robinson states that 'we have moved beyond the initial conclusion that the kerygmatized Gospels are incompatible with the historian's objectives, to the recognition that they in their way are doing something similar to what the modern historian in his way would like to do',[53] one could wish this were true of all Gospel critics. But sadly it is not. The evangelists are still too often placed in a special category, as propagandists who have no concern for factual accuracy.[54]

Add to this the sheer improbability of the view that a religious community which had found Jesus a Saviour and Leader worthy of their complete allegiance should not be interested in knowing what that Leader was really like, what he really said and what he really did. How many religious communities have so little concern for the details of their founder's life and teaching, even though they may regard that founder as no more than a fallible human teacher? Particularly in the milieu of Palestinian Judaism (where not only a rabbi's words but his significant actions as well were scrupulously memorized and passed on for the instruction of his followers), could the followers of Jesus have been blithely unconcerned about whether he said the words attributed to him or not?

Such a view is so improbable as to require very strong evidence to support it. Unfortunately, it is generally advanced not on the basis of evidence, but of Bultmann's conviction 'that the gospels as such are necessarily concerned with only one historical fact: the "that-ness" of Jesus and his cross. . . . Beyond this the synoptic gospels themselves are uninterested in the historical element as such'.[55] On the basis of this dogma we are asked to believe that the early Christians did not enquire about the facts of Jesus' life and teaching, that when they preached Christ as Saviour no-one challenged them to back up their message with these facts, and that their converts were content to worship and follow Jesus without knowing what he was really like and what he himself taught. Compare with this re-construction Luke's avowed purpose in writing for Theophilus, to provide, by means of careful research into the eye-witness tradition and the written accounts, the accurate facts (*asphaleia*) on which his catechetical instruction had been based,[56] and we may well ask who's kidding whom. Of course we are not dealing with biographies in the full modern sense, but we *are* dealing with 'a wholly natural and wholly unquenchable curiosity'[57] about what Jesus taught and did, and it is surely not improbable that *a* purpose of the Gospels (some scholars would say *the* main purpose[58]) is to satisfy this curi-osity, not with pious fiction, but with as accurate an account of the historical reality as the tradition made available to them.[59]

But what sort of material *did* the tradition make available to the evangelists? Did it bear any relation to what Jesus actually said (and our concern here will be with only the *sayings*-tradition), or was the tradition so freely inventive as to give evidence only of what a later generation thought the Christ of their faith would have said? It is on this question of the alleged 'freedom' of the tradition that we must now concentrate.

Probably the most ambitious attempt to defend the historical reliability of the Christian tradition is that of Riesenfeld and Ger-hardsson,[60] who argue for a method similar to the rigid memoriza-tion and verbatim transmission in the rabbinic schools. The analogy is not new,[61] but no-one had previously argued the case on the basis of so full an account of the rabbinic technique as Gerhardsson. Few scholars follow Gerhardsson all the way. A common critical reaction is to compliment Gerhardsson rather patronizingly on his handling of the rabbinic material,[62] but to dismiss as far-fetched his attempt to trace similar techniques in the Christian church. Until Gerhardsson applies his results in detail to the synoptic Gospels (as he apparently still intends to do) we shall not know how he will meet this criticism. Certainly the variations within the synoptic tradition make it patently obvious that they are *not* reproducing sayings verbatim, and that they exercise more selectivity in what they record than a rabbinic student could do. Gerhardsson has, apparently, exaggerated his case.

But an exaggerated case is not necessarily wholly false, as is too often assumed. What Gerhardsson has done is to call our attention to the milieu in which the Christian church began its life, that of Palestinian Judaism. The early Christians may not have copied every detail of the rigid technique of transmission in the scribal schools, with their use of trained memorizers of tradition and their insistence on verbal accuracy, but if we want an analogy for the nature of the early Christian tradition it would seem *a priori* more likely that we shall find it in this milieu than in Greek and oriental folk-literature.[63] The historical context in which the church originated places the presumption in favour of an accurate transmission of sayings-material unless there is evidence to the contrary. Jesus' *teaching* was new, certainly, but this does not demand a new *method* of teaching or of transmission; men brought up in Palestinian Judaism would not without good cause develop new and unrelated ideas and techniques of religious tradition.

W.D. Davies, one of the leading authorities on this subject, has made several penetrating criticisms of Gerhardsson's thesis, but concludes with an essentially positive verdict: 'We can no longer doubt that the process whereby the Christian tradition was transmitted is to be largely understood in the light of Pharisaic usage in dealing with Oral Tradition.'[64] It is, Davies concludes, 'far more historically probable and reasonably credible, over against the scepticism of much form-criticism, that in the Gospels we are within hearing of the authentic voice and within sight of the authentic activity of Jesus of Nazareth, however much muffled and obscured these may be by the process of transmission.'[65]

But it is not enough to make this point in the abstract, for the sceptic will not be slow to reply that there *is* evidence to the contrary and that the Gospels display a very considerable freedom in their handling of the sayings which is far removed from rabbinic literalism.[66]

But just what *does* the evidence indicate? Clearly the evangelists (and presumably the same will apply to the earlier transmitters of the tradition) felt free to select such of the material as was suitable to their purpose in writing, and to omit other sayings. Clearly, they rearranged this material into larger units. Clearly too, they were not aiming at exact verbatim reporting.* The verbal differences between two evangelists' record of what is apparently the same saying are evidence that it was the meaning rather than a particular form of words which was their main concern: they were apparently quite prepared to adapt the wording to bring out more clearly the particular bearing of a saying on the theological or practical issues of their own time. All this can be ascertained by an hour or two with a Gospel synopsis, and few scholars are likely to quarrel with it. But where is the evidence that the evangelists, or earlier transmitters of the material, felt free to *invent* sayings-material and attribute it to Jesus? This is a very different activity from selection and adaptation of received tradition, as we hope to make clear in the next section. To show that the early Christians were prepared to select and adapt is *not* to show that they also invented. Where is the *evidence* for this?

I stress the need for evidence because what we find in most sceptical writing is an *assertion* that the early church did not distinguish between what Jesus said on earth and what the risen Christ was saying through the church; an *assertion* that what is relevant to the needs of the apostolic church must be presumed to owe its origin to that church; an *assertion* (or more often an unexpressed

---

*It is suggested below (p. 128 f.) that the use of inverted commas in modern translations of the Bible may convey a misleading impression. To us, inverted commas imply a verbatim quotation, but it is questionable whether the formula 'Jesus said . . .' in the Gospels need have such an implication.

assumption) that a theological purpose in writing excludes a concern for historical accuracy and authenticity. Assertions without evidence are hard to refute, except by *asserting* even more loudly that you find them highly improbable. But what is the *evidence*?

I dare to suggest that, in addition to the *assertion* made above that the milieu of Palestinian Judaism is the most probable analogy for early Christian tradition (*mutatis mutandis*), there is also *evidence* that, for all their freedom in selecting, rearranging and adapting the wording of sayings to suit their own purpose, the early Christians *were* concerned to preserve essentially what Jesus said, because he said it. The following points may be noted:

a. The stylistic form of Jesus' sayings Very many of the sayings of Jesus in the synoptic Gospels fall into a poetic or otherwise easily memorizable form,[67] the sort of form one might expect to find in sayings intended to be carefully remembered and preserved. It is not apparent by what logic these characteristics are attributed to early Christian catechesis rather than to the one who was recognized as 'the Teacher' *par excellence*. It is interesting that, as M. Black has shown,[68] these poetic features are largely confined to the *sayings* element in the synoptic tradition. Moreover, certain markedly characteristic turns of phrase and features of style recur constantly in the sayings of Jesus, and hardly ever elsewhere; J. Jeremias begins his work on *The Proclamation of Jesus* with a detailed study of several such features, which he finds to be either peculiar to or particularly characteristic of the teaching of Jesus, and which he regards as sufficient to justify a presumption in favour of the authenticity of the synoptic tradition of the words of Jesus.[69]

b. The terminology of tradition Many scholars have commented on the use, particularly by Paul, of such terms as *paralambanein, paradidonai* and *paradosis* to denote those truths which he has received, either from the Lord or from men, and has passed on to his converts.[70] This terminology is parallel to that used in the rabbinic schools for the handing on of the authoritative tradition in the meticulous manner described by Gerhardsson. If Paul, a Pharisaic Jew, can use such language, this suggests that there was in the Christian church a concept analogous to the Jewish idea of transmission.[71]

c. The function of the apostles That the apostles were recognized as the guardians and transmitters of an authoritative tradition about Jesus is suggested not only by Paul's 'questioning' of Peter, and by his eagerness to gain the apostolic approval of his teaching (Gal. 1:18; 2:2-10), but also by the requirement that an apostle must be an eye-witness of the ministry and resurrection of Jesus (Acts 1:21, 22; *cf.* 1 Cor. 9:1), and by the concentration of the apostles on *didachē* (Acts 2:42) and *diakonia tou logou* (Acts 6:2,4). As Cullmann puts it in his important study of tradition, 'The *tanna* of the Jews is replaced by the *apostolos* of Christ.'[72]* It may also be relevant to remember Jesus' remarkable concentration during his ministry on the private instruction of his closest disciples, preparing them for their future role.

d. Respect for the sayings of Jesus   In 1 Corinthians 7 Paul makes a clear distinction between his own instructions and the words of *ho kyrios* (1 Cor. 7:8, 10, 12, 25, 40); his own words are authoritative (verses 25,40), but those of the Lord are on a higher plane. Where Paul has no saying of Jesus to quote, he does not presume to invent one.[73] The Epistles contain few sayings of Jesus, certainly not the free invention of a saying for every contemporary need as some Gospel criticism might lead us to expect. Conversely, T.W. Manson has pointed out that none of the sayings attributed to Jesus in the Gospels is known to have been culled from the Pauline Letters, some of which would have been available for the evangelists to use if they wished.[74] The words of Jesus are treated as *sui generis*.[75]

e. Dissimilarity of interests   We may appeal at this point to the criterion of dissimilarity. We shall not use it now in the illegitimate way criticized above; *i.e.* to *eliminate* sayings which display a similarity to either Jewish or Christian interests. Rather, we shall use it in a positive way to show that the Gospels do in fact preserve a good deal of material which is scarcely relevant to the needs of the church in AD 50 to 60 (so far as we can reconstruct those needs from Acts and the Pauline Letters), and that they fail to include material which would be relevant to those needs. In other words, the original *Sitz im Leben* of a good part of the synoptic tradition is in fact more plausibly found in the ministry of Jesus than in the concerns of the

---

*The *Tannaim* were the authoritative rabbinic teachers of the first two centuries AD, whose teaching was eventually gathered into the Mishnah.

apostolic church.[76] Used positively, to show that the synoptic Gospels *are* concerned with the preservation of the teaching of Jesus for its own sake, this criterion is not open to the criticisms levelled above against its use as a criterion of *exclusion.*[77]

Scholars have noted on the one hand the complete lack of material in the Gospels on such a burning issue of the apostolic church as circumcision, or the charismatic gifts which loomed so large in some of Paul's churches. Little is included on baptism, the Gentile mission, the food laws, or church/state relations, and that little refers to the concerns of the period of Jesus' ministry and not to the form in which these issues confronted the church thirty years later.[78] On the other hand, the synoptic Gospels abound in teaching on the Son of man and the kingdom of God (which were apparently little stressed in the apostolic church) and give prominence to Jesus' controversies with the Pharisees on Sabbath observance and the Corban question, which do not seem to have been live issues at a later period. The list could be extended,[79] but the point is that a positive use of the criterion of dissimilarity will show that, if the synoptic Gospels were compiled with a view only to answering contemporary questions and expressing contemporary theology, they were singularly inept attempts. In fact, this positive use will show that the presumption must be that their aim was to preserve what Jesus said and did, unless there is specific evidence to the contrary.

Our conclusion from all this is that while it is undeniable that the evangelists and their predecessors adapted, selected, and reshaped the material which came down to them, there is no reason to extend this 'freedom' to include the *creation* of new sayings attributed to Jesus; that in fact such evidence as we have points decisively the other way, to a respect for the sayings of Jesus as such which was sufficient to prevent any of his followers attributing their own teaching to him. If the Christian church did not share the rabbinic concern for verbatim transmission and reproduction of the tradition, there is every reason to believe that they did share the Jewish respect for the authoritative teaching of the Master. The sceptical assumption, repeated so often that it has become an axiom, that the early church saw no difference between what Jesus said on earth and what the risen Christ said through his church, is not only very improbable, given the milieu of Palestinian Judaism, but is contrary to such evidence as the New Testament provides.[80]

We thus conclude that to reject the burden of proof which the sceptic so confidently casts upon the historicist is not an act of blind obscurantism, but is the most responsible attitude to the evidence. We may still with a good conscience regard the synoptic tradition as intended to preserve the authentic teaching of Jesus, however much adapted and reshaped to the evangelist's purpose. We may count it innocent until proved guilty.

6. GUIDELINES FOR A HISTORICIST APPROACH TO THE QUESTION OF AUTHENTICITY

So far I have been arguing defensively, to show that we do have a right to adopt a historicist position. My concern in this final section is to show how we may advance from this position, once vindicated, to a study of the question of authenticity.

The essential question we must ask ourselves is: What were the evangelists trying to do? Too often the conservative student of the Gospels assumes that the answer is that they were trying to reproduce verbatim exactly what Jesus said, a correct transcription of the *ipsissima verba*, a sort of first-century Hansard.

It does not take much thought to see that this cannot be right. To begin with, our Gospels are in Greek, and most scholars agree that Jesus normally spoke in Aramaic.[81] What we have, therefore, is a translation, and no translation can be exact. This is perhaps too obvious to be mentioned, but it is not always remembered in discussions about authenticity. Whatever we have in the Gospels, it cannot be the *ipsissima verba Jesu*, unless Jesus spoke in Greek.

But this is only the beginning. Where one evangelist draws his material from another, he is clearly not aiming to reproduce it exactly. In the majority of cases the wording is altered, sometimes slightly, often quite considerably. The order and grouping of the sayings also undergoes quite large-scale modification. And if the evangelists were prepared to treat sayings derived from one another with this degree of freedom, presumably they were no more literalistic in their treatment of material derived from other sources, oral or written. In short, and again the point is old and obvious, there is every sign of a considerable fluidity in the order and wording of the sayings of Jesus in the synoptic tradition. We seem much further from the *ipsissima verba* than the mere fact of translation demands.

But it is here that the historicist must start drawing the line. He may freely admit that there are variations in the order and wording of the sayings—indeed he *must* admit it. But he must challenge the next step that scholars frequently make, which is to infer that the tradition was as free in invention as in adaptation, and that therefore we have to all intents and purposes lost sight of the authentic teaching of Jesus. This step is a *non sequitur*. As we have argued in the previous section, to say that the evangelist felt free to select and adapt the sayings of Jesus which he received from the tradition is not to say that he did not care whether Jesus said it or not, or that the evangelist made no distinction between the words of Jesus and other Christian teaching. It would be perfectly possible for the evangelists to be selective and relatively free in adapting the wording to their purpose, while at the same time preserving the essential sense of the sayings and refraining from adding any new sayings to the tradition.

Whoever doubts this would be well advised to listen to some contemporary evangelical expository preaching. The preacher's aim is to expound the Bible: it is his sole authority; its words are his sole source of teaching. But it is seldom that his quotations from the Bible will be verbatim. Sometimes he will quote freely from memory (and thus not strictly verbatim). Nobody objects to this, so long as he is reproducing the meaning of the text in other words. Sometimes he will summarize or paraphrase a passage from the Bible using indirect speech: 'Jesus taught that it is impossible to be loyal to two competing principles at once: a love for God must weaken a man's concern for material possessions, and vice versa.' His congregation would not expect to be able to look up Matthew 6:24 and find those exact words, but they would not therefore accuse him of distorting the teaching of Jesus. Sometimes he will deliberately expand and adapt the wording to make clear the contemporary application of a saying: 'Jesus said, "Let your light so shine out in the darkness of this materialistic twentieth-century world that those who are groping for truth may see the quality of your lives and recognize that your God is real." '

That may not be every preacher's style; but my point is that neither the preacher nor his congregation would regard such paraphrasing, even from a deliberate theological or apologetic motive, as betraying any lack of respect for the authority of the words of Scripture. It is because he believes that the Bible has authority for his hearers that he takes the trouble to adapt its wording so that they cannot miss the application. But the fact that he is selective in his use of Scripture and free in adapting its wording does not mean that he would be prepared to coin new teaching of his own and preface it by the words 'Jesus said'. Still less does it mean that he would take an acceptable saying of Muhammad, or even of John Wesley, and present it to his congregation as the words of Scripture.

This extended analogy is intended to show that freedom in handling the wording of sayings is not incompatible with an exclusive respect for the authority of those sayings and a desire to preserve and convey the sense of the original. An adapter is not necessarily an inventor. A parallel case would be the New Testament treatment of quotations from the Old Testament. The New Testament writers are freer than most of us would dare to be in their adaptation of the wording to bring out their intended application, but there is no doubt about their unqualified acceptance of the authority of the original, and no suggestion of their having invented sayings to suit their purpose and attributed them to the Old Testament. Why should the evangelists not have handled the tradition of the sayings of Jesus in much the same way? The Aramaic Targums on the Old Testament provide a further example of willingness to paraphrase quite freely despite the unique authority accorded to the original.[82] In fact, as R.H. Gundry points out, 'neither the historian in the Graeco-Latin classical tradition nor the Jewish targumist had the modern concept of the sacrosanctity of direct quotation. Rather, a certain freedom of interpretation and adaptation was expected in order to show one's grasp of the material, to bring out its inner meaning and significance, and to apply it to the subject at hand.'[83]

It is relevant here to note that we today make much more extensive use of reported speech than did the New Testament writers. Where we would say 'Jesus taught that . . .', and continue with a free paraphrase of his actual words, the evangelist would be much more likely to put that same paraphrase into direct speech. To us, direct speech generally implies exact reproduction of the *ipsissima verba*, and any less exact reproduction of the original we would put into reported speech. The New Testament writer, however, is much more likely to use direct speech for both. The use of inverted commas in translations of the Gospels may lead us to expect, on the basis of our own conventions in reporting speech, a degree of verbatim accuracy which the writer did not intend. So many of the sayings which the Gospels introduce with 'Jesus said' may in fact be paraphrases. But that does not mean they are inventions.

G.E. Ladd well summarizes the situation as follows:

> The Gospels *do not intend to provide us with a record of the precise literal words of Jesus.* On the contrary, the Evangelists feel free to expand, to interpret, to paraphrase, to bring out the meaning they see in Jesus' words; and they do this by varying His reported words, not by a technical apparatus of footnotes. . . . These changes are made deliberately under the guidance of the Holy Spirit. . . . To label such variations 'errors' is to view the Gospels from a false perspective and to misunderstand what the Evangelists obviously intended to do, namely, to report accurately the substance of Jesus' teaching in meaningful terms to their readers, not to record His precise words in every instance.[84]

So the Gospels are not 'objective' records in the sense of detached reports of Jesus' exact words, like Hansard. They are preaching, teaching documents, documents of faith, committed to the message they proclaim. To make that message as clear as possible, they are prepared to paraphrase Jesus' sayings in a way that brings out the meaning and application of what he taught. This does not make them dishonest, careless, or unhistorical; it merely shows that the evangelists were communicators, not stenographers.

We can never, therefore, assume that we have the *ipsissima verba Jesu*. His sayings have been translated, and in many cases paraphrased to bring out the interpretation of the evangelist and/or some earlier transmitter of the tradition. But this fact does not place upon us the burden of proof when we claim that a saying is the authentic teaching of Jesus. Its exact wording may well have been altered in transmission, but we have seen good reason to believe that the original saying may be taken as having come from Jesus himself, preserved with a truly Jewish respect for the authority of the Master's words, but handled with the freedom of the preacher, who is convinced that he is dealing with the words of life, and spares no pains to get the message across. The burden of proof, we believe, rests on the sceptic.

This does not mean, however, that we have comfortably eliminated all need for critical enquiry, and may look down with a superior smile on those who still toil in the bondage of form criticism, redaction criticism, and all other forms of criticism. A presumption in favour of the authenticity of the tradition as a whole does not mean that no individual saying must be ever be questioned. It simply means that our point of departure will be different: instead of insisting that a saying must satisfy stringent criteria of authenticity, we shall demand positive evidence of *un*authenticity before we accept that a saying originates from a source other than Jesus.

What, for instance, of a saying such as Matthew 28:19b, the trinitarian formula for baptism, pronounced unauthentic by practically all non-conservative scholars, and uneasily avoided by not a few conservatives? Did Jesus pronounce the formula or not? (And note that this is all that is meant by 'authentic'; to pronounce a saying 'unauthentic' is not to label it unchristian or heretical!) If you start with the assumption of unauthenticity, you will be hard put to it to find any means of rescuing this saying. But what is the evidence *against* these words as deriving from Jesus?

The textual argument against Matthew 28: 19b, based on the fact that some (not all) of Eusebius' apparent quotations of this verse do not include the trinitarian formula, carries little weight in the absence of support from any manuscript or version. Textual evidence would, of course, be a strong reason for doubting a supposed saying of Jesus, and conservative scholars are not slow to recognize this line of evidence. Few would want to support Luke 9:55b, 56a, for example. But in Matthew 28:19 the text is not seriously in doubt.

The case against Matthew 28:19b rests on the fact that its trinitarian formula stands out as apparently more stereotyped than anything else in the New Testament. If Jesus pronounced this baptismal formula, why was baptism in Acts apparently in the name of Jesus alone? Why does Paul speak of baptism into Christ, not into the threefold name? Above all, if Jesus had so clearly stated the formula 'the Father, the Son, and the Holy Spirit', why do the New Testament writers seem to be groping towards a clear trinitarian doctrine, mentioning the three persons in every possible permutation of order, and only in John 14-16 achieving anything like a thought-out statement of the relationship of the three persons? The formula of Matthew 28:19b looks much more like the end-product of this doctrinal process than its starting-point.[85]

These are strong arguments. They proceed not from any dogmatic assumption of a freely creative tradition, but from an observation of the phenomena of the New Testament itself. On the basis of such arguments, a historicist, for all his conviction that the tradition is basically preservative and not inventive, might well conclude that these words are an exception to the rule and that the formula in question is the evangelist's theological expansion of what Jesus actually said.* There is no question, of course, of introducing any radically new teaching. Jesus' teaching during his ministry had made clear his own unique relationship with the Father, and the role of the Holy Spirit in continuing his work. It may be that after the resurrection this relationship of the three persons formed an important theme of the risen Christ's instruction of his disciples. This teaching, which was later crystallized into the formal trinitarian language of the early church, Matthew summarizes by using the formula which was by now familiar to his readers. The formula may not have been used as such by Jesus, but it represents what was implicit in his teaching.[86]

This one example—perhaps an extreme one—is intended to show that the conservative scholar is not excused from the effort of critical study, and cannot assume that a positive verdict on authenticity will be returned in every case. Not even the fidelity of the Christian sayings-tradition can be assumed to be a rule without exceptions. But they *will* be exceptions, not the rule. So if a negative verdict is

---

*This conclusion would apply, of course, only to the trinitarian formula of the second half of Mt. 28:19, not to the whole saying in which it occurs.

returned, it will be on the basis of tangible evidence, not of an un-questioned assumption about the nature of the tradition, or an *a priori* rejection of all that falls outside normal secular experience.

And that evidence will need to be such as to affect the substance of the saying concerned, not just its outer clothing. Words which suggest a Greek background, or echoes of the LXX text form of an Old Testament quotation, can be admitted as evidence against the authenticity of a saying only if they affect its essential sense and application. If they are simply part of the process of translation and adaptation to a Greek readership, they create no presumption against the authenticity of the underlying saying.[87]

It will be noticed that such a historicist approach does not dis-pense with the need for form-critical and redaction-critical study. We recognize that sayings were considerably reshaped in the course of transmission, and if we are to discover the original form of a say-ing, it will be largely by a form-critical method. Where we shall part company with much form-critical work is in assuming, when we have tried to reconstruct the original saying, that this original is what it claims to be, a saying of Jesus, not an early Christian crea-tion. We may well be critical of many of the assumptions and meth-ods which form critics have traditionally employed, such as the inex-orable 'laws of tradition' on which they rely, and which have in several cases been shown to be quite illusory.[88] But a careful, un-dogmatic form criticism should enable us to trace how a saying has been adapted from its original form as Jesus said it to its use in the Gospel.

Moreover, the recognition of this element of deliberate adapta-tion of the wording gives full scope for a redaction-critical study. Some conservative scholars are strangely reluctant to recognize that the evangelists were no less interpretative historians, men with a clear theological purpose, than the historical writers of the Old Testament. We must give full weight to their role as careful com-municators, men with a message. A study of the way they have handled the sayings of Jesus will throw light on what they believed and what they were concerned to get across. A presumption in favour of the authenticity of the underlying sayings in no way rules out such study if it is recognized that the wording and order of these authentic sayings have in many cases been altered, and that these alterations were not made by acident, but are deliberate and significant. Such adaptations provide quite sufficient material for a fruitful redaction criticism, without our needing to accept the assumption of many redaction critics that the evangelists or their predecessors also *invented* 'sayings of Jesus'.[89]*

The object of this essay, then, is to urge that the scholar is obliged to take the Gospels as he finds them. He must reconstruct their aims and methods from what the Gospels themselves indicate, and interpret them in accordance with their intention, rather than from a dogmatic presupposition that the evangelists were either freely creative or rigidly literalistic. As we have seen, the evidence of the Gospels suggests that, while the evangelists were prepared to adapt the order and wording of the sayings of Jesus to bring out a particular interpretation or application, their intention was to preserve the authentic teaching of Jesus, which they regarded as uniquely authoritative. Thus, while the final wording gives scope for a fruitful study to discover the theology and concerns of the evangelists and their intended readers, the presumption must be that the underlying sayings are the authentic teaching of Jesus.

---

*In fact it could well be suggested that little about redaction criticism is new except its name: generations of scholars, not least conservatives, have studied the particular interests of the evangelists (*e.g.* Luke's concern for women and foreigners, Matthew's interest in the fulfilment of prophecy, *etc.*). In so doing they have recognized the evangelists as individuals, each with different interests and convictions of their own, which the evangelists were concerned to stress in the way they presented the life and teaching of Jesus.

NOTES

[1] The basic text-book for this subject is still Bultmann's *The History of the Synoptic Tradition*[2] (1921; Blackwell, 1968). Bultmann's detailed discussion of texts remains the foundation of later work within his school.

[2] See G.E. Ladd, *The New Testament and Criticism* (Hodder & Stoughton, 1970) for a useful conservative evaluation of the various critical disciplines which gives due weight to their positive value as well as to their abuse in some circles. See also pp. 132 f. of the present essay.

[3] On *Historie* and *Geschichte* cf. A. Richardson, *History: Sacred and Profane* (SCM Press, 1964), pp. 154 ff.

[4] *What is Redaction Criticism?* (SPCK, 1970), p. 78; *idem, Rediscovering the Teaching of Jesus*, p. 31, etc.

[5] *E.g.* R. Bultmann, *The History of the Synoptic Tradition*, p. 372; E. Käsemann, 'The Problem of the Historical Jesus' (1953) in *Essays on New Testament Themes* (SCM Press, 1964), especially pp. 19-24, 30. This view is strongly challenged by G.N. Stanton, *Jesus of Nazareth in New Testament Preaching* (Cambridge University Press, 1974).

[6] See, for instance, N. Perrin, *Rediscovering the Teaching of Jesus*, p. 21, on parables: 'There are a limited number of instances where the parable in very much its original form made a point of significance to the early Church... But these are exceptions.'

[7] *Ibid.*, p. 16.

[8] *Ibid.*, p. 24; *cf.* N. Perrin, *What is Redaction Criticism?*, p. 40, where a contrast is drawn between a 'redaction-critical approach' and 'the older way of regarding it as essentially a historical narrative'.

[9] B. Gerhardsson, *Memory and Manuscript* (Gleerup, Lund, 1961), p. 209. D.E. Nineham, replying to A.T. Hanson's criticism of his commentary on Mark in A. T. Hanson (ed.), *Vindications* (SCM Press, 1966), rejects the imputation of this view to himself and other Bultmannian scholars ('... *et hoc genus omne*', in W.R. Farmer, C.F.D. Moule, and R.R. Niebuhr (eds.), *Christian History and Interpretation*, Cambridge University Press, 1967, pp. 199-222, especially pp. 201-4). If Nineham himself is not open to this charge (and that is debatable), the above words show that the same could not be said of Perrin; and in fact the assumption that theological motivation excludes a concern for historical accuracy underlies much of the methodology of Bultmann's *The History of the Synoptic Tradition* and works derived from it.

[10] *What is Redaction Criticism?*, p. 69.

[11] D.E. Nineham *et al.*, *Historicity and Chronology in the New Testament* (SPCK, Theological Collections no. 6, 1965), p. 4.

[12] E. Käsemann, *Essays on New Testament Themes*, p. 34.

[13] N. Perrin, *Rediscovering the Teaching of Jesus*, p. 39.

[14] For similar descriptions and evaluations of the various criteria in use, see W. O. Walker, 'The Quest for the Historical Jesus: a Discussion of Methodology', *AThR* 51, 1969, pp. 38-56, especially pp. 41-50; N.J. McEleney, 'Authenticating Criteria and Mark 7:1-23', *CBQ* 34, 1972, pp. 431-60; R.S.

Barbour, *Traditio-Historical Criticism of the Gospels* (SPCK, 1972), pp. 3-13. Barbour introduces a helpful distinction between *formal* criteria (those concerned with the language and style of the sayings and with their distribution in the sources) and *material* criteria (those concerned with the content of the sayings, *i.e.*, the criteria of dissimilarity and of coherence).

[15]*Rediscovering the Teaching of Jesus*, p. 39. For a useful discussion and criticism of the criterion see F.G. Downing, *The Church and Jesus* (SCM Press, 1968), pp. 111-16.

[16]Perhaps the clearest statement is on p. 205, but the criterion may be seen in practice throughout; see, *e.g.*, pp. 101, 104, 105.

[17]*Encyclopaedia Biblica*, II (1899-1903); *s. v.* 'Gospels', paragraphs 139 f.

[18]*Rediscovering the Teaching of Jesus*, p. 43. *Cf.* also C.E. Carlston, 'A *Positive* Criterion of Authenticity', *BR* 7, 1962, pp. 33-44.

[19]*The History of the Synoptic Tradition*, p. 162. See also the present essay, pp. 113 f.

[20]*Rediscovering the Teaching of Jesus*, pp. 45-7.

[21]*E.g.*, the saying 'Whoever receives one such child in my name receives me; and whoever receives me, receives not me but him who sent me' (Mk. 9:37; Mt. 18:5; Lk. 9:48) recurs in a closely related converse form in Lk. 10:16 (L), as well as being partially repeated in Mt. 10:40 (M); the warning against causing little ones to stumble in Mk. 9:42 is combined in Mt. 18:6,7 with a parallel saying from Q material (*cf.* Lk. 17:1,2); the instruction not to worry about how to answer persecutors occurs both in Mark (13:11 = Lk. 21:14,15) and Q (Mt. 10:19,20; Lk. 12:11,12); the prediction that the Son of man must 'suffer many things and be rejected (*apodokimasthēnai*)' (Mk. 8:31) occurs in the Lucan parallel (9:22), but also independently in Lk. 17:25. Yet, despite their multiple attestation, none of these cases is included in Perrin's study of sayings which may have a claim to authenticity; and all are rejected by Bultmann, who uses various forms of the criterion of dissimilarity (*The History of the Synoptic Tradition*, pp. 163, 144, 122, 152 respectively). The last is commonly seen as an allusion to Ps. 118:22, and as such is classed by B. Lindars (*New Testament Apologetic*, SCM Press, 1961, pp. 170 f.) as reflecting a secondary application of the psalm, to 'the Passion apologetic'. (The earliest Christians, Lindars believes, applied this psalm to the resurrection, not to the passion.) See further N.J. McEleney, *CBQ* 34, pp. 434 f. for the authentication by this criterion of a saying widely regarded as secondary on other grounds. Thus multiple attestation, however valuable in theory, is accorded little weight in practice.

[22]R.H. Fuller, *The New Testament in Current Study* (SCM Press, 1963), pp. 41 f.; N. Perrin, *Rediscovering the Teaching of Jesus*, pp. 37 f.

[23]The point is well argued by E.P. Sanders, *The Tendencies of the Synoptic Tradition* (Cambridge University Press, 1969), pp. 190-209.

[24]*E.g.* T.F. Glasson, 'Mark xiii and the Greek Old Testament', *ExpT* 69, 1957-8, pp. 213-5; R.H. Fuller, *The Foundations of New Testament Christology* (Lutterworth, 1965), p. 19. This approach to the New Testament quotations is considered fully in chapter 2 of my *Jesus and the Old Testament*

(Inter-Varsity Press, 1971), with detailed discussion of all relevant examples.

[25]Since this essay was originally written, two useful articles have appeared which cover much the same ground as this section. M.D. Hooker (*NTS* 17, 1970-1, pp. 480-7) criticizes the standard Bultmannian criteria along much the same lines as the present section, and concludes that the probable origin and history of each saying must be decided by careful study of each in its own right, not by stereotyped criteria based on a dogmatic view about the burden of proof. D.G.A. Calvert (*NTS* 18, 1971-2, pp. 209-19) makes a useful distinction between the positive and negative use of the criteria (see the end of the present section), and concludes that 'there is no value in ruling out "unauthentic material" by means of the negative criteria'. More wide-ranging and searching criticisms are included in R.S. Barbour, *Traditio-Historical Criticism of the Gospels*, Part 1, pp. 1-27.

[26]*Rediscovering the Teaching of Jesus*, p. 43.

[27]*The New Testament in Current Study*, p. 41.

[28]See F.G. Downing, *The Church and Jesus*, p. 116, for the parallel point that to suppose that what distinguished Jesus from Jewish thought is 'most characteristic' of him is to beg the question.

[29]*Cf.* M.D. Hooker's comment on this approach to the 'Son of man' sayings: 'To discard the "possible" and use only the "probable" in making a decision regarding the meaning of "Son of man" is to distort the evidence by ignoring some of it' (*The Son of Man in Mark*, SPCK, 1967, p. 79; *cf.* pp. 6 f.).

[30]*Rediscovering the Teaching of Jesus*, p. 81.

[31]*Essays on New Testament Themes*, pp. 37 f.

[32]*Rediscovering the Teaching of Jesus*, p. 62.

[33]*Ibid.*, p. 198.

[34]The same rationale in other aspects of the sceptical approach is brought out by A.T. Hanson in *Vindications*, pp. 76 f.; *cf.* R.P.C. Hanson, *ibid.*, pp. pp. 39, 43 f. *Vindications* is a rather varied collection of essays edited by A.T. Hanson, essentially concerned to emphasize the historical character of Christianity, and in particular of the Gospels, in the face of Bultmannian scepticism. If not always completely fair to radical critics, the essayists succeed admirably in showing that the sceptical approach is not the only one open, or even the most probable. They provide a great deal of valuable ammunition for those eager to fight for the historicist cause.

[35]*The History of the Synoptic Tradition*, p. 205. See *ibid.*, p. 105, for a fuller list of 'characteristic emphases'.

[36]*Rediscovering the Teaching of Jesus*, p. 44.

[37]*Vindications*, p. 40. The same charge of subjectivity is levelled against Bultmann by, *e.g.*, V. Taylor, *The Formation of the Gospel Tradition* (Macmillan, 1933), pp. 108 ff.; G.B. Caird, *Jesus and the Jewish Nation* (Athlone Press, 1965), pp. 4 f.; and P.C. Hodgson, *JR* 41, 1961, pp. 91-108 (with reference to J. Knox as well as Bultmann). *Cf.* F.G. Downing, *The Church and Jesus*, p. 118 ff., who criticizes H.M. Teeple's essay in *JBL* 84, 1965, pp. 213-50. See further n. 51 below.

[38]*Cf.* the present essay, pp. 39 f., for this positive use.

[39](Mowbray, 1963.) The section discussed here is on pp. 73-8.

[40]'The Burden of Proof in Historical Jesus Research', *ExpT* 82, 1970-1, pp. 116-19.

[41]N. J. McEleney, *CBQ* 34, pp. 445-8, points out that this 'historical presumption' is in fact made, even if not acknowledged, by most historians, including those studying the Gospels.

[42]*New Testament Theology*, I, *The Proclamation of Jesus* (SCM Press, 1971), p. 37.

[43]*Jesus and the Kingdom* (SPCK, 1966), p. xiii. *Cf.* T.W. Manson in W.D. Davies and D. Daube (eds.), *The Background of the New Testament and its Eschatology* (Cambridge University Press, 1956), pp. 219 f.

[44]See, *e.g.*, V. Taylor, *The Formation of the Gospel Tradition*, pp. 31-43, 105-10; E.B. Redlich, *Form Criticism* (Duckworth, 1939), pp. 34-79; C.S.C. Williams, in A.H. McNeile (ed.), *An Introduction to the Study of the New Testament*[2] (Oxford University Press, 1953), pp. 52-8; T.W. Manson in *The Background of the New Testament and its Eschatology*, pp. 211-221; H. Riesenfeld, *The Gospel Tradition and its Beginnings* (Mowbray, 1957); J.A. Baird, *The Justice of God in the Teaching of Jesus* (SCM Press, 1963), pp. 17-34; D. Guthrie, *New Testament Introduction*[3] (Inter-Varsity Press, 1970), ch. 6, especially pp. 208-11; R.H. Gundry, *The Use of the Old Testament in St Matthew's Gospel* (Brill, Leiden, 1967), pp. 189-93. The points made in the present section are numbered for the sake of convenience. But this should not be taken to imply that the list is necessarily complete.

[45]V. Taylor, *The Formation of the Gospel Tradition*, pp. 106 f.; C.H. Dodd, *According to the Scriptures* (Nisbet, 1952), pp. 109 f.; D. Guthrie, *New Testament Introduction*, pp. 195-9. R.S. Barbour (*Traditio-Historical Criticism of the Gospels*, p. 13) rightly points out that this has become a rather sterile argument, as concepts such as 'creation by community' need careful definition. Recent emphasis on the supposed role of Christian prophets (see above, pp. 103 f.) has rather turned the edge of this argument.

[46]E.P. Sanders, in *The Tendencies of the Synoptic Tradition*, devotes his thesis to demonstrating this point. He examines in particular the supposed tendencies of the sayings to increase in length, to gain extra details, and to lose their Semitic character, in the course of transmission. A comparison with tendencies in textual corruption, and in the use of the synoptic tradition in the apocryphal Gospels and the early Fathers, indicates that these are far from being universal tendencies, and detailed study of the synoptic parallels themselves reveals no clear 'laws of tradition' in operation. The whole book is an important corrective to the facile generalizations of some form critics. *Cf.* also R.P.C. Hanson in *Vindications*, pp. 42-53.

[47]The classic statement, frequently echoed since, is by V. Taylor (*The Formation of the Gospel Tradition*, pp. 41-3, 107). N. Perrin, in *Rediscovering the Teaching of Jesus*, pp. 26-30, questions whether an 'eye-witness' need be any more concerned with factual accuracy or verbal authenticity than an evangelist. (This point is more fully argued by D.E. Nineham in a series of articles in *JTS* 9, 1958, pp. 13-25, 243-52; 11, 1960, pp. 253-64.) This is a

necessary corrective to the modern quasi-legal idea of an eye-witness as one who is concerned to give an exact account of what actually happened; but the argument is not thereby destroyed, even though it has sometimes been incautiously stated. Those who had heard Jesus teach would hardly be prepared to sanction any radical departure from his teaching, purveyed in his name, however little they may have been concerned about the *ipsissima verba*.

[48] *Cf.* W.L. Knox, *The Sources of the Synoptic Gospels* (Cambridge University Press, 1953-7), particularly the summary of his findings in vol. II, p. 139. *Cf.* J.A. Baird, *The Justice of God in the Teaching of Jesus*, pp. 23-5; R.H. Gundry, *The Use of the Old Testament in St Matthew's Gospel*, pp. 182 f.

[49] J.A. Baird, *The Justice of God in the Teaching of Jesus*, pp. 30-2. *Cf.* C.H. Dodd, *History and the Gospel* (Nisbet, 1938), pp. 101-3.

[50] R.P.C. Hanson in *Vindications*, pp. 38 f.

[51] See especially L. Cerfaux, ' "L'Histoire de la Tradition Synoptique" d'après R. Bultmann' (1932), in *Recueil Lucien Cerfaux*, I (J. Duculot, Gembloux, 1954), pp. 353-67. *Cf.* Bultmann's own statement in *The History of the Synoptic Tradition*, p. 47: 'Naturally enough, our judgement will not be made in terms of objective criteria, but will depend on taste and discrimination.' The following pronouncements are typical of many: 'The logion would have been originally unattached (unless, which I cannot believe, the Church found it complete with the situation)' *(ibid.,* p. 19); 'The saying did not originally refer to Jesus in this connection, though the evangelist might well have thought so' *(ibid.,* p. 109); 'It cannot remain among the sayings of Jesus; yet, on the other hand, I see no compelling reason for denying it to him' *(ibid.,* p. 160). See further above, p. 113. R.S. Barbour *(Traditio-Historical Criticism of the Gospels*, pp. 10-13) points out the frequent failure of Bultmannian critics to give any account of the supposed origin and transmission of the sayings which they label 'secondary'.

[52] See, *e.g.,* A.N. Sherwin-White, *Roman Society and Roman Law in the New Testament* (Oxford University Press, 1963), pp. 186-92; A.W. Mosley, 'Historical Reporting in the Ancient World', *NTS* 12, 1965-6, pp. 10-26; R.P.C. Hanson in *Vindications*, pp. 34-7.

[53] *A New Quest of the Historical Jesus* (SCM Press, 1959), p. 40.

[54] The Hanson brothers have pointed out in *Vindications* (pp. 41 f., 94 f.) that form critics of the NT tend to come to their documents with a far more sceptical presumption about their historicity than students of Greek and Roman history, or form critics of the OT. A.T. Hanson *(ibid.,* p. 94) draws a distinction between 'the historians' and 'the Form Critics, a peculiar group who have evolved criteria of evidence all their own'.

[55] N. Perrin, *Rediscovering the Teaching of Jesus*, p. 221.

[56] See C.F.D. Moule, *The Phenomenon of the New Testament* (SCM Press, 1967), p. 103.

[57] R.P.C. Hanson in *Vindications*, p. 33; *cf.* W.L. Knox, *The Sources of the Synoptic Gospels*, I, p. 5.

[58] See especially the important essay by C.F.D. Moule, 'The Intention of the Evangelists', in A.J.B. Higgins (ed.), *New Testament Essays: Studies in Mem-

ory of T.W. Manson (Manchester University Press, 1959), pp. 165-79; reprinted in Moule's *The Phenomenon of the New Testament*, pp. 100-14. More briefly, see *idem*, *The Birth of the New Testament*[2] (A. & C. Black, 1966), pp. 86 f. See also E.F. Scott, *The Validity of the Gospel Record* (Nicholson & Watson, 1938), pp. 1-24; N.A. Dahl, 'Anamnesis: mémoire et commémoration dans le christianisme primitif', *STh*, I (1947), pp. 69-95, especially pp. 90-5.

[59]T.W. Manson, in *The Background of the New Testament and its Eschatology*, pp. 214 f.; H.G. Wood, *NTS* 4, 1957-8, pp. 175-7; A.M. Ramsey, in *SE*, I (*TU* 73, 1959), pp. 35-42. See also G.N. Stanton, 'The Gospel Traditions and Early Christological Reflection', in S.W. Sykes and J.P. Clayton (eds.), *Christ, Faith and History* (Cambridge University Press, 1972), pp. 191-204. Stanton has now presented his case more fully in *Jesus of Nazareth in New Testament Preaching*, where he argues that the life and character of Jesus formed an integral part of the missionary preaching of the church from the beginning, and that this was the *Sitz im Leben* of much of the 'biographical' material in the Gospels. He argues that the deeds and the words of Jesus were inextricably linked in this preaching tradition.

[60]H. Riesenfeld, *The Gospel Tradition and its Beginnings*; B. Gerhardsson, *Memory and Manuscript*.

[61]See, *e.g.*, L. Cerfaux, 'La probité des souvenirs évangéliques' (1927), in *Recueil Lucien Cerfaux*, I, 369-87; P. Carrington, *The Primitive Christian Catechism* (Cambridge University Press, 1940), pp. 67-73; O. Cullmann, 'The Tradition' (1953), in *The Early Church* (SCM Press, 1956), pp. 59-99, especially pp. 63-6; J.W. Doeve, 'La rôle de la tradition orale dans la composition des évangiles synoptiques', in J. Cambier *et al.*, *La formation des évangiles* (Desclée & Brouwer, 1957), pp. 70-84; N.A. Dahl, *STh*, I (1947), especially pp. 73-4; and more recently, J.J. Vincent, 'Did Jesus Teach his Disciples to Learn by Heart?', in *SE*, III (*TU* 88, 1964), pp. 105-18; W.D. Davies, *The Setting of the Sermon on the Mount* (Cambridge University Press, 1964), pp. 416-25.

[62]See *contra*, however, M. Smith in *JBL* 82, 1963, pp. 169-76. Gerhardsson has replied to this criticism in *Tradition and Transmission in Early Christianity* (Gleerup, Lund 1964).

[63]For some of the analogies used by form critics, see R. Bultmann, *The History of the Synoptic Tradition*, pp. 6 f.; M. Dibelius, *From Tradition to Gospel* (Nicholson & Watson, 1934), pp. 133-77; R.H. Lightfoot, *History and Interpretation in the Gospels* (Hodder & Stoughton, 1935), pp. 32 f.

[64]*The Setting of the Sermon on the Mount*, p. 466.

[65]*Ibid.*, p. 480.

[66]*E.g.* N. Perrin, *Rediscovering the Teaching of Jesus*, p. 31.

[67]See especially C.F. Burney, *The Poetry of Our Lord* (Oxford University Press, 1925); also H. Riesenfeld, *The Gospel Tradition and its Beginnings*, pp. 24 f.

[68]*An Aramaic Approach to the Gospels and Acts*[3] (Oxford University Press, 1967), pp. 185, 276 f.

[69]*New Testament Theology*, I, pp. 8-37. The conclusion is quoted on p. 116

above. *Cf.* Jeremias' *The Prayers of Jesus* (SCM Press, 1967), pp. 108-15, for a brief discussion of 'Characteristics of the *Ipsissima Vox Jesu*'.

[70]See especially 1 Cor. 11:2, 23; 15:1-3; 2 Thes. 2:15; 3:6. For the idea see Gal. 1:1—2:10; 2 Tim. 2:2.

[71]O. Cullmann, *The Early Church*, pp. 63 f.; in detail, B. Gerhardsson, *Memory and Manuscript*, pp. 288-301.

[72]O Cullmann, *op cit.*, p. 65; *cf.* the argument of the whole article. Also P. Carrington, *The Primitive Christian Catechism*, pp. 69-73 ('Tannaite Elders in Christianity').

[73]For a full account of Paul's attitude to the tradition see B. Gerhardsson, *Memory and Manuscript*, pp. 302-23. *Cf.* also G.N. Stanton, *Jesus of Nazareth in New Testament Preaching*, pp. 96-8.

[74]In *The Background of the New Testament and its Eschatology*, p. 214 f.

[75]See B. Gerhardsson, *Tradition and Transmission in Early Christianity*, pp. 41-4.

[76]G.N. Stanton, in *Jesus of Nazareth in New Testament Preaching*, ch. 6, isolates a number of aspects of the life and character of Jesus preserved in the Gospels from 'biographical' interest rather than to meet the later needs of the church.

[77]For this positive use of the criterion, see especially F.F. Bruce, *Tradition Old and New* (Paternoster Press, 1970), pp. 48-54; also J.A. Baird, *The Justice of God in the Teaching of Jesus*, pp. 32-4. It is so used, though not explicitly mentioned, in E.F. Harrison's essay, *'Gemeindetheologie*: the Bane of Gospel Criticism', in C.F. Henry (ed.), *Jesus of Nazareth: Saviour and Lord* (Inter-Varsity Press, 1966), pp. 165-73.

[78]H.E.W. Turner, *Historicity and the Gospels*, p. 49; E.F. Harrison, *op. cit.*; F.F. Bruce, *op. cit.*, pp. 48-51. *Cf.* C.S.C. Williams, in A.H. McNeile (ed.), *Introduction to the Study of the New Testament*,[2] p. 55.

[79]See C.F.D. Moule, *The Phenomenon of the New Testament*, pp. 56-76, for a detailed discussion showing that 'aspects of Jesus' attitude and ministry have survived in the traditions, despite the fact that the early Christians do not seem to have paid particular attention to them' (p. 76).

[80]For a useful summary along similar lines see W.D. Davies, *The Setting of the Sermon on the Mount*, pp. 415-18, 422-4.

[81]Debate on the languages of first-century Palestine is still lively. Some have argued in favour of Hebrew as the language of Jesus (*e.g.* H. Birkeland, *The Language of Jesus*, Det Norske Videnskaps Akademie, Oslo, 1954); others have argued for Greek (particularly N. Turner, *Grammatical Insights into the New Testament*, T. & T. Clark, 1965, pp. 174-88). But most scholars remain convinced that Aramaic was the common language which Jesus would have spoken in his normal teaching. For a recent brief statement of the case see J. Jeremias, *New Testament Theology*, I, *The Proclamation of Jesus*, pp. 3-8. The question is more fully surveyed by J.A. Fitzmyer, *CBQ* 32, 1970, pp. 501-31; J.A. Emerton, *JTS* 24, 1973, pp. 1-23.

[82]On the method of the Targums, see *e.g.* M. McNamara, *Targum and Testament* (Irish University Press, 1972), pp. 69-78.

[83]R.H. Gundry, *The Use of the Old Testament in St Matthew's Gospel*, p. 171.

[84]*The New Testament and Criticism*, pp. 121 f.

[85]The case is well stated by A.W. Wainwright, *The Trinity in the New Testament* (SPCK, 1962), pp. 238-41.

[86]*Cf.* the conclusion of P.W. Evans in the Tyndale New Testament Lecture for 1946, *Sacraments in the New Testament* (Tyndale Press, 1946), p. 21. Following an extensive review of opinions he writes: 'We suggest, then, that the evidence is indecisive as to whether our Lord used the exact phrase reported in Matthew xxviii. 19. But even were it finally proved that we have not here Christ's *ipsissima verba*, we may still have His intention correctly reported.' The authenticity of the formula is defended, however, by R.V.G. Tasker, *The Gospel According to St Matthew* (Inter-Varsity Press, 1961), pp. 275 f.

[87]This case is argued fully in ch. 2 of my *Jesus and the Old Testament* (Inter-Varsity Press, 1971).

[88]See above, n. 46, with reference to the work of E.P. Sanders.

[89]See further B. Van Elderen, in C.F. Henry (ed.), *Jesus of Nazareth: Saviour and Lord*, pp. 111-19.

BIBLIOGRAPHY

For detailed references on the various subjects treated in this essay, see the notes. The following works are particularly recommended for the attention of those who wish to pursue the subject further.

Baird, J.A., *Audience Criticism and the Historical Jesus* (Westminster Press, Philadelphia, 1969). A bold attempt to break out of the traditional methods and presuppositions. With the aid of a computer, Baird argues statistically for a high degree of authenticity in the synoptic accounts of Jesus' teaching.

Barbour, R.S., *Traditio-Historical Criticism of the Gospels* (SPCK, 1972). Some cautionary remarks on the 'new quest of the historical Jesus', and particularly on the standard 'criteria of authenticity'.

Bruce, F.F., *Tradition Old and New* (Paternoster Press, 1970). Wide-ranging, containing a valuable discussion of tradition in Judaism and in the New Testament.

Bultmann, R., *The History of the Synoptic Tradition*[2] (Blackwell, 1968). The foundation of the whole edifice of radical form criticism.

Cullmann, O., 'The Tradition', in *The Early Church* (SCM Press, 1956), pp. 59-99. An important study, partly anticipating the 'Scandinavian approach'.

France, R.T., *Jesus and the Old Testament: His Application of Old Testament Passages to Himself and his Mission* (Inter-Varsity Press, 1971). See notes 24 and 87 of the present essay.

Fuller, R.H., *The New Testament in Current Study* (SCM Press, 1963). Concentrates particularly on Bultmann and the 'new quest of the historical Jesus'.

Gerhardsson, B., *Memory and Manuscript* (Gleerup, Lund, 1961). The *magnum opus* of the Scandinavian school to date.

Hanson, A.T. (ed.), *Vindications* (SCM Press, 1966). See above, n. 34.

Jeremias, J., *New Testament Theology*, I, *The Proclamation of Jesus* (SCM Press, 1971). Jeremias first justifies an optimistic estimate of the reliability of the synoptic tradition, and then applies this estimate in a detailed study of the teaching of Jesus.

Käsemann, E., 'The Problem of the Historical Jesus' (1953), in *Essays on New Testament Themes* (SCM Press, 1964), pp. 15-47. The essay which started the 'new quest of the historical Jesus' within the Bultmannian school.

Ladd, G.E., *The New Testament and Criticism* (Eerdmans, 1967; Hodder & Stoughton, 1970). A careful evaluation of recent trends in New Testament criticism, especially of the Gospels, by a conservative scholar. Of great value to the student perplexed by destructive criticism.

Manson, T.W., 'The Life of Jesus: Some Tendencies in Present-Day Research', in W.D. Davies and D. Daube (eds.), *The Background of the New Testament and its Eschatology* (Cambridge University Press, 1956), pp. 211-21. A plea for common sense, aimed at radical form criticism.

Moule, C.F.D., *The Phenomenon of the New Testament* (SCM Press, 1967). Notice especially the reprint of an essay on 'The Intention of the Evangelists' (1959) on pp. 100-14; an important attempt to rehabilitate a biographical motive in the writing of the Gospels.

Perrin, N., *Rediscovering the Teaching of Jesus* (SCM Press, 1967). Probably the most thorough recent study in English of the synoptic tradition by a Bultmannian scholar.

Idem, *What is Redaction Criticism?* (SPCK, 1970). A brief, popular introduction to redaction criticism as seen and practised by a convinced Bultmannian.

Riesenfeld, H., *The Gospel Tradition and its Beginnings* (Mowbray, 1957). The original manifesto of the 'Scandinavian approach'. Brief, but important. This essay also appears in *The Gospels Reconsidered: A Selection of Papers Read at the International Congress on the Four Gospels in 1957* (Blackwell, 1960), pp. 131-53; in *Studia Evangelica*, I (*Texte und Untersuchungen zur Geschichte der altchristlichen Literatur* 73, 1958), pp. 43-65; and in H. Riesenfeld, *The Gospel Tradition* (Blackwell, 1970), 1-29.

Rohde, J., *Rediscovering the Teaching of the Evangelists* (SCM Press, 1969). A painstaking, if rather laboured, study of all the significant practitioners of redaction criticism in Germany up to 1966.

Stanton, G.N., *Jesus of Nazareth in New Testament Preaching* (Cambridge University Press, 1974). See note 59 of the present essay.

Turner, H.E.W., *Historicity and the Gospels* (Mowbray, 1963). A defence of historicist presuppositions and methods.

III
HISTORY &
THE
BELIEVER

4. HISTORY &
THE BELIEVER

COLIN BROWN

The eighteenth-century German dramatist, literary critic and amateur theologian, Gotthold Ephraim Lessing, once remarked that 'Accidental truths of history can never become the proof of necessary truths of reason'.[1] The dictum was propounded in the heat of argument, but it has been remembered long after the particular argument has been forgotten, because it focuses on a problem. History—both in the sense of what happened in the past and in the sense of accounts of the past—seems to be so much less solid than, say, Pythagoras' theorem or the proposition that two and two make four. It is not self-evident like the latter. Nor can it be proved like scientific theories. The scientist verifies his hypotheses in a laboratory by controlled experiment. His findings and his methods can be checked by anyone capable of understanding what is involved and performing similar experiments. Compared with that, history seems so insecure with its dependence on witnesses, second-hand and third-hand evidence, documents whose survival seems to depend so much on chance, and the rival interpretations of historians. To bring God into it only seems to make the whole undertaking doubly dubious.

Yet we cannot get away from history. What William the Conqueror, Christopher Columbus and Adolf Hitler did in their different ways has affected the lives of all of us in the western world. The more we understand the past, the better we are able to find our way about the present. But how are we to understand the past? Are we to see history through the eyes of a Marxist? And if so, which brand of Marxist? The Christian talks about seeing things in a Christian perspective. But are not these terms loaded, and are not the various slants that people bring to history all more or less arbitrary? The Christian talks about God in history. But can any self-respecting historian today bring himself to use such language without throwing overboard the very rules of the game?

It is with this kind of question that the present essay is concerned. In particular, we shall look at four areas of debate:

1. God in history
2. Rules, principles and explanations
3. What does the historian achieve?
4. How does history affect belief?

We shall begin with a preliminary survey of the question of 'God in history'. For this is the crunch question for the Christian and for anyone looking at the Christian faith. We shall ask what this implies and shall offer some reflections on miracles and history. This leads to the question of criteria and method under the heading 'Rules, principles and explanations'. Here too the main interest lies in asking what bearing these have on taking seriously the idea of God and the supernatural in history. The third section asks, 'What does the historian achieve?' The question here relates to what has been loosely called historical reconstruction and its use. Finally we shall ask, 'How does history affect belief?' In so doing we shall focus on two issues: (1) history and revelation, and (2) the importance of history to the believer. All four sections are interlocking, and the argument of the whole is cumulative.

1. GOD IN HISTORY
Kierkegaard's paradox
Books and papers on the question of God in history might almost all open with 'In the beginning Kierkegaard . . .'. Like no-one else before him, Kierkegaard throws into sharp relief the problems of thinking about God in history, as seen from the standpoint of the Christian believer. But alongside this we might set the famous (and true) saying about liberty: 'What crimes are committed in thy name . . .'. For the nineteenth-century Danish philosopher is regularly credited with being the grandfather of secular existentialism

and the advocate of an extremely sceptical attitude to history in general and to Christian origins in particular. After all, there is the frequently quoted statement in his *Philosophical Fragments* about the first generation of Christians:

> If the contemporary generation had left nothing behind them but these words: 'We have believed that in such and such a year the God appeared among us in the humble figure of a servant, that he lived and taught in our community, and finally died,' it would have been more than enough. The contemporary generation would have done all that was necessary; for this little advertisement, this *nota bene* on a page of universal history, would be sufficient to afford an occasion for a successor, and the most voluminous account can in all eternity do nothing more.[2]

It looks as if Kierkegaard is saying that history does not matter much. What counts is how you react and what you believe. And this can very easily lead to a *Wizard of Oz* situation. In the modern American fairy story the straw man, the tin man, the cowardly lion and the little girl, Dorothy, go off in search of the famous wizard who, they believe, will help them get what they want most—a heart, a brain, courage and the security of home. Unfortunately, when they find him, the wizard turns out to be an ordinary man with no special powers. But in the course of their adventures the companions acquire by themselves the things that they thought could be given to them only supernaturally. Well, there is a moral in all this. But is there no more than this to Christianity? And is this the kind of religion that Kierkegaard really had in mind?

As in all things, it is dangerous to take statements out of context. It is doubly so with Kierkegaard. For if we study Kierkegaard in his own words (as distinct from what people have said that he said) the picture that emerges is not that of the incipient sceptical existentialist philosopher but that of a deeply committed Christian. If labels are to be attached to him, it would be more accurate to describe him as a dialectical theologian[3] with a fairly conservative (indeed, uncritical) approach to history. Basic to Kierkegaard's whole outlook (as it is to the biblical writers) is the thought that God is *other*. The significant point is the way in which Kierkegaard develops the idea. God exists on a different plane and in a different way from ourselves. As he put it in one of his *Christian Discourses*,

> If the difference is infinite between God who is in heaven and thee who art on earth, the difference is infinitely greater between the holy One and the sinner.[4]

There is both a metaphysical and a moral distinction here. It expresses the fundamental disjunction between God and the world which underlies Kierkegaard's entire thought. This disjunction is radical and complete. It cannot be overcome on man's side, but it is overcome on God's. How? Kierkegaard explains this by invoking the notions of *paradox* and even *absolute paradox*. Finite reason can grasp only what is finite and rational. It cannot, therefore, grasp God. Paradoxically, even to obtain the knowledge that God is unlike him man needs the help of God.[5] The gulf between man and God is bridged from God's side supremely in the incarnation. Thus in the *Philosophical Fragments* Kierkegaard puts forward the suggestion that

> in order to be man's Teacher, the God proposed to make himself like the individual man, so that he might understand him fully. Thus our paradox is rendered still more appalling, or the same paradox has the double aspect which proclaims it as the Absolute Paradox; negatively by revealing the absolute unlikeness of sin, positively by proposing to do away with the absolute unlikeness in absolute likeness.[6]

We should notice what this involves. Not only is God absolutely unlike man, but in the incarnation as 'the Teacher' he is absolutely *like* man. This means that in Christ—as in nature[7]—God is *incognito*. What we see is a man, human actions, events in time and space, but not the divine directly.[8] The thought is taken a step further in those passages where Kierkegaard speaks of being contemporary with Christ. To be a contemporary with Christ is not to have lived at the same time as Jesus in close physical proximity. Rather the contemporary is one who transcends the limitations of time by perceiving the eternal in the temporal. For on the plane of time and space the eternal is hidden.

> It is Christ's free will and determination from all eternity to be incognito. So when people think to do Him honour by saying or thinking, 'If I had been contemporary with Him, I should

have known Him directly', they really insult Him, and since it is Christ they insult, this means that they are blasphemous. . . . Oh, loftiest height of self-abnegation when the incognito succeeds so well that even if He were inclined to speak directly no one would believe Him. . . . And now in the case of the God-Man! He is God, but chooses to become the individual man. This, as we have seen is the profoundest incognito, or the most impenetrable unrecognizableness that is possible; for the contradiction between being God and being an individual man is the greatest possible, the infinitely qualitative contradiction.[9] In his private papers Kierkegaard expressed the point geometrically:

> Christ veritably relates tangentially to the earth (the divine cannot relate in any other way): He has no place where to lay his head. A tangent is a straight line which touches the circle at only one single point.[10]

The conclusion to be drawn from this position is that there is no 'direct communication' between man and God. To be directly recognisable is the mark of an idol. The God-man—which is Kierkegaard's term for expressing the reality of Jesus Christ—is known only as 'the object of faith'. 'Direct recognizableness is paganism.'[11]

In making these points, Kierkegaard is saying more than Lessing in his dictum that the accidental truths of history can never become the proof of the necessary truths of reason. Lessing was concerned with the uncertainty of historical assertions which lack the compulsion of self-evident truth. Kierkegaard was concerned with the question of God in history. For him it was not a matter of evidential or logical certainty. Faith in God involves a realm which lies beyond evidence and logic. But this does not make Kierkegaard a radical in the modern sense of the term. Although he called his *Concluding Unscientific Postscript to the Philosophical Fragments* 'An Existential Contribution', he had no desire to reduce the gospel to existential self-awareness. He was certainly concerned with the elements of choice and decision in man's apprehension of reality. But Kierkegaard's scheme of reality was not one of purely immanent structures. Indeed, it could be said that his primary concern was to recognize and express the transcendence of God. Moreover, he was doing this in the face of idealist philosophy and contemporary churchmanship which were dominated by immanentism.

Nor was Kierkegaard sceptical about the historical authenticity of the biblical records. Although he was acutely aware of what was going on in the intellectual world, his writings betray a profound lack of interest in the criticial debates of his time. In both his philosophical and his devotional writings he consistently takes Scripture at its face value. The quotation about a minimal belief, with which we began, comes in the context of a discussion not of critical history but of the relationship between the temporal and the eternal. The text goes on to say:

> If we wish to express the relation subsisting between the contemporary and his successor in the briefest possible compass, but without sacrificing accuracy to brevity, we may say: The successor believes *by means of* (this expresses the occasional) the testimony of the contemporary, in virtue of the condition he himself receives from God.[12]

History for Kierkegaard is thus the *occasion* for encounter with God. But God is not to be identified with anything in history even when he is present. For since God is other, he remains incognito.

To many of Kierkegaard's readers this defence of God's presence in the world, in Christ and in history has seemed a Pyrrhic victory. Kierkegaard seems to come perilously close to saying that God is there but he is unknowable. The difficulties may be stated in a variety of ways, but they come back to the same point. If God is so wholly *other*, and touches the world only tangentially even in Christ (and that in a hidden way), it seems perfectly possible to give an account of nature and history (including gospel history) without reference to God.[13] If so, why do we need to bring God into it at all? Indeed, are there any grounds for a 'Christian' interpretation of history? It is but half a step from a Kierkegaardian interpretation of reality in which the transcendence of God is fundamental, to an atheistic, existential one which does without God altogether.

History: sacred and secular

Kierkegaard's standpoint and that of the secularist are like the two sides of the same coin. In both cases it is only the finite that is directly observed. But saying this is not the same as saying that all events have to be understood *exclusively* in secular terms. Nor does it mean that we shall *automatically* adopt a sceptical outlook on everything.[14] The secular historian takes a high view of the historicity of some accounts and documents and a low view of others. It all depends on his evaluation of the evidence. We may even (like the secular historian) be predisposed to accept the historicity of some accounts and not of others. Such a predisposition may be perfectly proper in the same sense in which a jury may be properly predisposed to accept the testimony of one witness and reject that of another, on the grounds that it has reason to believe that the one witness is competent and trustworthy whereas the other is not.

We shall return to these questions later on. In the meantime it is important to notice that a good deal can be said for Kierkegaard's approach. When we look at history—including our own personal histories and biblical history—it can be described continuously in finite, not to say secular, terms. We might instance the crossing of the Red Sea, the entry into Canaan, the message of the prophets, the fall of Jerusalem and the exile, much of the teaching of Jesus, or Paul's missionary journeys. When we look back at 'God's hand' in our lives, we see a succession of events which are *isomorphic* with those of the rest of mankind—only we see certain conjunctions to which we give a religious interpretation. We do not experience a suspension of natural, social, economic or historical causes. We do not experience the direct, pure presence of God. Nor, for that matter, did the biblical personalities.[15](We leave aside as possible exceptions such experiences as Isaiah's vision in the temple, the transfiguration and the encounters with the risen Christ. It is not that these are unimportant, but that they seem to involve factors which are not present in normal biblical experience.) We might know 'the peace of God which passes all understanding', but it is always contained in this or that event or experience, and is apprehended in a normal psychological way.

Why then do we give to our experiences a religious interpretation, and attribute this or that to God and perhaps that or the other to Satan? One reason is that we use certain histories as paradigms. And these serve as presuppositions for our understanding and as models for our interpretation of other events and experiences. They may be psalms, parables, pronouncements, or incidents. We identify ourselves and our situations with them. What was previously a hard or confused situation is seen by the believer in a different light. It is not that he has had a *direct* experience of God in it, but he has gained a new perspective and with it an indirect apprehension of God.

But if this is all that there is to it, are we not open to the charges of fideism, primitive pre-scientific thinking, and naive believism? The answer to this will turn partly on whether what we are doing is *reading into* both past and present factors which are not really there, or whether we are genuinely *reading them out of* parallel situations.[16] And it will also turn on whether we have good grounds for belief in God, and for the kind of God we believe in. We may have certain arguments from the natural world. If so, we must show that these hold good not only for a God of nature but also for the God of history. It may be that in some of our interpretations of history God is presupposed. That is, he is not seen directly, nor does he figure as one actor alongside of the other actors. On the other hand, our account of the given situation would be incomplete without God.

In their very different ways Francis Schaeffer[17] and Alan Richardson[18] see the Christian faith as involving an element of presupposition. They see the Christian interpretation of history as an explanation or hypothesis. Schaeffer's apologetic charges the atheistic and agnostic view of the world with irrationalism and presents a biblical, theistic view of God and the world as a radical alternative which alone is able to give coherence and meaning to history. God is a metaphysical, moral and epistemological necessity. Only by adopting this explanation of the world and history can man be saved from relapsing into meaninglessness and despair. Schaeffer's approach involves a confrontation of world-views in which the Christian one is vindicated by its ability to make sense of the universe. The Christian is justified in introducing God into his account of history and experience, when occasion warrants it, because God is warranted by his general frame of reference.

Richardson's approach is more directly concerned with history itself. For him, biblical theology involves 'the framing of an hypothesis concerning the content and character of the faith of the apostolic

Church, and the testing of this hypothesis in the light of all available techniques of New Testament scholarship, historical, critical, literary, philological, archaeological, and so on'.[19] It thus involves recognition that biblical events are capable of explanation in terms of these various scientific disciplines. But it also involves an element of faith on the part of the investigator.[20] It is 'scientific' in the same way that any other science is scientific. The scientist never starts with an empty mind. He does not go around collecting facts in the expectation that when he has discovered enough of them he will find that they conform to an orderly pattern or law. The reverse is the truth. The scientist gets a hunch, frames a hypothesis, and then devises experiments to see whether the observable data can be seen better in this new way.

A Newton or an Einstein has a hunch about a wider uniformity in the behaviour of falling apples or revolving planets. Its verification lies in devising means of testing the hypothesis. There are obvious limitations to the parallel of the scientist and the historian.[21] But in both cases an explanation or hypothesis is validated by its capacity to account for something in a way which takes into account the relevant facts and which also accords with the body of accepted truth. Its rivals are excluded by their failure to do this in one or another respect. Thus Richardson defends the 'hypothesis' that

> Jesus himself is the author of the brilliant re-interpretation of the Old Testament scheme of salvation ('Old Testament theology') which is found in the New Testament, and that the events of the life, 'signs', passion and resurrection of Jesus, as attested by the apostolic witness, can account for the 'data' of the New Testament better than any other hypothesis current today. It makes better 'sense', or better history, than, for instance the hypothesis that St Paul (or someone else) transformed the simple ethical monotheism of a young Jewish carpenter-rabbi into a new mystery-religion of the dying-and-rising god pattern with the crucified rabbi as its cult-hero.[22]

The contention here is that the 'religious', theistic interpretation of Jesus does not mean that we must ignore the social, economic, political and other secular factors in his history. They are valid on their particular level, and an adequate understanding of Jesus requires them. But Richardson's contention is that the history itself contains elements which point beyond such factors, and that these elements can best be accounted for on the hypothesis that they represent valid aspects of reality. Conversely, the hypothesis that the world is a closed system of finite causes which preclude the notions of God and of the supernatural means that these elements have to be ignored or explained away in a manner which does violence to the data at our disposal.

To make these points is not to dispose of all problems at a single stroke. Whether Richardson's hypothesis is borne out depends upon detailed investigation of the data available. But to make them is to indicate the general shape of the question and the kind of argument that it involves.

We shall return to the question of God in history in section 2 on 'Rules, principles and explanations', where we shall also look at the question of the interpretation of history and experience; and again in section 4 on 'How does history affect belief?' In the meantime, we shall attempt to bring into focus the question which for many presents the problem of thinking about God in history in its acutest form—the question of miracles.

Miracles

It falls outside the scope of this study to attempt an extensive survey of the miraculous or even to examine detailed evidence for any particular miracle. We shall confine our attention to two aims: (a) to clarify what is involved in the concept of the miraculous; and (b) to ask whether the miraculous and supernatural can legitimately be entertained as history.

a. The concept of miracle   It is sometimes said that it is impossible to define miracles. Certainly, if all the factors involved in any alleged instance could be explained, it may be asked what there is to distinguish the event from any other event. On the other hand, the New Testament writers regarded certain actions of Jesus, taken in the context of his teaching and Old Testament prophecy, as signs of his relationship with the Father.[23] These signs form an integral part of the New Testament witness. Traditionally, Christians have regarded the biblical miracles as (to use John Locke's phrase) *above reason,* though they were not necessarily *contrary to reason.*[24] Moreover, they would go on to say with Locke that 'Where the miracle is admitted, the doctrine cannot be rejected; it comes with the assurance of a divine attestation to him who allows the miracle, and he cannot question its truth'.[25] In short, miracles are like the credentials of an ambassador, guaranteeing his authority. Broadly speaking, miracles fall into two categories. On the one hand, there is what has been called the 'contingency concept'[26] or 'coincidence concept'[27] of miracle. In this case, there is no apparent violation of the laws of nature but a conjunction of circumstances which is so unexpected and improbable according to the expected course of events, and so beneficial to at least one of the parties involved, that some would see in it a supernatural ordering of circumstances. Cases in point would be the 'miracle' of Dunkirk, or the instance of a child playing with its pedal car on an unmanned level crossing, heedless of the approach of an express which stopped suddenly for a reason unconnected with the child.[28] Some of the biblical signs might come under this category. It would not detract from their significance if we saw in some of the healings psychosomatic factors, [29] or attributed the temporary drying up of the Red Sea to the 'strong east wind' that blew all night.[30] In such cases it is possible to suggest a historical explanation in terms of medical, natural, scientific or other factors. We are in the realm of natural phenomena. A religious person might see in it the work of providence, because he sees it in the framework of belief. An unbeliever might put it down to extraordinary luck, because he is inclined to see things in the framework of chance or superstition. But it is also possible that a previously uncommitted person might see in it some indication of a higher ordering of events. It is not that a divine agency has directly intervened, suspending ordinary causes. Rather it is the circumstances and conjunction of ordinary causes which make the event unique.

But not all miracles fall into this category. Many of the major signs of the New Testament appear to be violations of the laws of nature. With R.F. Holland we may say that this 'violation concept' of miracle involves 'two incompatible things: (1) that it is impossible, and (2) that it has happened.'[31]

A miracle, though it cannot only be this, must at least be something the occurrence of which can be categorized at one and the same time as empirically certain and conceptually impossible. If it were less than conceptually impossible it would reduce merely to a very unusual occurrence such as could be treated (because of the empirical certainty) in the manner of a decisive experiment and result in a modification to the prevailing conception of natural law; while if it were less than empirically certain nothing more would be called for in regard to it than a suspension of judgment.[32]

There are two main lines of objection to this—one philosophical and logical and the other historical. The philosophical one asks whether this concept of miracle is not self-contradictory and thus nonsensical in the same way that the notions of a round square or a female father are self-contradictory and nonsensical. The answer is that there is more than one kind of conceptual impossibility. The founding fathers of America could not have conceived how it would be possible for someone to watch a screen in London and see events taking place in the New World (and still less on the moon) as they actually happen. Nowadays even children know that such occurrences are possible by television satelite.

It may be objected that such events are not miracles in that they are now recurrent and are explicable in terms of laws now known to modern science. The concept of miracle that I would wish to defend, however, would not preclude the possibility of explanation. If an explanation were found, the miracle would then turn out to be an instance of the contingency concept. Its justification would not rest on a vague appeal to indeterminacy.[33] Nor need it be unrepeatable. The traditional Christian belief in resurrection involves belief that we shall be raised like Christ.[34] The sign-like character of the New Testament miracles is just as important as their inexplicability.[35] Indeed, the former remains even when a conceivable explanation has been found. What I am contending for is the legitimacy of believing in what to us at present is unique and conceptually impossible, provided that there are adequate reasons for doing so. And this leads us to the question whether the miraculous and supernatural can legitimately be entertained as history.

b. The legitimacy of the miraculous and supernatural in history   Since the eighteenth-century Age of Enlightenment there has been a strong tradition in western thought which would rule out the miraculous from serious consideration on a combination of scientific and historical grounds. The classic text setting out these objections is David Hume's study 'Of Miracles' in his *Enquiry Concerning Human Understanding* (1748), section X. Hume defined miracle as 'a transgression of a law of nature by a particular volition of the Deity or by the interposition of some invisible agent'.[36] His argument fell into two parts. The first and major part claimed that 'a miracle is a violation of the laws of nature; and as a firm and unalterable experience has established these laws, the proof against a miracle, from the very nature of the fact, is as entire as any argument from experience can possibly be imagined'.[37]

The second and subsidiary argument noted four further lines of objection. (i) Miracles generally lack competent witnesses.

> There is not to be found, in all history, any miracle attested by a sufficient number of men, of such unquestioned good-sense, education, and learning, as to secure us against all delusion in themselves; of such undoubted integrity, as to place them beyond all suspicion of any design to deceive others; of such credit and reputation in the eyes of mankind, as to have a great deal to lose in case of their being detected in any falsehood; and at the same time, attesting facts performed in such a public manner and in so celebrated a part of the world, as to render the detection unavoidable: All which circumstances are requisite to give us a full assurance on the testimony of men.[38]

(ii) It is only human nature to love gossip and to enlarge upon the truth. Enthusiasts for religion are not unknown to perpetrate falsehoods 'with the best intentions in the world, for the sake of promoting so holy a cause'.[39] (iii) Miracles 'are observed chiefly to abound among ignorant and barbarous nations', and where they are admitted among civilized people they will be found to have been received 'from ignorant and barbarous ancestors, who transmitted them with that inviolable sanction and authority, which always attend received opinions'.[40] (iv) The miracles of rival religions cancel each other out.[41] The claim to miracles by rival religions means that they cannot be used to establish the truth of any given religion.[42] From all this

Hume concluded that, if miracles are to be accepted at all, they are to be accepted on the basis of faith. In reaching this conclusion, Hume inverted the traditional approach exemplified by Locke, but at the same time made it clear that any faith that accepted miracles was a groundless faith.[43]

The plausibility of Hume's case owes not a little to the fact that many alleged instances of the miraculous are open to his objections. But it may be asked whether his sweeping criticisms are not in fact too wholesale. We take first his four subsidiary arguments. If argument (i) were applied rigorously, it would preclude not only the miraculous but also the possibility of accepting as historical anything at all that happened outside the urban centres of western Europe prior to the sixteenth century. Even so, it may be asked whether Hume would be willing to accept testimony to the miraculous on such a basis. For he goes on to admit an instance of miracles wrought in France in modern times which 'were immediately proved upon the spot, before judges of unquestioned integrity, attested by witnesses of credit and distinction, in a learned age, and on the most eminent theatre that is now in the world'.[44] Nevertheless, Hume refuses point-blank to credit such testimony on the grounds of 'the absolute impossibility or miraculous nature of the events, which they relate'.[45] In other words, no amount of historical testimony would suffice. And with this we are brought back to Hume's major argument, that miracles are violations of the laws of nature and as such are impossible.

With regard to argument (ii), it has been pointed out that not all people are credulous and gullible, with a natural penchant for embroidering the truth. There are plenty of others who are natural sceptics. As a general criterion for assessing testimony to the unusual and miraculous, Hume's argument will not do, as it stands. In assessing any given testimony, we have to assess the character and motivation of the testifier. As Richard Swinburne has pointedly remarked, 'How many people are in each group, and in which group are the witnesses to any alleged miracle are matters for particular historical investigation'.[46]

Argument (iii) is as imprecise as argument (i), and is open to similar objections. It is absurd to demand as a test of historicity that those who testify to an event should subscribe to the same meta-physical beliefs and *Weltanschauung* as oneself. Moreover, the argument does not distinguish sufficiently between the testimony to any given event and the explanation that the witnesses to the event may or may not offer. We may be competent to revise the latter in the light of superior understanding. But the validity of the testimony *that* a given event happened depends rather on the honesty, capacity not to be deceived, and proximity of the witnesses of the event. Nor does Hume's argument take into account other forms of evidence, such as physical traces and changed behaviour patterns which may be connected with events.[47]

Hume's argument (iv) also has less substance than might appear at first sight. Swinburne has commented:

> In fact evidence for a miracle 'wrought in one religion' is only evidence against the occurrence of a miracle 'wrought in another religion' if the two miracles, if they occurred, would be evidence for propositions of the two religious systems incompatible with each other. It is hard to think of pairs of alleged miracles of this type. If there were evidence for a Roman Catholic miracle which was evidence for the doctrine of transubstantiation and evidence for a Protestant miracle which was evidence against it, here we would have a case of the conflict of evidence which Hume claims occurs generally with alleged miracles. . . . But . . . most alleged miracles do not give rise to conflicts of this kind. Most alleged miracles, if they occurred as reported, would show at most the power of a god or gods and their concern for the needs of men, and little more specific in the way of doctrine. A miracle wrought in the context of the Hindu religion and one wrought in the context of the Christian religion will not in general tend to show that specific details of their systems are true, but, at most, that there is a god concerned with the needs of those who worship, which is a proposition accepted in both systems.[48]

We might add that the New Testament writers never claim that God shows goodness only to those who share their doctrines.[49] On the other hand, they do recognize that people habitually persist in defective notions of God when they ought to have known better.

Reflection on natural phenomena around them, Paul argued, ought to have been sufficient to show men that God should not be thought of as a thing or an animal.[50] The healing of a lame man should have been seen by the inhabitants of Lystra in the context of 'the good news' that they should turn from vain, superstitious practices 'to a living God who made the heaven and the earth and the sea and all that is in them'.[51] Instead, the populace jumped to the conclusion that 'the gods have come down to us in the likeness of men'. Barnabas they called Zeus, the chief god (because he remained silent) and Paul they called Hermes, the messenger of the gods (because he was doing most of the talking).

Like any other occurrence, an event of this kind is open to different interpretations. As a sheer matter of fact, people are able to remain content with whatever interpretation they put on the event. It is not that the event in itself is necessarily ambiguous and that there are no indications in its context as to its significance. Rather, historical events (like natural phenomena) have a significance that is latent rather than overt. They challenge us to reflect on their meaning. This is supremely true of the signs of the New Testament and, in particular, of the Easter message of resurrection.

In the last analysis, Hume's decisive argument is his first and major one, that miracles are contrary to the established laws of nature and therefore no amount of testimony will suffice as proof of their factuality. Now, as Hume recognized, natural laws are statistical and their predictive character is based on past observation.[52]. As such, they are open to correction and modification. The force of any given formulation depends upon the degree of its corroboration. The point may be accepted that whatever can be explained is not a violation of a law,[53] and that any established violation of a given law would simply show that the law has been inadequately formulated.[54] We would thus be back with the contingency concept of miracle. Nevertheless, such an event would still retain its sign-like character in its historical context.[55] The crucial question that Hume raises, however, is: Are we justified in accepting testimony to a unique event which has no obvious parallel in our experience, especially when it rests on the word of one or two witnesses who may not even be eye-witnesses?

We shall return to the question of assessing evidence, and in particular to the question of assessing this kind of testimony, in section 2 on 'Rules, principles and explanations'. In the meantime, we shall notice two lines of thought which have a bearing on this subject and which have been put forward by Richard Swinburne and Alan Richardson respectively.

Swinburne observes that such evidence as is currently available about the occurrence of violations and the circumstances of their occurrence is not on balance strong enough to render very probable the existence of a divine agency which intervenes in human affairs. The case is radically different, however, if we have evidence of other types for or against the existence and character of God.[56] Such evidence (as in the natural sciences) would be cumulative, and may derive from reflection on nature, on providence, on history, on the testimony of Scripture, and on personal experience. As such, its validity and relevance will itself be the subject of appropriate investigation. Swinburne's point, however, remains:

> If any of these arguments have any weight, we would need only slender historical evidence of certain miracles to have reasonable grounds to believe in their occurrence, just as we need only slender historical evidence to have reasonable grounds for belief in the occurrence of events whose occurrence is rendered probable by natural laws. We take natural laws to show the improbability of violations thereof because they are well-established parts of our overall view of how the world works. But if they are relevant for that reason, then so is any other part of our overall view of how the world works. And if from our study of its operation we conclude that we have evidence for the existence of a God of such a character as to be liable to intervene in the natural order under certain circumstances, the overall world-view gives not a high prior improbability, but a high prior probability to the occurrence of miracles under those circumstances.[57]

Swinburne's approach to the question turns therefore on the general presuppositions that we bring to each particular case. It leaves open the question of what are the ultimate grounds on which one can base belief. But on his premises they cannot include the miraculous. For whether one accepts the miraculous depends in part on precisely these grounds. This is not to say that the miraculous could play no part at all in shaping one's view of God, any more than one would say that a scientific hypothesis which is dependent on the validity of other hypotheses cannot yield valid insights into the nature of things. But as such, it cannot serve as an ultimate basis. This may not deter the believer, as it may be questioned whether the biblical writers ever regarded signs as an ultimate basis for belief. Rather, they are signs pointing beyond themselves *within* the given context of theistic belief.

We have already had occasion to note Alan Richardson's use of the concept of hypothesis in historical explanation. He applies it specifically to the question of the resurrection of Jesus. There are three possible types of explanation here. The first is that it happened in some sense as a historical fact. We need not be able to say precisely how it happened, any more than historians are able to say how Hannibal achieved the feat of crossing the Alps complete with elephants, cavalry and a large army. The historian need not be able to reconstruct in detail how those things happened which he accepts as facts. Nor need he be able to observe the events in question. In fact, the historian is never an observer of events, unless he happens to have been a personal eye-witness. Historical 'facts' are inferences from pieces of testimony and other evidence which the historian has good reason to accept. The second alternative is that the claim that Jesus was raised was deliberately fraudulent. Richardson rejects this on the grounds that 'it is incredible that a faith which brought reconciliation with the all-holy God and peace and charity amongst men could have originated in a fraudulent conspiracy'.[58] The third possible explanation is that the disciples were mistaken. It is a view which involves dismissal of the claims of the first disciples to have encountered the risen Christ and to have found that the tomb was empty,[59] and it involves devising a different explanation from the one given by the first Christians for the origin of the church.

Against these latter alternatives Richardson puts the view that 'either Christ's resurrection called the Church's faith into being or we must give some more rationally coherent account of how that faith with all its tremendous consequences arose'.[60] He cannot remain content with Günther Bornkamm's view that 'the last historical fact' available to scholars is 'the Easter faith of the first disciples'.[61] Underlying such a view is the implicit contention that the historian can deal with questions such as 'Did the disciples believe that God raised Jesus from the dead?' (since this involves purely human terms), but he cannot deal with a question such as 'Did God raise Jesus from the dead?' (since this involves the metaphysical and the supernatural). But Richardson insists that Bornkamm's 'attitude involves the abandoning of historical method altogether, for the historian cannot admit that there are any "last facts" in history, for they would be causeless events. . . . History is a causal nexus in which there can be no breaks, no events which are in principle inexplicable. The historian, if he is to be true to his calling, is bound to go on to consider the various possible explanations of the alleged happening or, if he can, to find a new and better one'.[62] It is not a question of how Jesus was raised, or whether he had a 'spiritual' or a 'physical' body, since in our present state of knowledge we know so little about 'spirits' and 'bodies'.[63] But that Jesus was raised is for Richardson the hypothesis which best explains the date available.

Richardson (like Swinburne) holds that an element of faith is involved in such a judgment. It may be observed that he is using 'faith' not necessarily in the sense of commitment and trust, but in the sense of settled convictions about God and the world.[64] But it may be asked whether such a predisposing faith is a necessary condition. Does Richardson's approach require it? Did the first Christians approach the resurrection with such a prerequisite faith? In both cases the answer would seem to be in the negative. On the one hand, a hypothesis can be entertained as an explanation without any special commitment other than a willingness to see whether it fits the case. The case itself determines whether the hypothesis is adequate. On the other hand, it would seem that the thing the first Christians least expected was the resurrection of Jesus. It was encounter with the risen Christ that awakened faith; not faith that created resurrection belief.[65]

2. RULES, PRINCIPLES AND EXPLANATIONS
The debate whether history is an art, a craft or a science is at least as

old as the present century and will probably go on much longer. I do not propose to attempt a settlement here. I would like, however, to take as a text for this section the pronouncement of R.G. Collingwood that

> History has this in common with every other science: that the historian is not allowed to claim any single piece of knowledge, except where he can justify his claim by exhibiting to himself in the first place, and secondly to any one else who is both able and willing to follow his demonstrations, the grounds upon which it is based.[66]

Van Austin Harvey has remarked that philosophers of history tend to divide into two groups:

> (1) those who have maintained that entitlement to credence is directly proportionate to the degree to which historical explanations approximate to scientific explanations; and (2) those who have argued that historical explanations are of a unique sort and require no reference whatever to the hallmark of scientific explanations, the subsumption of a statement under a law.[67]

Harvey himself (and I would agree with him) is reluctant to lay down rigid laws and criteria in advance. At most, one can indicate the general structure of historical argument, which Harvey does as follows:[68]

key		given D ————————————————→ so (Q), C
D	=	data
W	=	warrant
B	=	backing
Q	=	qualifier
C	=	conclusion
R	=	rebuttal

given D ——————|——————————→ *so (Q), C*

since W

on account of B   *unless R*

Thus the reasons for the crucifixion would take the form: Jesus was crucified (D); since crucifixion was reserved by the Romans for political prisoners (W) which is supported by the following considerations . . . (B), so Jesus was presumably (Q) judged to have been a political enemy (C), unless, in this particular case, an exception was made to please the Jewish authorities (R).[69]

In historical judgments there are so many kinds of argument, considerations and disciplines involved that Harvey prefers to speak of history as a 'field-encompassing field'.[70] Here, as in other disciplines (including law, medicine and the natural sciences) much depends upon the skill and discernment of the investigator. There are certain procedures in looking at evidence, and certain types of question that the historian puts to himself and to others when he evaluates their work. I myself would say that in general these are to be defended and justified in retrospect rather than established a priori. Sir Lewis Namier has commented:

> A dilettante is one who takes himself more seriously than his work; and doctrinaires enamoured of their theories or ingenious ideas are dilettanti in public affairs. On the contrary, the historical approach is intellectually humble; the aim is to comprehend situations, to study trends, to discover how things work: and the crowning attainment of historical study is a historical sense—an intuitive understanding of how things do not happen (how they did happen is a matter of specific history).[71]

Harvey speaks of establishing certain presumptions in a field, and it is in the light of these presumptions that subsequent workers in the field frame and answer their questions.

> By virtue of their exhaustive work, certain presumptions have been established, and these presumptions cast something like the 'burden of proof' of legal argument on those who would establish a different thesis. This burden alters the dynamics of argument in subtle ways, conveying a certain weight to this or that argument and lending special importance to this or that rebuttal. The skill of the historian is manifested in his degree of sensitivity to these dynamics. He must know what the crucial questions are, where the weak links in other interpretations lie, which data need to be challenged, and which have been misinterpreted.[72]

All this does not mean that history is an entirely subjective affair. As Harvey goes on to say, 'Although there is this almost intangible element in historical judgment, it does not follow that these judgments cannot be justified, or that it is meaningless to ask for evidence and warrants in each case.'[73] But we have to recognize that there are different types of historical judgments and correspondingly varying degrees of verifiability. The American archaeologist W.F. Albright has drawn up the following table of historical judgments in a descending scale of verifiability:

1. Judgments of (about) Typical Occurrence
   The logical basis is inductive and statistical.
2. Judgments of (about) Particular Facts
   Based on public observation and report, subject to repeated testing, or on verifiable evidence of scientific nature—e.g., astronomically fixed dates, medically established cause of death, etc.
3. Judgments of (about) Cause and Effect
4. Judgments of (about) Value
   Subjective ancient or modern, personal or public opinion.
5. Judgments of (about) Personal Reactions.[74]

Some might object that such a tabulation is too rigid, or that there are other possibilities and categories, or that the final two categories are too vague to admit objective judgment. Within these categories there is room for degrees of certainty, even in judgments concerning typical occurrence. Inferences from statistics may vary wildly— as can be seen all too clearly in the realm of economics, to the embarrassment of the politicians and the economists alike. On the other hand, it is normally easier to establish what happened and why in the case of a single, well-documented, recent event than in that of something remote and complex. Thus, one can say why Edward Heath resigned as prime minister in 1974; it was because his party lost the general election, and under the British parliamentary system defeated prime ministers tender their resignations to the sovereign who invites the leader of the majority party to form a government. It is a much more difficult business to say why the Roman Empire declined and finally fell, or to specify and assess the relative strengths of the causes of the First World War. Nevertheless, there must have been causes, however complex and heterogeneous, for there are no causeless events. If history is to rise above mere antiquarianism, fascinated by the quaintness of isolated objects, such attempts have to be made.[75]

We may repeat what has already been said, that historical facts are not items of information to which the historian has direct access, but are inferences drawn often from a widely diverse range of information.[76] Similarly, the explanations of the historian are not propositional statements about directly observable events, but hypotheses put forward to account for data at hand. As such, they may be tested by seeing whether they fit the data of the case in question and whether at the same time they agree with other accepted knowledge. The historian may be compared to a detective testing theories against evidence[77] or to a shoe salesman trying pairs of shoes on people's feet. The process is neither purely inductive nor purely deductive.[78] The historian needs imagination and sense in the framing of his theories (as does the salesman in selecting suitable shoes). He then tests *the theory* against the data which he is evaluating. It is possible for the theory (like the shoes) to be too tight or too slack. In the former case the data (like our toes) are pinched. Something has to be manipulated or even left out. In the latter case, the explanation takes account of the data, but is not precise enough. It lacks the elegance which is the goal not only of fashion but also of scientific theory. It is the duty of the historian to go on trying his theories until he is satisfied that the theory fits all the data before him in a way which is consonant with his wider view of reality and which is appropriate to the subject-matter involved.[79] (Or, if we are to keep the picture of the shoe salesman, he must find shoes which not only fit the feet of the customer but also suit the customer's general requirements.)[80]

It may be that no such account can be produced. In that case, he has to suspend judgment as a historian, though he may still entertain his beliefs and views, acknowledging them for what they are. It may be that no single explanation can be established to the exclusion of others. In such cases the historian has to keep before himself the various possibilities and probabilities. Here the believer is no exception. Although he may be convinced of the fundamental truth of his beliefs, there may be many aspects of the latter where he has to suspend academic judgment, admitting that he is not in a position to demonstrate the point, and granting the possibility of alternative explanations.[81] On the other hand, this procedure may be applied to judgments of cause and effect, value and personal reaction. In some cases, the interpretation may fit the data so well as to be beyond all reasonable doubt. In either case, the historian comes before his public not as one whose reputation suffices to guarantee truth but as one whose work is open to public verification. This applies as much in the realm of theological criticism as in secular history. By their hypotheses and methods of verification ye shall know them.

We have talked in very general terms about verifiability. How this works out in practice depends upon the subject in question. The discussions by Professor Bruce and Dr France in this volume exemplify methods of historical and critical reasoning in the field of New Testament studies. Because the Christian revelation is a historical revelation, whatever means and techniques are appropriate to the study of history are in principle relevant here. This is not to say that, when this has been done, every question will be solved. Christianity is more than historical reconstruction. To know its meaning involves repentance, faith, love and hope. Only in this way can one become, as Kierkegaard would have said, a 'contemporary' of Christ. On the other hand, to understand the Christian revelation in its concrete, historical expression, we must study it in the light of the disciplines of textual criticism, linguistics, and literary and historical criticism. The latter involves not only questions of authorship and date of documents, but their background, form and tendencies.

This is not the place to attempt to survey this ground.[82] On the other hand, the point must be underlined that to say this is not to endorse each and every technique favoured by whatever happens to be the most vocal school of thought at the time. The same hard-headed caution has to be applied here as in any other academic discipline. What today might seem to be an impressive discovery may tomorrow turn out to be a blind alley. A case in point is the vogue for redaction criticism as a method of determining historicity. As Dr France has shown in discussing the sayings of Jesus, the criteria employed by some of the redaction critics just will not stand up to close scrutiny. Here, as anywhere else, the validity of the results depends upon the validity of the methods.

Nowhere is this point more crucial than in the contemporary debate on hermeneutics.[83] Here the central question is that of the interpretation of Jesus and the gospel. The traditional Christian approach, as represented by Reformed theology down to the present day, sees Scripture as the record of God's revelation of himself in the history and writings of the people of Israel and supremely in Jesus Christ. This record was written by men inspired by the Holy Spirit, who guided their insights and writing. The ultimate basis for this view is the testimony of the writers themselves and the teaching of Jesus, acknowledged by the believer not only as historically authoritative but as the Word of God in his own life and experience. The same authority is the basis for taking the perspectives of Scripture not only as decisive and normative for our perspectives and understanding of life but also for the theistic interpretation of history. God acts in history, and supremely in the life, death and resurrection of Jesus, which constitute God's decisive revelation of himself to man.

The Bultmann school, on the other hand, refuses to admit divine revelations and regards such accounts as belonging to the primitive perspectives of the pre-scientific era. The notions of heaven, hell, atonement and of a divine redeemer are mythological expressions of man's understanding of his own existence.[85] Professor Bruce has already examined the question of myth in some detail. Our concern here must be with the fundamental differences of principle which underlie these conflicting interpretations and their radically different world-views. Basic to Bultmann's approach are the premises that the world is to be explained in terms of a closed system of natural, historical and psychological causes which does not admit exceptions or interventions, and that all history must be reinterpreted in the light of contemporary understanding. This view received classical exposition from the pen of Ernst Troeltsch in an essay dating back to 1898, 'Ueber historische und dogmatische Methode in der Theologie'.[86] For Troeltsch there must be universal correspondence of all historical phenomena and thus the acceptance of causal relations between them. A fundamental part is played here by the methodological principle of analogy.

> For the use of analogy is the means by which criticism is only really possible. Analogy with what happens before our eyes and comes to pass in us is the key to criticism. Deception, pro-

crastination, fabrication of myth, fraud and party spirit which we see before our eyes are the means by which we recognize the same kind of thing in the material which comes to us. Agreement with normal ordinary, repeatedly attested modes of occurrence and conditions, as we know them, is the mark of probability for the occurrences which criticism can acknowledge as having really happened or leave aside. The observation of analogies between similar occurrences of the past makes it possible to ascribe probability to them and to interpret what is unknown in the one by the known of the other.[87]

Clearly, Troeltsch is saying something important here. Comparison of the new and unknown with the known plays an important part in human knowledge. If we have not the remotest experience of a thing, it is impossible to conceive what that thing is like. I do not think that the historian can or should try to avoid interpreting new data in the light of his present understanding. But it seems to me wrong to say that the historian must have had precisely the same passions and ambitions as Genghis Khan or Adolf Hitler or even as Lloyd George or Franklin D. Roosevelt in order to understand these men. Still less does he need to have suffered personally at their hands. Indeed, too close a personal involvement can also distort. But he does need sympathetic imagination to try to put himself in their place and in the place of those with whom they came into contact. We must also ask another question, however: Does not the rigid application of the doctrine of analogy actually preclude the apprehension of the unique—even before we have looked at it?

It seems to me that Wolfhart Pannenberg is nearer the mark when he redefines the use of analogy as follows:

The cognitive power of analogy depends upon the fact that it teaches us to see contents of the same kind in *nonhomogeneous things* [*das Gleichartige im Ungleichartigen*]. If the historian keeps his eye on the nonexchangeable individuality and contingency of an event, then he will see that he is dealing with nonhomogeneous things, which cannot be contained without remainder in any analogy.[88]

This is not to say that we must weave our net with holes so wide that they let in each and every myth and legend. To quote Pannenberg again:

> That a reported event bursts analogies with otherwise usual or repeatedly attested events is still no ground for disputing its facticity. It is another matter when positive analogies to forms of tradition (such as myths and even legends) relating to unreal objects, phenomena referring to states of consciousness (like visions) may be found in the historical sources. In such cases historical understanding guided by analogy can lead to a negative judgment about the reality of the occurrences reported in the tradition. Such a judgment will be rendered not because of the unusualness of something reported about, but rather because it exhibits a positive analogy to some form of consciousness which has no objective referent.[89]

So then we must look for analogies between our present understanding of history and the data we are examining. But we must be careful not to overpress them and reject that which does not fit.

This applies on a secular level as well as when dealing with the allegedly supernatural. Sir Lewis Namier has some timely warnings here. In answer to the question 'Can men learn from history?' he replies:

> That depends on the quality and accuracy of the historian's perceptions and conclusions, and on the critical faculties of the reader—on the 'argument,' and on the 'intellects' to comprehend it. When erudition exceeds intelligence, past results are rigidly applied to radically changed situations and preparations are completed for fighting the previous war.... The price paid ... in the trench-warfare of 1914-18 produced in turn the Maginot mentality among the French public and politicians.... The time lag in disciplined military thought is aggravated on the victorious side by the glory which attaches to past success and by the prestige of their ageing artificers. Yet in all spheres alike, even in the freest, false analogies, the product of superficial knowledge and reasoning, are the pitfall of history as *magistra vitae*.[90]

Here, of course, Namier is talking about secular history in secular terms.

To my mind two points stand out in all this. (1) We need to be extremely sensitive and careful in seeing and applying analogies; and (2) our present understanding needs to be perpetually revised and enlarged in the light of new knowledge. The latter must be allowed to include new knowledge of the past. Unless our understanding is broadly based and open-ended, progress in knowledge is impossible.

In reading biblical history, the ordinary Christian, no less than the critical historian, repeatedly makes use of analogy, whether he is conscious of doing so or not. When he identifies himself with this or that character, sees a contemporary situation paralleled by something in Scripture, or draws some lesson, he is implicitly employing the principle of analogy. But in believing (say) in the resurrection of Jesus, even though he has no experience of the dead being raised, he is doing what Pannenberg recommends. He is affirming his belief in the unique which bursts analogies with present experience. In the last analysis the issue between the traditional understanding of Christianity and that of Bultmann and the radicals comes down to the question of analogy. The Bultmann school insists that the witness of the New Testament must be understood in the light of the closed scientific world-view which it holds, and hence must be 'demythologized.' Traditional Reformed theologians reply that this rigid use of analogy has prevented Bultmann from recognizing the unique.

Professor T.F. Torrance goes even further, accusing the Bultmann school of a lack of objectivity. In any science the object studied must determine the methods employed. In the case of Christian theology we are concerned with the revelation of God. It is this revelation in all its concreteness which must determine our methods and modify our presuppositions.[91] For the Bultmann school the problem is: How do we think of Jesus Christ in the light of our scientific world-view and closed view of history which do not admit supernatural interventions? Torrance inverts the question. How do we think of space and time, *given* the incarnation and modern physics? He holds that the former view which preconceives and thus misconceives the question may be traced back to Greek philosophy. This in turn affected the medieval West and thence Lutheranism which set the pace for modern theology. Bultmann, and his way of posing the problem, is pre-eminently an heir to this tradition. It views space and time as a receptacle in which things exist and happen, and which thus predetermine their shape and possibility. Torrance traces his own view back through Reformed theology to the Nicene fathers, Athanasius, and Origen. In connection with the latter he declares:

> The incarnation means that He by whom all things are comprehended and contained by assuming a body made room for Himself in our physical existence, yet without being contained, confined or circumscribed in place as in a vessel. He was wholly present in the body and yet wholly present everywhere, for He became man without ceasing to be God![92]

Space is a *differential* concept that is essentially *open-ended*, 'for it is defined in accordance with the interaction between God and man, eternal and contingent happening'.[93] In an objective and disciplined theology

> the scientific function of theological statements is to offer a rational account of knowledge beyond the limits of mere this-wordly experience through the use of acknowledged concepts taken from this world, and so to help our minds to lay hold upon it even though it is more than we can grasp within the limits of these concepts. Theological statements properly made are thus by way of being operational statements directing us towards what is new and beyond but which cannot be wholly indicated or explained in terms of the old.... Theological statements operate ... with essentially *open concepts*—concepts that are relatively closed on our side of their reference through their connection with the space-time structures of our world, but which on God's side are wide open to the infinite objectivity and inexhaustible intelligibility of the divine Being.[94]

There is a sense in which the Jews and the biblical writers have a concept of analogy. But in one way at least it seems to invert that of Troeltsch. Whereas Troeltsch measures the past in the light of his understanding of the present, the biblical writers measure the present in the light of their understanding of the past.[95] The Psalmist strengthens faith and builds up hope by calling to mind the great deeds of God.[96] Peter seeks to put the plight of his readers in perspective by addressing them as 'exiles of the Dispersion', 'a chosen race, a royal priesthood, a holy nation, God's own people', and as 'aliens and exiles'.[97] The history and the imagery of the past is applied to the present in order to reveal diminsions of the situation which would otherwise be concealed.

A particular case of this is the notion of fulfilment which in the hands of the New Testament writers is not simply a case of noting predictions which have come off.[98] Indeed, if we treat some of their examples as such instances, we may conclude that they look rather forced and trivial. The context of Hosea 11: 1 ('Out of Egypt I called my son') does not suggest that the prophet foresaw the holy family returning as refugees from Egypt (*cf*. Mt. 2: 15). And similarly the context of Jeremiah 31: 15 does not suggest that the prophet predicted the slaughter of the innocents at Bethlehem so many hundreds of years after his death (*cf*. Mt. 2:18). But the passages in question demand a more profound interpretation. Matthew is saying, in effect, that these new events which fulfil prophecy are to be understood in the perspective of the original event. In a sense they reduplicate the latter. Whereas the believing Jew regarded the exodus as a great landmark in history, this apparently insignificant event of a single family returning from Egypt is just as much the work of God and in fact is even more significant.

In biblical history the concept of God is continually being enlarged and modified. If we wish to know God and understand what he is doing, the biblical writers tell us to reflect on his dealings with Israel. There is a kind of continuous, reciprocal modification of the past by the present and of the present by the past. This operates within biblical history itself. The history of Jesus completes and modifies earler understanding. Pannenberg comments:

> This concept of God will become a proper concept of a theology based on revelation only . . . by the correction and transformation it undergoes in its application to the God of Israel: that is, by its referral to the history in which the character of this God first disclosed itself step by step, then finally and with ultimate validity in the presence of the eschaton in the fate of Jesus of Nazareth. True knowledge of God is obtained from this history for the first time, and therefore cannot be presupposed as something that makes it possible to grasp this knowledge. It is

this history which first corrects the preliminary (and distorted) representations of God—indeed, even Israel's representations of its God! Thus, all statements about the redemptive event remain bound to analogies 'from below', whose applicability is subject to the procedures of historical criticism.[99]

The use of analogy works both ways in understanding biblical history, as it does in understanding secular history. We understand the past in the light of the present, but we also understand the present in the light of the past. Understanding grows by a process of successive approximation. To comprehend history, we need to make use of whatever techniques are appropriate for the historian; but history itself and the reality it contains must determine our techniques and modify our presuppositions.

3. WHAT DOES THE HISTORIAN ACHIEVE?

Sooner or later almost every writer on this subject cites (usually with a view to debunking) the celebrated pronouncement of the nineteenth-century German historian von Ranke, that the task of historian is to show *'wie es eigentlich gewesen'* (as [or how] it actually was). To be fair to von Ranke, the sentence should be quoted in full.

People have assigned to history the office of judging the past and instructing the present generation for the benefit of future ages: the present attempt does not aspire to such high offices: it merely wants to show how it actually was.[100]

In context this is not a statement of presumption but of modesty. It is a declaration that the primary goal of the historian is to get at the truth as it happened.

Since Ranke's day historians who are usually labelled relativists have seriously questioned whether Ranke's goal is realistic. This questioning has taken two main lines. On the one hand, it is urged that it is naive to suppose that history is a matter of presenting 'all the facts' and letting them 'speak for themselves'.[101] Indeed, history involves value-judgments. On the other hand, we are reminded that the historian never has access to all the facts. And from those which he has, he has to select. History, it is therefore said, is relative to the historian who himself reflects a particular culture and particular interests and standpoints.

The thesis that history involves value-judgments has been argued convincingly by Sir Isaiah Berlin in his lecture on *Historical Inevitability*. History involves moral judgments, because it is dealing with human beings, and as such it should not be confused with the natural sciences.

The invocation to historians to suppress even that minimal degree of moral or psychological evaluation which is necessarily involved in viewing human beings as creatures with purposes and motives (and not merely as causal factors in the procession of events), seems to me to rest upon a confusion of the aims and methods of the humane studies with those of natural science. It is one of the greatest and most-destructive fallacies of the last hundred years.[102]

Against such a position it has been argued by Herbert Butterfield that 'moral judgments on human beings are by their nature irrelevant to the enquiry and alien to the intellectual realm of scientific history'. For the latter is concerned with 'just the observable interconnections of events'.[103] William H. Dray argues that, in so far as history is concerned with the study of human actions and therefore may be expressed in *purposive* terms, moral evaluation is not necessary.[104]

Against Butterfield and Dray, it may be said that human interconnections cannot be described without invoking moral terms, however covertly. As Dray himself concedes, to describe an act as 'murder' involves a moral value-judgment. From a purely physical point of view, the same act could be described as a 'killing.' But as a matter of practice, historians do not go through their writings crossing out the word 'murder' in those cases which they think require it. In so doing, they are making an implicit moral judgment, implying moral responsibility. Moreover, to suspend a moral judgment is just as much a moral act as to make a positive moral judgment. The same applies to the whole range of words covering human activities. Some, of course, are neutral in that they do not involve moral judgments. But to use a neutral one, instead of one expressing some kind of evaluation, may itself involve making a moral judgment.

The decision whether to use the word 'murder' or the word 'kill' depends upon one's perspective. Some moral judgments (like psychological judgments) will depend upon the standpoint of the observer. In this sense, they are relative to his judgment and criteria. They may be subjective in that they represent a purely personal attitude. But they may be objective in so far as they represent values which are independent of the individual thinker. Ranke's reaction to didactic history (which is more interested in drawing morals and using the past for propaganda purposes) was a healthy one. But if the above argument is valid, neither the past nor the present can be rid of values. We cannot expunge moral issues from the past, nor can we avoid making moral judgments in trying to discern what they were. What we have said about moral judgments applies as well to the assessment of other factors, such as psychological, economic, sociological and religious causes. Our assessment of these factors will be relative to our standpoint. This is not to say that they will necessarily be arbitrary. That will depend on the over-all validity of our standpoint, on its relevance to the subject we are considering, and on the use we make of it. But it does mean that the account we give will represent a perspective or a combination of perspectives.

There is an element of selection in the choice of our standpoints. There is also an element of selection (both voluntary and involuntary) in the historian's handling of his material. One of the most important statements of the relativist case here is a paper by the American historian, Charles A. Beard, entitled 'That Noble Dream' (1935).[105] Beard argues, for example, that 'the historian is not an observer of the past that lies beyond his own time. He cannot see it *objectively* as the chemist sees his test tubes and compounds. The historian must "see" the actuality of history through the medium of documentation. That is his sole recourse.' But many events and personalities 'escape the recording of documentation', and 'in very few cases can the historian be reasonably sure that he has assembled all the documents of a given period, region, or segment'. Thus the 'total actuality is not factually knowable to any historian'. The historian is never 'a neutral mirror'. 'Whatever acts of purification the historian may perform he yet remains human, a creature of time, place, circumstance, interests, predilections, culture.' 'He may search for, but he cannot find, the "objective truth" of history, or write it, "as it actually was." '

We cannot but agree with Beard that history involves selection. It is a selection that is partly done for him by the preservation (conscious and unconscious) of other material. But out of this material the historian will select what is significant to him in the light of the questions he is asking. It is this process which led Jakob Burckhardt to describe history as 'the record of facts which one age finds remarkable in another'.[107] But whether a fact is remarkable depends on why it is remarkable. When seen within one framework of thought a fact may not be particularly significant, but when it is seen within another it may take on quite a different meaning.[108] To the Roman historian Tacitus, Christ was a man who 'suffered the extreme penalty during the reign of Tiberius at the hands of one of our procurators, Pontius Pilate'.[109] He is noted only because his followers happened to suffer abominable torments at the hands of Nero who is the immediate object of Tacitus's interest. To the evangelists and other New Testament writers Christ's death has a quite different significance. It is not that there is any difference of opinion as to what happened. It is the framework or perspective which is decisive here.

History books differ, not only because some historians are more diligent and perceptive than others, but also because they write from different perspectives. It is not necessarily a case that one perspective is right and another wrong. Just as geographical text-books contain some maps which give the physical features of a region and others which give political ones, and some a combination of both, so historical subjects are capable of being studied from different and complementary standpoints. Moreover, just as there are different kinds of projections and conventions which are made necessary by the attempt to reduce a multi-dimensional reality to two dimensions, so inevitably the attempt to reduce people and events to verbal narrative means the employment of conventions and projections.[110]

No single account can show exhaustively the course of history as it happened. The resources and the perspectives are too limited. In the period of which Ranke was speaking when he made his celebrated remark, it is doubtful whether it is possible to write a biography of any single person, because the materials for a biography in the modern sense are just not there.

I myself think that it is inappropriate to describe the work of the historian as reconstructing the past. It is not reconstruction in any normal sense of the word. There are those who reconstruct old cars, aeroplanes, trams, railway engines and houses. In such cases one has certain fragments of the original, and by use of original plans, research and hard work, one makes something *like* the original in as much detail as possible and *on the same scale*. But the events and personalities of the past cannot be reconstructed in this way. We may get fragments from the past (artefacts, records, clothes, *etc*.), but we cannot go back into the past. Nor do we usually have sufficient continuous record to be able to make a full-scale reconstruction. The nearest we get to this is the historical tableau and television documentary in which actors speak the lines originally spoken. But if such a tableau consists merely in repeating recorded lines and actions, it lacks the interpretative element which is an essential feature of critical history. And if the tableau is so arranged as to bring out this or that emphasis, an element of selection and interpretation is clearly involved, so that it ceases to be a mere reconstruction.

But most history-writing does not take such a form. Most of it takes the form of written historical judgments based upon evaluation of data and opinions.[111] What then is involved? Sir Lewis Namier has put forward the thesis that

> As history deals with concrete events fixed in time and space, narrative is its basic medium—but guided by analytic selection of what to narrate. The function of the historian is akin to that of the painter and not of the photographic camera: to discover and set forth, to single out and stress that which is of the nature of the thing, and not to reproduce indiscriminately all that meets the eye. To distinguish a tree you look at its shape, its bark and leaf; counting and measuring the branches would get you nowhere. Similarly what matters in history is the great outline and the significant detail; what must be avoided is the deadly mass of irrelevant narrative.[112]

This, of course, is not an open invitation to take short cuts and to make impressionistic caricatures instead of doing painstaking investigation. Accuracy, as A.E. Housman remarked, 'is a duty, not a virtue'.[113] Namier's own work was characterized by tremendous industry and attention to detail. Rather, Namier is saying that the aim which the historian should keep before him is to discern what is significant, and he sees this as 'the great outline and the significant detail'.

It may be remarked how closely the biblical writers come in their own particular ways to the notion of history as 'the great outline and the significant detail'. Admittedly, they do not set out to produce pieces of critical history in the modern sense. But to demand this of any ancient writing is to set up an arbitrary criterion. Any ancient— or for that matter any modern—writing must be understood in terms of what it is trying to do and in the light of its particular conventions. These writings had their conventions and operated on the basis of what we have called their 'projections'. Different conventions and projections are to be found in different parts of the Bible. They are not all written on the same scale. The kind of reporting that the synoptic Gospels give of the sayings and actions of Jesus is different from that of the early chapters of Genesis, which report cosmic events in terms of words and actions. The standpoint of the Fourth Gospel is different from that of the Synoptics, and the standpoint of each of the latter is markedly different from that of the others. To say this is not to say with the nineteenth-century critics that one of them was right and that the others are later elaborations. Rather, it is to say that each must be understood in its own terms before anything further can be said. The biblical writers do not ask psychological and economic questions. They see events and people in terms of righteousness, and the will of God. Consequently the New Testament writers see events and people within the framework of law, prophecy, apocalyptic imagery and messianic expectation.

We should not expect ancient writers to observe the same distinctions between direct speech and indirect speech as we would today. There are no quotation marks in the ancient languages and, in my opinion, it is misleading when modern translations insert them. For they give the impression of an intended verbatim precision in recorded speech, which was not present in the original.[114] What is given by the evangelists is not a series of verbatim quotations but a report of the main thrust of a speaker's utterance, as seen in relation to the event being described. If we look at the Gospels we do not find a balanced biography in the modern sense. Rather, each evangelist gives, from his own standpoint, a general outline and significant detail. What determines the composition of that outline and detail is each writer's particular perception of his subject.[115]

Namier compares the work of the historian with that of the painter. It could also be compared with that of the model-maker.[116] Like scientific theory, historical construction is not a literal description of what is observed. As we have already seen, it is not exactly a reconstruction of reality. It is more like a model or a series of models. The historian may have incorporated things from the past, such as fragments of utterances, observations and records. But he will have had to use his own skill, insight and ingenuity in its construction. What he has made will not be identical with the original thing. It will have its particular scale and conventions. Some things will be represented and not others, depending partly on the material available and partly on the purpose of the model. But if it is well done, it will enable the onlooker to have some idea of what the original was like and what significance it has. It will enable him to perceive that original, not directly, but indirectly.

In history-writing this model-making process is a continual one. The initial accounts, say of the life of Jesus in the Gospels, provide one set of models. The accounts of critical historians provide another. The reader's understanding presents yet another set. The process of understanding involves an interaction between the models and the historian (whether he is a professional critical historian or just an ordinary person thinking about history). It is not that the latest critical reconstruction necessarily supersedes all earlier models, or that the primary accounts can ever be dispensed with. But neither can we avoid making our reconstructions, whether they be technical and critical or unreflective. What critical reconstruction does is to attempt to correct unreflective understanding and to see earlier accounts in new perspective and depth. It proceeds by what we earlier called successive approximation as it seeks to discern the intelligible structure of the events with which it deals.

The goal of the study of history is not this model-making as an end in itself but the apprehension and understanding of reality through it.[119] It was this that led R.G. Collingwood to see history as 'the re-enactment of past experience'.[118] In so far as God is involved in an event in the past, reflection on that event is the means not only of consciously apprehending God but of apprehending God in a way which reaches beyond the limits of our immediate experience. Some sixty years ago Wilhelm Dilthey observed how understanding opens up possibilities which are just not present within the restrictions of one's normal life.

> The possibility of experiencing religious states in my own existence is narrowly restricted for me as it is for most people today. But when I run through the letters and writings of Luther, the reports of his contemporaries, the records of the religious confrontations and councils, and his activity as a minister, I experience a religious process of such eruptive force, such energy, in which it is a matter of life and death, that it lies beyond all possibility of actually being lived by a man of our time. But I can relive it. I transpose myself into the circumstances: everything in them drives towards such an extraordinary development of the religious temperament. . . . Unknown objects of beauty in the world and regions of life, which could never be reached personally by a man in his limited circumstances, are opened up before him. To put it in general terms: man, bound and determined by the reality of life, is set free not only by art—as has often been argued—but also by the understanding of history. And this effect of history, which its most modern detractors have not seen, is broadened and deepened in the further stages of historical consciousness.[119]

What Dilthey says here of Luther may be applied to any historical personality, whether they are connected with Christianity or with any other religion. In this sense Christianity is on the same footing as other religions. But to make this point is simply to recognize that all religions have histories. The decisive difference between them—as between different historical figures—is what they embody in history. Whether new experiences, insights and horizons are opened up for us depends on two factors: on the one hand the man or the event and what they embody, and on the other, our understanding of them. The medium by which this is mediated is history and in particular our historical models.

4. HOW DOES HISTORY AFFECT BELIEF?

In this final section we shall focus on two issues: (1) history and revelation, and (2) the importance of history to the believer.

History and revelation

Since the eighteenth century there has been an on-going debate about the nature of revelation in the light of the attempt to understand the Bible as history. Broadly speaking, there are two opposing camps: those who see revelation as revelation of the Word of God and those who see revelation as history. But to leave it at that would be to oversimplify. For the theologians of the Word range from the Reformers to Bultmann. And the protagonists of revelation in history include those who see it as Israelite history and those who see it as universal history. At least one contemporary theologian would like to scrap the idea of revelation altogether. But there are others, including myself, who believe that a Christian view of revelation must embrace revelation in history (both biblical and universal history), revelation through the Word of God and revelation in on-going human experience.

It is a commonplace among biblical theologians to say with G. Ernest Wright that one of the distinctive characteristics of the Bible is to see history and historical tradition 'as the primary sphere in which God reveals himself'.[120] Wright goes on to say, 'To be sure, God also reveals himself and his will in various ways to the inner consciousness of man, as in other religions. Yet the nature and content of this inner revelation is determined by the outward, objective happenings of history in which individuals are called to participate. It is, therefore, the objectivity of God's historical acts which are the focus of attention, not the subjectivity of inner, emotional, diffuse and mystical experience.'[121] This view of history in the Old Testament found expression in the concept of God's 'election of a special people through whom he would accomplish his purposes'.[122] This belief in election provided the framework for understanding not only the exodus deliverance and the migration of Abraham to Canaan, but life in Palestine, prophetic eshatology and the apocalyptic of the book of Daniel. It was confirmed and clarified on Sinai. Israel's subsequent sin was seen as a breach of the covenant which enabled the faithful to see that election was unalterable. Wright's view represents a fairly conservative approach to Old Testament history. Revelation is mediated through history, the revelation being the significance of events as indicative of the mind and character of God.

But others have denied that revelation has any factual content. In his Gifford Lectures in the 1930s, William Temple put forward a view of revelation which drove a sharp wedge between encounter with God and any empirical content that such an encounter might have. 'What is offered to man's apprehension in any specific Revelation is not truth concerning God but the living God Himself.'[123] Temple was particularly concerned to get away from the idea of revealed truth. 'There is no such thing as revealed truth. There are truths of revelation, that is to say, propositions which express the results of correct thinking concerning revelation; but they are not themselves directly revealed.'[124]

Rudolf Bultmann is equally concerned to remove all factual content from revelation. He answers the question 'What then has been revealed according to the New Testament?' by saying: 'Nothing at all, so far as the question concerning revelation asks for doctrines—doctrines, say, that no man could have discovered for himself—or for mysteries that become known once and for all as soon as they are communicated. On the other hand, however, everything has been revealed, insofar as man's eyes are opened concerning his own existence and he is once again able to understand himself.'[125] 'Revelation is an act of God, an *occurrence,* and not a communication of supernatural knowledge.'[126] The demand to say what the Word of God is must be rejected, because it rests on the idea that it is possible to designate a complex of statements that can be found and understood with respect to 'content'. Formal clarification of what is meant by the Word of God in Scripture, Bultmann claims, shows us only that 'no "content" of the Word of God can be exhibited, but rather can only be heard in the immediate moment.'[127] Faith, for Bultmann, does not have an object. It 'does not relate itself to historical or cosmic processes that could be established as free from doubt, but rather to the *preaching* behind which faith cannot go and which says to man that he must understand the cross as God's act of salvation and believe in the resurrection'.[128] The context of Bultmann's thought makes it clear that the 'cross' and 'resurrection' are not to be understood as empirical, historical events, but as symbols designating the limits of man's existence and thought.[129] Faith is a *venture*. It is a decision to let my concrete existence here and now 'be determined by the proclamation and faith in it'.[130]

F.G. Downing goes on to take the final step. Whereas Bultmann at least retained the idea of revelation, Downing proposes to abandon it altogether. 'If God intended to "reveal himself" in Christ, in the events of his life and death and resurrection and in his teaching, he failed. It seems more faithful to assume that this was not his intention. . . . A "revelation" of what cannot now be seen is not a "revelation". We may believe, trust, that Christ has made the "revealing of God" a possibility in some sort of future. It is surely nonsense, even pernicious nonsense, to pretend that it is a present fact.'[131]

Over against Temple, Bultmann and Downing, with their stress on a factually contentless (and in Downing's case, a non-existent) revelation, we may turn back to others who see revelation as having some objective content (whether it be in event or word). Oscar Cullmann, for example, insists that faith must have an object:

> The basis for this separation between an objective event on the one hand, and my faith in it and my decision on the other, is not an 'unconscious', antiquated philosophy of the separation between object and subject, outdated by existentialism, as the theologians influenced by Heidegger assert. It is the plain and simple New Testament concept of faith as it is developed especially clearly in Paul. *The act of faith itself requires this distinction.* Faith means that in humility I turn away from myself and look only to the radiant light of an event in which I am totally uninvolved, so that I can only fall down in worship before him who has brought about this event (Rom. 1.21). As I humbly turn away from myself and look to the event, I appropriate the event in faith. Faith means excluding myself and thus including myself. *So I gain my self-understanding when I am not observing my self-understanding.* Therein lies the paradox of New Testament faith.[132]

Few theologians have more vigorously defended the otherness of God than Karl Barth. With William Temple he could insist that

'What God utters is never in any way known and true in abstraction from God Himself. It is known and true for no other reason that He Himself says it, that He in person is in and accompanies what is said by Him'.[133] Barth's view of revelation is personal and dynamic. But Barth held that just as we do not know people fully apart from their utterances,[134] so we do not know God by a purely mystical illumination. 'God reveals Himself in propositions by means of language, and human language at that, to the effect that from time to time such and such a word, spoken by the prophets and apostles and proclaimed in the Church, becomes His Word. Thus the personality of the Word of God is not to be played off against its verbal character and spirituality.'[135] Barth spoke of the Word of God in its threefold from: Jesus Christ, the revealed Word of God, who is the revelation of the Father; Scripture, the written Word; and the proclaimed Word of God. The three forms are inter-related: 'The *revealed Word of God* we know only from the Scripture adopted by Church proclamation, or from Church proclamation based on Scripture. The *written Word of God* we know only through the revelation which makes proclamation possible, or through the proclamation made possible by revelation. The *proclaimed Word of God* we know only by knowing the revelation attested through Scripture, or by knowing the Scripture which attests revelation.'[136] In this way Barth preserved the otherness of God and the dynamic character of revelation, while at the same time showing that revelation has an objective, knowable content. 'We can indeed say what the Word of God is; but we must say it indirectly. We must recall the forms in which it is real for us and from these forms which it takes infer *how* it is. That "how" is the reflected image, attainable by man, of the unattainable nature of God.'[137] It is with this reflected image that all thought about God is concerned.

Barth's teaching contains important insights into the personal, dynamic and verbal character of revelation.[138] But is revelation wholly confined to the Word? In the past decade Wolfhart Pannenberg has sought to bring theology back from theologies of the Word (whether they be Barth's or Bultmann's) and ground it once more in history.[139] It is through history that God is known. In bringing Israel out of Egypt and giving them the land God 'has proved himself to be

their God, for he has acted on *their* behalf. The exodus and the occu-
pancy of the land are established as the decisive factor in the knowledge of God, and this is so stated in Hosea and later in Jeremiah'.[140]
The same applies to subsequent biblical history. The resurrection of
Jesus and his pre-Easter life, seen in the light of prophetic and
apocalyptic expectation, are a 'reflection of the eschatological self-
vindication of Jahweh'.[141]

However, 'revelation is not comprehended completely in the
beginning, but at the end of revealing history'.[142] Since revelation is
mediated by events and is thus indirect, it is only after their occurrence that God's deity is perceived.[143] From our present vantage-
points we cannot see the whole of history. The full revelation of God
is known only at the end of history. This concept, Pannenberg holds,
not only corresponds to the truth of Hegel's insight into history but
also to the broadening perspective of the biblical writers themselves.
In apocalyptic thought,

> the destiny of mankind, from creation onward, is seen to be the
> unfolding according to a plan of God. . . . That the end will
> make manifest the secrets of the present is also the presupposi-
> tion of primitive Christianity. The history that demonstrates
> the deity of God is broadened to include the totality of all
> events. This corresponds completely to the universality of
> Israel's God, who is not only the God of Israel, but will be the
> God of all men. This broadening of the *Heilsgeschichte* to a uni-
> versal history is in essence already accomplished in the major
> prophets of Israel in that they treat the kingdoms of the world
> as responsible to God's commands.[144] . . . the apocalyptic view-
> point conceived of Jahweh's Law as the ground of the totality of
> world events. It is at the end of this chain of world events that
> God can for the first time be revealed with finality as the one
> true God.[145]

Now for Pannenberg, 'the historical revelation is open to anyone
who has eyes to see. It has a universal character'.[146] It is no Gnostic
secret, shared only by a select band of initiates. But this is not to say
that all events are equally revealing. Rather, the history of Israel consists of a series of special events which 'communicate something
special which could not be gotten out of other events. This special

aspect is the event itself, not the attitude with which one confronts the event.'[147] Faith is not something which can leap over the gap between the believer and the historical fact by serving as a substitute for the latter.[148]

> Faith has to do with the future. This is the essence of trust. Trust primarily directs itself toward the future, and the future justifies, or disappoints. Thus a person does not come to faith blindly, but by means of an event that can be appropriated as something that can be considered reliable. True faith is not a state of blissful gullibility. The prophets could call Israel to faith in Jahweh's promises and proclaim his prophecy because Israel had experienced the dependability of their God ·in the course of a long history. The Christian risks his trust, life, and future on the fact of God's having been revealed in the fate of Jesus. . . . The proclamation of the gospel cannot assert that the facts are in doubt and that the leap of faith must be made in order to achieve certainty. If this sort of assertion were allowed to stand, then one would have to cease being a theologian and Christian. The proclamation must assert that the facts are reliable and that you can therefore place your faith, life, and future on them.[149]

From here Pannenberg goes on to argue that 'the universal revelation of the deity of God is not yet realized in the history of Israel, but first in the fate of Jesus of Nazareth, insofar as the end of all events is anticipated in his fate'.[150] We noted earlier how Pannenberg regards the resurrection of Jesus as a historical fact.[151] It is also the historical event which illuminates the rest of history and anticipates the end of history and the eschatological manifestation of God.

> With the resurrection of Jesus, the end of history has already occurred, although it does not strike us in this way. It is through the resurrection that the God of Israel has substantiated his deity in an ultimate way and is now manifest as the God of all men. It is only the eschatological character of the Christ event that establishes that there will be no further self-manifestation of God beyond this event. Thus, the end of the world will be on a cosmic scale what has already happened in Jesus. It is the eschatological character of the Christ event as

the anticipation of the end of all things that alone can establish this development so that from now on the non-Jew can acknowledge the God of Israel as the one true God, the one whom Greek philosophy sought and the only one who could be acknowledged as the one true God from that time on.[152]

What then is the relationship between revelation-history and what Scripture presents as 'the Word of God'? Pannenberg's reply is that the Word relates itself to revelation as foretelling, forthtelling, and report'.[153] It foretells in the sense that 'Israel experienced the self-vindication of Jahweh in the given events of history largely as a confirmation of words of promise or threat that are still in the future. Nevertheless, the prophetic word is the vehicle of proclamation and thus is not of itself the self-vindication of God. If it is to found in visions and auditions, these were not understood as the direct self-disclosure of God.'[154] It forthtells, Pannenberg maintains, in the sense that 'the Israelite Law of God presupposed the knowledge of the deity of Jahweh and also his self-vindication as demonstrated. Law and commandment follow as a result of the divine self-vindication. They do not themselves have the character of revelation.'[155] The same applies to the declarations of Jesus that are characterized as the Word of God. 'The authority of Jesus as the bearer of the authority of God himself is thus already presupposed.'[156] The Word of God as proclamation or kerygma appears for the first time in the New Testament.

The message of the apostles is called the Word of God, because it is decisively set in motion (1 Thess. 2: 13) through the appearances of Jesus (Gal. 1: 12, 15 f.). This is not because of human effort, but because of God himself. . . . The issuing of the kerygma, as the report of the revelation of God in the fate of Jesus, is itself an element in the accomplishment of the revelation of God in the fate of Jesus, is itself an element in the accomplishment of the revelation event. The self-vindication of God before all men cannot be thought of apart from the universal notification. However, the kerygma is not by itself a revelatory speech by virtue of its formal characteristic, that is, as a challenge or call. The kerygma is to be understood solely on the basis of its content, on the basis of the event that it reports and explicates. In this sense, the kerygma is not to be thought of as bringing something to the event. The events in which God demonstrates his deity are self-evident as they stand within the framework of their own history. It does not require any kind of inspired interpretation to make these events recognizable as revelation.[157]

Some students of biblical theology feel that Pannenberg comes in that category of men whom Coleridge described as being mostly right in what they affirm and wrong in what they deny. After all, the positive affirmation of revelation in history does not depend upon a denial of God's self-disclosure through spoken or written word. But is Pannenberg really saying this? To adapt Pannenberg's own language, in so far as history is related to the Word of promise it is an extension of that Word, and in so far as the Word proclaims revelation-history it is an extension of that history. Or as Conzelmann puts it with reference to Romans 1: 16 f., 'The historical saving event is actualized in the word.'[158] It is the concrete means by which past history is known and appropriated in the present. To use the language that we used earlier in describing what the historian achieves, the Word presents us with a model or series of models which enables us to grasp the reality it describes.

We need not be detained by Pannenberg's inclination to see the influence of Gnosticism in early Christian thought about revelation. Pannenberg himself draws attention to fundamental differences between the biblical and the Gnostic outlook.[159] The evidence for Gnosticism proper is in any case later than the New Testament period. More serious is Pannenberg's apparent double assumption that revelation is to be thought of in general terms rather than in personal and individual ones, and that words and utterances have some kind of secondary status in history. On the one hand, his discussions of revelation tend to focus on public events to the exclusion of what happens between God and the individual. And on the other hand, he seems to overlook the fact that an utterance can be no less historically significant than an act. Indeed, most historical events are combinations of acts and utterances. It is not only 'performative utterances' that have an event-like character, although some biblical utterances appear to belong to this category.[160] The words of Jesus were not something secondary to his ministry and 'fate' but part and parcel of them. As Joachim Jeremias observes with regard to Jesus' proclamation of the kingdom, 'The return of the spirit of God is manifested not only in actions, but also in words of authority.'[161] It would seem odd to deny to the parables a revelatory role. This is not to say that they must be understood to communicate propositions which could not otherwise be known. The communication of propositions is an important but only one function of language. The parables work by bringing the hearer to the point of seeing himself in the light of an eschatology that is 'in process of realization', and acting accordingly.[162] They take the form of a language-event which brings about a disclosure situation[163] in which existence is seen in relation to God. And to see existence in relation to God is of the essence of revelation.[164]

A point to be underlined is that such a disclosure can take place through reflection on history (both in the sense of events and accounts of events) and on words which have no immediate connection with history at all. It is the occupational hazard of the theologian with important insights to overstate his case. Barth did this, when he so stressed revelation through the Word that he felt obliged to deny any revelation in nature.[165] It would be equally wrong to treat history and language as mutually exclusive media of revelation. One of the great theological needs today is for a coherent account of revelation as it occurs in the Word, history, nature and experience.

In the past, evangelicals have sometimes lapsed into a way of speaking about the Bible as the Word of God which gave the impression of a monophysitism in which the divine absorbed the human. Just as in a docetic christology in which Jesus only appears to be a man but is not one really, so the humanity of the Bible is treated merely as the superficial clothing of what is essentially divine. No doubt this is all part of a reaction against the liberalism which went to the opposite extreme of seeing the Bible as a collection of purely human writings reflecting certain phases of the history of middle-eastern religion. But this liberal understanding of Scripture is at variance not only with the claims of the biblical writings themselves but also with the attitude of Jesus to the Scriptures and with their revelatory role in Christian experience.[166] The study of the christological controversies of the early church shows that truth was not served either by coming down in favour of one extreme to the exclusion of the other or by seeking a middle-course compromise. What is required in our contemporary understanding of revelation is recognition of both the divine and the human elements together. Because revelation is a historical revelation in word and event, it is to be understood precisely in its historicity. Whatever means are appropriate to the understanding of it in its historicity are therefore to be used. At the same time any approach which does not understand it in its revelatory aspect falls short of understanding it as a historical reality.

There is a second and kindred danger to which Christians are prone in speaking of Scripture as the Word of God. That is to confine revelation merely to the verbatim pronouncements of the text. But to accept this would mean, for example, that in preaching, revelation takes place only when texts of Scripture are actually quoted. The logical conclusion would be that sermons (or for that matter, any form of Christian witness) should consist of nothing but a compilation of texts. In its extreme form it would give the Bible a quasi-magical character, making it operate regardless of our faculties of cognition and understanding, merely by the performance of the appropriate act.

But this is not the view of the biblical writers themselves. There is a sense in which for them the whole of life and reality is sacramental.[167] Natural events and human actions, while still remaining natural events and human actions, point beyond themselves and have a significance that is wider than the dimensions of time and space. In so doing, they bring God right into the midst of life. 'The heavens are telling the glory of God; and the firmament proclaims his handiwork,' the psalmist wrote (Ps. 19: 1). Paul held that 'ever since the creation of the world his invisible nature, namely, his eternal power and deity, has been clearly perceived in the things that have been made. So they are without excuse' (Rom. 1: 20; cf. Acts 14: 17; 17: 26 ff.). For Paul this knowledge of God that men have as creatures is the reason why they are accountable to God. Similarly, an act of sin is like an inverted sacrament. It affects not only our fellow men on the human plane, but also our relationship with God.

For Amos, crimes against humanity are not confined to the level of humanity but are worthy of the judgment of God (Am. 1 and 2). Matthew 25 depicts the judgment of the nations by the Son of man. The decisive factor in his condemnation of them is failure to serve the stranger, the naked, the sick and the prisoner, and thus failure to serve the Son of man. Conversely, the King will say to the righteous who *have* done these things, 'Truly, I say to you, as you did it to one of the least of these my brethren, you did it to me' (Mt. 25: 40).

This last passage suggests that not all such situations are revelatory at the time. For the righteous may well be unaware of what they were doing. And similarly the unrighteous protest that they never saw the Son of man in these situations. There is in life a kind of divine incognito which may cease to be incognito only in retrospect. In making this point we are brought back to the point made early on in the discussion of Kierkegaard, that from one point of view historical events can be described in secular terms, but from another point of view the same events can be seen in relation to God. It was said earlier on that in this process the believer interprets events and actions in the light of other events and actions.[168] The purpose of the parable of Matthew 25 is to teach disciples to see ordinary, secular events and situations in God's perspective.

John Hick has called attention to the interpretative aspect of faith. The discovery of God is not like finding a new fact. It arises from 'interpreting in a new way what was already before us. It is epistemologically comparable, not to the discovery of a man concealed behind a screen, or of inferred electrons underlying the observed behaviour of matter, but to what Wittgenstein called "seeing as".'[169] As Hick goes on to illustrate, when the Chaldeans were at the gates of Jerusalem, the prophet Jeremiah experienced the event not simply as a foreign political threat but also as God's judgment upon Israel.

This act of 'seeing as' or 'experiencing as' may operate at different levels and in different areas of experience. A savage who finds a piece of paper covered with writing may interpret it as something made by man. A more educated man may realize that it is something written in a foreign language. A person who knows that language may be able to read it. An expert may be able to understand its significance. Thus, each of these people may answer the question 'What is it?' correctly, but at different levels. Each of the more adequate attributions of significance presupposes the less adequate ones. As Hick observes, 'The significance of an object to an individual consists in the practical difference which that object makes to him, the way in which it affects either his immediate reactions or his more long-term plans and policies'.[170]

Broadly speaking, there are three main levels of significance: the physical world, the human world and the world in relation to God. Both within these three levels and between them there is a kind of reciprocal action in our interpretation. We approach new items of knowledge with an existing framework of knowledge and interpretation. The savage may recognize the piece of paper to be the work of a man because he already has some idea of the works of nature and of the works of men. The expert, likewise, is able to interpret the paper because he already knows something of the language and of the kind of thing indicated by the writing on it. But in turn the new experience adds to or modifies previous experience, and thus also modifies the existing framework of knowledge and interpretation.

My contention is that all experience (and with it, of course, history) is in principle capable of being revelatory. This is not to say that we see the significance of it at the time or even that we shall necessarily come to see the revelatory significance of any particular event. Rather, it is to say that events are in principle capable of being understood at the three levels of significance just noted: at the levels of nature, of man and of God. It is on this last level that revelation, in the Christian sense, takes place. When we see the significance of an event as disclosing something about our relationship with God, and with each other in relation to God, revelation takes place. Whether we see significance at any of these levels depends on the interplay between the individual, the event or thing in question, and his frame of reference. When there is obscurity in any of these factors, the significance will be correspondingly obscure. This may be due to a variety of factors, such as lack of knowledge, inadequate perception, being content with inadequate explanations, or inadequate frame of reference. These factors operate at all levels of significance, no less on the level of revelation than in the study of nature and history. But in revelation, history comes in at two points. It is the raw material or medium of revelation. And it also forms an essential part of the frame of reference by which that raw material is interpreted.

The importance of history to the believer

In his celebrated Eddington Memorial Lecture for 1955, on *An Empiricist's View of the Nature of Religious Belief*, R.B. Braithwaite claimed: 'A man is not, I think, a professing Christian unless he both proposes to live according to Christian moral principles and associates his intention with thinking of Christian stories; but he need not believe that the empirical propositions presented by these stories correspond to empirical fact.'[171] We may accept the first of these propositions, but the second does not necessarily follow. Underlying Braithwaite's view is the contention that such stories are not empirically verifiable, but what can be verified is the way in which they are used. On his analysis, the Christian's assertion that God is love, which Braithwaite takes 'to epitomize the assertions of the Christian religion', is reduced to a declaration of 'his intention to follow an agapeistic way of life'.[172]

If Braithwaite means that God is not a term capable of historical explanation in that God is not a historical figure like Napoleon or Julius Caesar, the point is true but relatively trivial. We have gone further and said with Kierkegaard that there is a sense in which in history God is incognito. He is not seen directly even in the figure of Jesus Christ for much of his life. We have also argued that historical explanations (whether or not we bring God into them) are not literal descriptions of certain empirical facts, but hypotheses or models which join together, explain, and put constructions on empirical facts. They are validated by their ability to put them together in a way which seems best to fit these facts and to make a coherent explanation. Such explanations may be given at different levels, depending on the frame of reference or level of significance. A secular explanation is possible and valid within a secular frame of reference. But it may not be exhaustive. If there is something in history which bursts this frame of reference (such as the resurrection of Jesus), we are justified in seeking a wider one. This in turn means that our frame of reference for looking at other events on their deeper levels of significance will be wider.

In so far as historical propositions are expressed in language, we may agree with Braithwaite in saying that our understanding of them must be determined by the way in which they are used and that this is a matter for empirical investigation. But we take issue with him over the suggestion that it is immaterial in what sense the Christian stories are true. The propositions associated with the stories of Christian origins take a variety of forms. Some are expressly parabolic. If they are about conduct and attitudes in a more general sense (like the parable of the Good Samaritan) their truth does not depend upon the demonstration of the historicity of a unique event. On the other hand, a parable may have bearing on the historical claims of Jesus, showing that the messianic age has arrived in the person of Jesus.[173] In such a case, its truth and bearing are bound up with the historical validity of those claims. So too is the response demanded by the parable. If an event such as the exodus is seen as a paradigm of God's care for his people,[174] the comfort and hope that the believer is exhorted to draw from it are surely ill founded if there is no corresponding historical base. Similarly, the Christian hope for the future and his view of the shape of history are grounded in the historicity of the resurrection of Jesus.[175] 'If Christ has not been raised, then our preaching is in vain and your faith is in vain' (1 Cor. 15: 14).

In making this point we must be careful not to mistake symbolic propositions for factual, empirical assertions. No end of controversies have been generated by the failure to understand symbolic dimensions of the early chapters of Genesis.[176] In the same way, pious and well-meaning people have attempted to interpret the book of Revelation as a literal programme for the future course of history, identifying its visions with particular people and events and failing to appreciate its eschatological and apocalyptic universe of discourse. These attempts have been fertile in the production of fanaticism and sects.[177] A particular case in point of the failure to appreciate the appropriate universe of discourse is the way in which Matthew 24: 29-31 is taken to refer to the end of the world. But as J. Marcellus Kik has shown, the imagery here is drawn from the apocalyptic language of the Old Testament which is used to describe this-worldly events like the fall of Babylon.[178] In context it is much more likely that the words refer to the fall of Jerusalem and the downfall of Israel which did, in fact, occur within the lifetime of 'this generation' (Mt. 24: 34). These points are not made in the interests of emptying biblical pronouncements of their factual, historical content. Rather the reverse. It is precisely because the Christian revelation is grounded in and mediated through history that its precise historical form is important. And in turn it is precisely this that makes important the study of it as history.

Does this then mean that faith must always be at the mercy of the historian and critical expert? The American liberal theologian John Knox has replied in the negative.[179] So too, despite (or because of) its scepticism, has the Bultmann school on the continent.[180] An answer more in line with the convictions of the biblical writers themselves is that of Walter Künneth: 'Revelation is . . . always more than history, not only history, but not without history'.[181] If our faith is of the kind that would persist regardless of evidence and regardless of historical models, it is an unanchored faith. Its utterances might be indicative of the believer's particular mental states, but they would not be informative about anything that is the case outside them. If it could be shown that (say) the Gospel accounts of Jesus were without historical foundation in his life, it is conceivable that I could go on having religious experiences, but the explanation of them would be different. I would have to look beyond the Christian explanation.

For the Christian the question of 'belief in' is inseparable from the question of 'belief that'. It is precisely the Christian's belief that God has acted in certain ways in history that determines his belief about the character of God and the destiny of the world. We might echo the words of R.P.C. Hanson, 'If we ignore the significance of history, we leave the field open to the fanatic, the fraud and the fool.'[182] But if we reflect on the character of the Bible, it is not a kind of promise box or a means of administering a kind of spiritual LSD which sends people on 'trips'. In fact, it is full of arguments, demonstrations, appeals to history and interpretations of history. Examples are the prologue of Luke's Gospel with its stress on the historicity of the story of Jesus as the basis of faith, or 1 Corinthians 15: 1 ff., where Paul stresses the historical foundation of his preaching. It is on the basis of such arguments that the validity of Christian faith rests. The ordinary believer is not required to work out all the arguments for himself any more than the average motorist needs to understand the scientific basis of the workings of his car. Nor indeed need every item of belief be demonstrably true. It is legitimate to accept with integrity unverified assertions on the basis of the credit and authority of the person who makes them. But it is important to be able to establish that credit.

We all have beliefs about the past, which are arrived at consciously or unconsciously, critically or uncritically. The historical models that we make in our minds for understanding the past may be crude and inaccurate, but we cannot help making them. It is the job of the expert—whether he be a professional historian, or in the case of Christian belief the minister and teacher—to show what is wrong with the misleading models and to help build more accurate ones and to interpret them correctly. But without the models we cannot grasp the reality they signify, and in the end each of us is responsible for what we make of them. In that sense, everyone must be his own historian.

NOTES

[1]'On the Proof of the Spirit and of Power' (1777), quoted from H. Chadwick (ed.), *Lessing's Theological Writings* (A. & C. Black, 1956), p. 53. Lessing was replying to critics who objected to his publication of the notorious *Wolfenbüttel Fragments* which had attacked the historical credibility of Christianity. *Cf.* Reimarus, *Fragments*, ed. by C.H. Talbert (SCM Press, 1971).

[2]*Philosophical Fragments* (1844), ed. by N. Thulstrup (Princeton University Press, 2nd edn. 1962), pp. 130 f.

[3]The term applies, of course, to the movement associated with Karl Barth in the twenties and thirties which stressed the otherness of God and the sole possibility of knowing him in Christ. In this, Barth was consciously indebted to Kierkegaard. *Cf.* K. Barth, *The Epistle to the Romans* (1921; Oxford University Press, 1933), pp. 10, 99, *et passim; idem, God, Grace and Gospel* (*SJT* Occasional Papers no. 8, 1959), pp. 34 ff.; *idem, Fragments Grave and Gay* (Fontana, 1971), pp. 102 ff.; C. Brown, *Karl Barth and the Christian Message* (Inter-Varsity Press, 1967), pp. 17 ff., 44 f.

[4]*Christian Discourses* (Oxford University Press, New York; 2nd edn. 1961), p. 368.

[5]*Philosophical Fragments*, pp. 57 f.

[6]*Ibid.*, pp. 58 f.

[7]*Ibid.*, p. 52; *cf. Concluding Unscientific Postscript to the Philosophical Fragments* (1846; Princeton University Press, 1941), pp. 485, 501 f.

[8]*Philosophical Fragments*, pp. 39 f.

[9]*Training in Christianity* (1850; Princeton University Press, 1944), pp. 128 ff.; *cf. Journals* (Oxford University Press, 1938; reprinted with alterations, 1959), no. 1021, p. 355; *Philosophical Fragments*, pp. 83 f.

[10]In H.V. and E.H. Hong and G. Malantschuk (eds.), *Søren Kierkegaard's Letters and Papers*, I (Indiana University Press, Bloomington, 1967), no. 327, p. 138.

[11]*Training in Christianity*, pp. 142 f.

[12]*Philosophical Fragments*, p. 131.

[13]The thought of the *otherness* of God requires further clarification. If God is wholly other in the strict sense of the term, nothing significant can be said about him. I would meet this point by arguing that the biblical view of revelation involves a doctrine of analogy. Although God is *other* than the created order, the latter is so constituted that it is capable of reflecting the character of God. Thus, in teaching truth about God and man, Jesus could say that the kingdom of God is *like* this or that natural phenomenon or human occurence. The truth was mediated indirectly. For a statement and defence of this view see C. Brown, *Karl Barth and the Christian Message*, pp. 47-54; *idem, Philosophy and the Christian Faith* (Inter-Varsity Press, 1969), pp. 30 ff., 176-81, 255 f.; see also the present essay, p. 188.

It may be noted that such a view of revelation does not entitle us to speak of 'absolute' or 'eternal' truth. For even in revelation man does not have absolute and timeless perspectives. They are relative to his historical position and conditioned by his situation. This is not to say that they are not true. The truth condition of a statement is met when the statement is seen to express the realities of the situation that it purportes to describe.

[14]On the question of scepticism, see P. Carnley, 'The Poverty of Historical Scepticism', in S.W. Sykes and J.P. Clayton (eds.), *Christ, Faith and History* (Cambridge University Press, 1972), pp. 165-90.

[15]*Cf.* Ex. 33:20 ff.; Mt. 5:8; 1 Cor. 13:12; Heb. 12:14; 1 Jn. 3:2, Rev. 22:4; see further C. Brown, *Philosophy and the Christian Faith*, pp. 30 ff., 176-81.

[16]*Cf.* G. Wenham's discussion of the relationship between theology and history in the OT, pp. 16 ff.; and the discussion in the present essay, pp. 174 ff.

The unhistorical use of the past to interpret the present has come under valid criticism from J.H. Plumb in *The Death of the Past* (Pelican, 1973). Nevertheless, Plumb himself is anxious to draw lessons from the past, and even as a historian with strong rationalistic inclinations he permits himself to pass moral judgments on history (p. 113).

'Historians can use history to fulfil many of the social purposes which the old mythical pasts did so well. It can no longer provide sanctions for authority, nor for aristocratic or oligarchical élites, nor for inherent destinies clothed in national guise, but it can still teach wisdom, and it can teach it in a far deeper sense than was possible when wisdom had to be taught through the example of heroes' (pp. 113 f.). It may be noted that Plumb appears to confine human achievement in history and in general to reason and rationalism, though these are somewhat ill defined. His concept of rationalism seems to oscillate between that which he attributes to Gibbon and the Enlightenment on the one hand, and to the valid application of reason wherever it can be found on the other hand. In the latter case reason is hardly a monopoly of any particular school or outlook.

[17]*Cf. Escape from Reason* (Inter-Varsity Press, 1968), and *He is There and He is not Silent* (Hodder & Stoughton, 1972).

[18]On Richardson's approach to history, see especially his *The Miracle Stories of the Gospels* (SCM Press, 1941); *Christian Apologetics* (SCM Press, 1947), pp. 89-109; *The Bible in the Age of Science* (SCM Press, 1961), pp. 54-76; *An Introduction to the Theology of the New Testament* (SCM Press, 1958), pp. 1-15; *History: Sacred and Profane* (SCM Press, 1964); and J.J. Navone, *History and Faith in the Thought of Alan Richardson* (SCM Press, 1966).

[19]*An Introduction to the Theology of the New Testament*, p. 9; *cf. Christian Apologetics*, pp. 104-9. *Cf.* the 'perspectivism' of Karl Heussi *(Die Krisis des Historismus*, Mohr, Tübingen, 1932) and Bernard Lonergan *(Method in Theology*, Darton, Longman & Todd, 1972), pp. 214-20.

[20]*An Introduction to the Theology of the New Testament*, p. 13.

[21]Scientific theories are about recurrent phenomena, not isolated events. The historian cannot test his theories by controlled experiment. Nor has he direct access to his subject-matter. On the other hand, his work is open to repeated public testing by himself or anyone else who has the necessary knowledge and skills.

Richardson's account may be compared with the following description by the philosopher of science C.G. Hempel: 'Scientific hypotheses and theories are not *derived* from observed facts, but *invented* in order to account for them. They constitute guesses at the connections that might obtain between the phenomena under study, at uniformities and patterns that might underlie the occurrence. "Happy guesses" of this kind require great ingenuity, especially if they involve a radical departure from current modes of scientific thinking, as did, for example, the theory of relativity and the quantum theory. The inventive effort required in scientific research will benefit from a thorough familiarity with current knowledge in the field. A complete novice will hardly make an important scientific discovery, for the ideas that may occur to him are likely to duplicate what has been tried before or to run afoul of well-established facts or theories of which he is not aware' (*Philosophy of Natural Science*, Prentice-Hall, Englewood Cliffs, 1966, p. 15).

[22]*An Introduction to the Theology of the New Testament*, p. 12.

[23]*E.g.* Mk. 2:1-12; Jn. 2:11; 20:30 f.; Acts 2:22; Rom. 1:4.

[24]J. Locke, *Essay Concerning Human Understanding* (1690), ed. by L.A. Selby-Bigge (Oxford University Press, 1902), IV.17.23.

[25]'A Discourse of Miracles' (1706), in I.T. Ramsey (ed.), *The Reasonableness of Christianity with a Discourse of Miracles* (A. & C. Black, 1958), p. 82; *cf.* J. Calvin, *Institutes of the Christian Religion* (1559), I, 8, 5.

[26]*Cf.* R.F. Holland, 'The Miraculous' (*APhQ*, II, 1965), reprinted in D.Z. Phillips (ed.), *Religion and Understanding* (Blackwell, 1967), pp. 155 ff.

[27]R. Swinburne, *The Concept of Miracle* (Macmillan, 1970), pp. 4 f. For H.H. Farmer it is the revelatory aspect of miracles in answering prayer for succour at a critical stage in personal destiny that constitutes the essence of the miraculous. It is wrong, he maintains, to start by discussing it in relation to natural law (*The World and God²*, Nisbet, 1936, pp. 107-27). Whereas Farmer gives the impression of trying to avoid a clash between science and religion by focusing on the revelatory dimensions of the natural, M. Polanyi holds the two apart. 'It is illogical to attempt the proof of the supernatural by natural tests, for these can only establish the natural aspects of an event and can never represent it as supernatural' (*Personal Knowledge: Towards a Post-Critical Philosophy*, Routledge & Kegan Paul, 1958, p. 284). He appears to deny the coincidence concept altogether, whilst allowing what we shall call the 'violation concept'.

[28]R.F. Holland, 'The Miraculous', in D.Z..Phillips (ed.), *op. cit.*, pp. 155 f.

[29]*E.g.* Mk. 1:23 ff.; 2:1-12; 3:3 ff.; Acts 3:1-10.

[30]Ex. 14:21.

[31]'The Miraculous', *op. cit.*, p. 163.

[32]*Ibid.*, p. 167.
[33]On this, see *ibid.*, pp. 163 f.; E.L. Mascall, *Christian Theology and Natural Science: Some Questions in their Relations* (Longmans, 1957), pp. 167-107; I. J. Barbour, *Issues in Science and Religion*[2] (SCM Press, 1968), pp. 173-316; A.R. Peacocke, *Science and the Christian Experiment* (Oxford University Press, 1971), pp. 35-53; M. Hesse, 'Miracles and the Laws of Nature', in C.F.D. Moule (ed.), *Miracles; Cambridge Studies in their Philosophy and History* (Mowbray, 1965), pp. 35-42.
[34]1 Cor. 15:12-22, 49 ff., Col. 3:1-4; 1 Jn. 3:2.
[35]*Cf.* A. Richardson, *The Miracle Stories of the Gospels; L.* Morris, *The Gospel According to John* (Marshall, Morgan & Scott, 1971), pp. 684-91; M.E. Glasswell, 'The Use of Miracles in the Markan Gospel', and G.W.H. Lampe, 'Miracles in the Acts of the Apostles', in C.F.D. Moule (ed.), *Miracles*, pp. 151-78.
[36]*Op. cit.*, X, ¶ 90, n. 1, cited from the edn. of Hume's *Enquiries* by L.A. Selby-Bigge (2nd edn., Oxford University Press, 1902). pp. 115. On Hume's discussion of miracles, see also N. Smart, *Philosophers and Religious Truth*[2] (SCM Press, 1969), pp. 25-49.
[37]*Op. cit.*, X, ¶ 90, p. 114.
[38]*Ibid.*, X, ¶ 92, p. 116.
[39]*Ibid.*, X, ¶ 93, p. 118.
[40]*Ibid.*, X, ¶ 94, p. 119.
[41]*Ibid.*, X, ¶¶ 95 ff., pp. 121 ff.
[42]*Ibid.*, X, ¶ 99, p. 127.
[43]*Ibid.*, X, ¶ 101, pp. 130 f.
[44]*Ibid.*, X, ¶ 96, p. 124.
[45]*Ibid.*, X, ¶ 96, p. 125.
[46]*The Concept of Miracle*, p. 17.
[47]*Ibid.*, pp. 33 ff.; A. Richardson, *History: Sacred and Profane*, pp. 209 f.
[48]*The Concept of Miracle*, pp. 60 f.
[49]Mt. 5:43 ff.; Acts 14:16 ff.; 17:24-31; Rom. 13:1 ff.; 1 Pet. 2:13 ff.; Rev. 22:2.
[50]Rom. 1:19-23.
[51]Acts 14:15.
[52]*Enquiry Concerning Human Understanding*, X, ¶ 81, p. 110.
[53]*Cf.* P. Nowell-Smith, 'Miracles', in A. Flew and A. MacIntyre (eds.), *New Essays in Philosophical Theology* (SCM Press, 1955), p. 253.
[54]A. McKinnon, ' "Miracle" and "Paradox" ', in *APhQ*, IV, 1967, pp. 308-14; *cf.* R. Swinburne, *The Concept of Miracle*, pp. 19 f., 23-32.
[55]See above, n. 35.
[56]*Op. cit.*, p. 65.
[57]*Ibid.*, pp. 68 f.
[58]*History: Sacred and Profane*, p. 206.
[59]*Ibid.*, pp. 206 f. On the question of the empty tomb, see H. von Campenhausen, 'The Events of Easter and the Empty Tomb', in *Tradition and Life in the Church: Essays and Lectures in Church History* (A. & C. Black, 1968), pp. 42-89; J. Orr, *The Resurrection of Jesus* (Hodder &

Stoughton, 1908), pp. 113 ff.; W. Künneth, *The Theology of the Resurrection* (SCM Press, 1965), p. 97; C.F.D. Moule (ed.), *The Significance of the Message of the Resurrection for Faith in Jesus Christ* (SCM Press, 1968), pp. 7 ff.

[60]*History: Sacred and Profane*, p. 209; *cf.* W. Pannenberg, *Basic Questions in Theology*, I (SCM Press, 1970), p. 8: 'Only the resurrection of Jesus, conceived in the framework of the cultural situation of primitive Christianity, renders intelligible the early history of Christian faith up to the confessions of Jesus' true divinity. If the resurrection of Jesus cannot be considered to be a historical event, then the historical aspect of the primitive Christian message and its different forms, both of which have crystallized into the New Testament, fall hopelessly apart.'

[61]G. Bornkamm, *Jesus of Nazareth* (Hodder & Stoughton, 1960), p. 180; *cf.* A. Richardson, *History: Sacred and Profane*, p. 196.

[62]*History: Sacred and Profane*, pp. 196 ff.

[63]*Ibid.*, p. 212. To some, this last point might seem to beg the whole question. But Richardson's point remains, that the phenomenon of resurrection faith requires explanation and that this in turn invites hypotheses to account for it. The NT data themselves provoke the question whether the resurrection belief described in it entails a physical resuscitation of the corpse of Jesus and no more, or whether it entails some form of transformation and theological illumination of the significance of Jesus. Some kind of transformation seems to be suggested by the narratives which indicate that disciples who had known Jesus well failed at first to recognize their risen Lord (*e.g.* Lk. 24:16, 31; Jn. 20:14) and by the way in which he came and went. Theological illumination may also be suggested by the Emmaus road narrative and by Paul's statement of belief in 1 Cor. 15:4. At the same time there was a continuity of identity between the historical Jesus and the risen Christ.

[64]*History: Sacred and Profane*, p. 212.

[65]*Cf.*, *e.g.*, Mk. 16:6 ff.; Mt. 28:1-10; Lk. 24:1-43; Jn. 20:1-29; Acts 9: 1-9; 26:12-19; 1 Cor. 15:3-11; 1 Pet. 1:3; W. Pannenberg, *The Apostles' Creed in the Light of Today's Questions* (SCM Press, 1972), p. 97.

Cf. the debate between C.F.D. Moule and D. Cupitt, who argues that 'seeing the risen Lord becomes more like seeing the conclusion of an argument than like seeing Edward Heath. . . . In the case of a *religious experience of a transcendent* object, the interpretative work precedes the vision, and does not follow it. So I claim that the Easter faith—the theological affirmation of Jesus' exaltation—must be, logically as well as chronologically, prior to the Easter experiences. That is why only a believer could see the risen Lord: or, to put it more exactly, the Christophany-experience focuses and crystallizes the fact that this man now does beyond doubt "see" and believe in the exaltation of Jesus as Christ' (C.F.D. Moule and D. Cupitt, 'The Resurrection: A Disagreement', *Theology*, vol. LXXV, no. 628, 1972, p. 514).

Moule replies: 'I still find it difficult, if not impossible, to believe that the disciples had, in the scriptures and the life, teaching and death of

Jesus and their own circumstances, all that was necessary to create the Easter-belief. Granted that they were thrown into an ecstasy of astonishment by what Jesus was and did, something more than this is needed (so it seems to me) to lead to the conclusion that Jesus had been not merely a superlatively great prophet, nor simply a man of the Spirit, nor just Messiah (the latter is an almost impossible conclusion, anyway, after the Crucifixion, without something to suggest it), but that he was alive in a unique and hitherto unexemplified way, and *therefore* Son of God (in a far more than Messianic sense), and "Lord," and the climax and coping-stone of God's plan of salvation' (*ibid.*, p. 515. *Cf.* C.F.D. Moule (ed.), *The Significance of the Message of the Resurrection for Faith in Jesus Christ*).
[66]*The Idea of History* (Oxford University Press, 1946; reprinted with alterations, 1961), p. 252.
[67]*The Historian and the Believer* (SCM Press, 1967), p. 45. *Cf.* P. Gardiner, *The Nature of Historical Explanation* (Oxford University Press, 1961), pp. 28 ff.; *idem* (ed.), *Theories of History* (Free Press, Glencoe, 1959), pp. 344-475; W.H. Dray, *Philosophy of History* (Prentice-Hall, Englewood Cliffs, 1964), pp. 4 ff.; *idem* (ed.), *Philosophical Analysis and History* (Prentice-Hall, Englewood Cliffs, 1966); A.C. Danto, *Analytical Philosophy of History* (Cambridge University Press, 1965); W.H. Walsh, *An Introduction to the Philosophy of History* (Hutchinson, 1951), pp. 30-71; M. White, *Foundations of Historical Knowledge* (Harper & Row, New York, 1965); J.H. Hexter, *Doing History* (Allen & Unwin, 1971).

The debate may be illustrated by J.H. Hexter's rebuttal of C. G. Hempel's attempt to assimilate history to the procedures of natural science. In a seminal article on 'The Function of General Laws in History' (*JPh* 39, 1943, pp. 35-48; reprinted in P. Gardiner (ed.), *Theories of History*, pp. 344-55), Hempel argued that historical research should be conducted by reference to general laws analogous to those of the natural sciences. This involves linking events with general laws. It is precisely this which distinguishes genuine explanations from false. 'Historical explanation ... aims at showing that the event in question was not "a matter of chance", but was to be expected in view of certain antecedent or simultaneous conditions. The expectation referred to is not prophecy or divination, but rational scientific anticipation which rests on the assumption of general laws' (*Theories of History*, pp. 348 f.).

Writing as a practising historian, Hexter also claims that history is 'a rule-bound discipline', but contends that the process of writing history is not something secondary and incidental but is essential to conveying the inward character of the past as it really was. Moreover, the vocabulary and syntax that constitute the appropriate response of the historian to his data are not identifiable with those of the scientist. 'The historian's goal in response to his data is to render the best account he can of the past as it really was' (*Doing History*, p. 68). To do this he must employ a language which sacrifices generality, precision and control to evocative force and scope. It implies that the language of history contains embedded in itself assumptions about the nature of knowing, understanding, meaning and truth which are not completely congruent with those of the sciences, at least in so far as the philosophy of science has so far identified them.

[68]*The Historian and the Believer*, p. 54. *Cf.* Swinburne's discussion of principles for weighing conflicting evidence: 'The most basic principle is to accept as many pieces of evidence as possible. If one witness says one thing, and five witnesses say a different thing, then, in the absence of further evidence (e.g. about their unreliability) take the testimony of the latter. If one method of dating an artefact gives one result, and five methods give a different result, then, in the absence of further information accept the latter result. The first subsidiary principle is— apart from any empirical evidence about their relative reliability—that evidence of different kinds ought to be given different weights. How this is to be done can only be illustrated by examples. Thus one's own apparent memory ought as such to count for more than the testimony of another witness (unless and until evidence of its relative unreliability is forthcoming).... The second subsidiary principle is that different pieces of evidence ought to be given different weights in accordance with any empirical evidence which may be available about their reliability, obtained by a procedure which I may term narrowing the evidence class.... If the testimony of Jones conflicts with the testimony of Smith, then we must investigate not the worth of testimony in general, but the worth of Jones' testimony and of Smith's testimony. We do this by seeing if on all other occasions when we can ascertain what happened Jones or Smith correctly described what happened. In so far as each did, his testimony is reliable.... The third subsidiary principle is not to reject coincidence evidence (unless the evidence of its falsity is extremely strong) unless an explanation can be given of the coincidence; and the better substantiated is that explanation, the more justified the rejection of the coincident evident' (*The Concept of Miracle*, pp. 37 ff.).

[69]*The Historian and the Believer*, pp. 51 ff. It is interesting to note that O. Cullmann uses a similar argument as proof of Jesus' messianic consciousness against the contention of the Bultmann school that Jesus did not think of himself as the messianic Son of man, or figure in his own preaching. 'The historical fact that Jesus was condemned by the Romans (of course in complete misunderstanding of his "self-consciousness") as a Zealot, as a pretender to the throne (cf. the "titulus" on top of the cross), seems to me to be almost irrefutable proof that Jesus in some way made himself the subject of his preaching on the Kingdom of God soon to come' (*Salvation in History*, SCM Press, 1967, p. 109; *cf. idem, The State in the New Testament*, SCM Press, 1957, pp. 8-49).

[70]*The Historian and the Believer*, pp. 54 ff.

[71]'History', in *Avenues of History* (Hamish Hamilton, 1952), cited from F. Stern (ed.), *The Varieties of History: From Voltaire to the Present*[2] (Macmillan, 1970), p. 375; *cf.* also M. Polanyi, *Personal Knowledge: Towards a Post-Critical Philosophy*, p. 321.

[72]*The Historian and the Believer*, p. 61.

[73]*Ibid.*, p. 61.

[74]*History, Archaeology and Christian Humanism* (McGraw-Hill, New York, 1964), p. 26.

[75]*Cf.* E.H. Carr, *What is History?* (Pelican, 1964), pp. 87 ff.; A. Richardson, *History: Sacred and Profane*, pp. 97 ff., 170.

[76]E.H. Carr, *op.cit.*, pp. 7-30; A. Richardson, *op.cit.*, pp. 154 ff., 190-4; R. G. Collingwood, *The Idea of History*, pp. 252 ff.

[78]In a valid deduction the conclusion is related to the premises in such a way that, if the premises are true, the conclusion must also be true. In induction inferences are drawn from a number of cases which point to a general conclusion. C.G. Hempel strongly repudiates the idea that the natural sciences are based on pure induction, involving observation of all facts without prior selection or guesses as to their relative importance, followed by analysis and classification, inductive derivation of generalizations from them and further testing of these generalizations (*Philosophy of Natural Science*, pp. 10 ff.). For him there are no general rules of induction. 'The transition from data to theory requires creative imagination. Scientific hypotheses and theories are not *derived* from observed facts, but *invented* in order to account for them' (*ibid.*, p. 15; *cf.* above, n. 21).

This may be compared with E.H. Carr's account of the historian's procedure. 'The historian starts with a provisional selection of facts, and a provisional interpretation in the light of which that selection has been made—by others as well as by himself. As he works, both the interpretation and the selection and ordering of facts undergo subtle and perhaps unconscious changes, through the reciprocal action of the one or the other. And this reciprocal action also involves reciprocity between the present and past, since the historian is part of the present and the facts belong to the past. The historian and the facts are necessary to one another. The historian without his facts is rootless and futile; the facts without their historian are dead and meaningless. My first answer therefore to the question "What is history?" is that it is a continuous process of interaction between the historian and his facts, an unending dialogue between the present and the past' (*What is History?*, pp. 29 f.).

[79]In the natural sciences it is not enough to produce a hypothesis which might explain certain phenomena but which is at variance with accepted thought (*cf.* C.G. Hempel, *Philosophy of Natural Science*, p. 15; quoted above, n. 21).

R.G. Collingwood has drawn attention to the way in which an established view may be used to test the veracity of a piece of testimony in cases where there is no contradictory testimony. 'The web of imaginative construction is something far more solid and powerful than we have hitherto realized. So far from relying for its validity upon the support of given facts, it actually serves as the touchstone by which we decide whether alleged facts are genuine. Seutonius tells me that Nero at one time intended to evacuate Britain. I reject his statement, not because any better authority flatly contradicts it, for of course none does; but because my reconstruction of Nero's policy based on Tacitus will not allow me to think that Suetonius is right. And if I am told that this is merely to say I prefer Tacitus to Suetonius, I confess that I do: but I do so just because I find myself able to incorporate what Tacitus tells me into a coherent and continuous picture of my own, and cannot do this for Suetonius' (*The Idea of History*, p. 244).

Recognition of this process, which often operates for good or ill at a subconscious level, is important. It has a positive value, but it is also open to abuse if one clings to a theory regardless of empirical data. The viability of a theory depends upon its ability to account for both instances and counter-instances. When the latter are sufficiently strong there must come a point when the theory must be modified or abandoned.

[80]See further C.L. Becker, in P. Snyder (ed.), *Detachment and the Writing of History: Essays and Letters of Carl L. Becker* (Cornell University Press, 1958), pp. 34 f.; B. Lonergan, *Method in Theology*, pp. 203 ff.; R.G. Collingwood, *The Idea of History*, pp. 249-82.

[81]'An evangelical criticism as well as rationalistic criticism must often be satisfied with hypotheses, probabilities, possibilities, rather than in dogmatic certainties, as distasteful as this may be to the uncritical mind which insists on "thus saith the Lord" in every detail of Bible study. Such questions as the original ending of Mark, the precise meaning of *dokimon*, . . . the authorship of the first Gospel, the *Sitz im Leben* of the Gospel of John, the nature of the problem Paul faced in the church in Corinth (whether Jewish or Gnostic), the degree to which God in redemptive history has made use of elements from the Jewish and Hellenistic environments—all these do not constitute the content of revealed truth but are aspects of the historical media through which revelation has been given' (G.E. Ladd, *The New Testament and Criticism*, Hodder & Stoughton, 1970, p. 216).

[82]For a survey of these disciplines, see G.E. Ladd, *op. cit.*

[83]On the background to this debate see J.M. Robinson and J.B. Cobb, *The New Hermeneutic: Discussions among American and Continental Theologians* (Harper & Row, New York, 1964); C.E. Braaten, *History and Hermeneutics* (Lutterworth, 1968); R.W. Funk (ed.), *History and Hermeneutic (Journal for Theology and the Church*, 4, Harper & Row, New York, 1967).

[84]*Cf.* J.W. Wenham, *Christ and the Bible* (Inter-Varsity Press, 1972); C. Brown, *Karl Barth and the Christian Message*, pp. 30-62.

[85]*Cf.* R. Bultmann, 'New Testament and Mythology', in H.-W. Bartsch (ed.), *Kerygma and Myth*, I (SPCK, 1953), pp. 1-44; *idem, Jesus Christ and Mythology* (SCM Press, 1960); *idem, History and Eschatology:The Presence of Eternity* (Harper & Row, New York, 1957); W. Schmithals, *An Introduction to the Theology of Rudolf Bultmann* (SCM Press, 1968), pp. 249-72; D. Cairns, *A Gospel without Myth?* (SCM Press, 1960), pp. 112-35; S.M. Ogden, *Christ without Myth* (Collins, 1962), pp. 24-50; C. Brown, 'Bultmann Revisited', *The Churchman* 88, 1974, pp. 167-87.

[86]First published in *Studien des rheinischen Predigervereins* (1898) and reprinted in E. Troeltsch, *Gesammelte Schriften*, II[2] (Mohr, Tübingen, 1922), pp. 729-53; *cf. idem*, 'Historiography', in J. Hastings (ed.), *Encyclopaedia of Religion and Ethics*, IV (T. & T. Clark, 1914), pp. 716-23; and *idem*, *The Absoluteness of Christianity and the History of Religions* (SCM Press, 1972).

[87]*Gesammelte Schriften*, II, p. 732.

[88]*Basic Questions in Theology*, I, p. 46; *cf.* C.E. Braaten, *History and Hermeneutics*, pp. 98-101; J. Moltmann, *Theology of Hope* (SCM Press, 1967), pp. 172-82.

[89]*Basic Questions in Theology*, I, p. 49.

[90]Cited from F. Stern (ed.), *The Varieties of History: From Voltaire to the Present*, p. 378.

[91]'Our primary task, epistemologically, is to focus our attention on the area where God is actually known, and to seek to understand that knowledge in its concrete happening, out of its own proper ground, and in its own proper reference to objective reality. Scientific procedure will not allow us to go beyond the boundary set by the object, for that would presume that by the inherent powers of our "autonomous reason" we can gain mastery over it. We have to act within the limits imposed by the nature of the object, and avoid self-willed and undisciplined speculative thinking. It would be uncontrolled and unscientific procedure to run ahead of the object and prescribe just how it shall or can be known before we actually know it, or to withdraw ourselves from actual knowing and then in detachment from the object lay down the conditions upon which valid knowledge is possible' (T.F. Torrance, *Theological Science*, Oxford University Press, 1969, pp. 25 f.).

'Hence even though we know God in the givenness of faith, it is not faith that is the given subject-matter of theology but the God in whom we have faith' (*ibid.*, p. 28).

[92]*Space, Time and Incarnation* (Oxford University Press, 1969), p. 13.

[93]*Ibid.*, p. 18.

[94]*Ibid.*, pp. 20 f.

[95]This process is not, of course, confined to the biblical writers. We do this in everyday life. The plain, old-fashioned name for it is wisdom. The obvious danger is to read into situations false parallels (see Namier's strictures above, p. 173). Nevertheless, dangers and misapplication do not invalidate proper use.

[96]*Cf., e.g.*, Pss. 105-7.

[97]1 Pet. 1: 1; 2: 9, 11.

[98]The question of the use of the OT in the NT has received considerable attention in recent years. *Cf.* E.E. Ellis, *Paul's Use of the Old Testament* (Oliver & Boyd, 1957); K. Stendahl, *The School of St Matthew and its Use of the Old Testament*[2] (Gleerup, Lund, 1967); B. Lindars, *New Testament Apologetic* (SCM Press, 1961); F.F. Bruce, *This is That: The New Testament Development of Some New Testament Themes* (Paternoster Press, 1968); R. T. France, *Jesus and the Old Testament* (Inter-Varsity Press, 1971); R.H.

Gundry, *The Use of the Old Testament in St Matthew's Gospel with Special Reference to the Messianic Hope* (Brill, Leiden, 1967); R.N. Longenecker, 'Can we Reproduce the Exegesis of the New Testament?', *TB* 21, 1970, pp. 3-38; D.M. Smith, Jr, 'The Use of the Old Testament in the New', in J.M. Efird (ed.), *The Use of the Old Testament in the New and Other Essays* (Duke University Press, Durham, NC, 1972), pp. 3-65.

[99]*Basic Questions in Theology*, I, p. 53.

[100]*Geschichte der romanischen und germanischen Völker, 1494-1535* (Reimer, Berlin, 1824), preface (*Sämtliche Werke*, Leipzig, XXXIII, p. vii). A translation of the preface is given in F. Stern (ed.), *The Varieties of History: From Voltaire to the Present*, pp. 55-8.

[101]Such a notion of history was denounced as 'preposterous' by C.L. Becker, 'first, because it is impossible to present all the facts; and second, because even if you could present all the facts the miserable things wouldn't say anything, would just say nothing at all' (*Detachment and the Writing of History*, p. 54; *cf.* B. Lonergan, *Method in Theology*, p. 203).

[102]*Op. cit.* (Oxford University Press, 1954), p. 53.

[103]*History and Human Relations* (Collins, 1951), p. 103. *Cf.* E. Nagel: 'It is an obvious blunder to suppose that only a fat cowherd can drive fat kine. It is an equally crude error to maintain that one cannot inquire into the conditions and consequences of values and evaluations without necessarily engaging in moral or aesthetic value judgements' ('The Logic of Historical Analysis', in H. Meyerhoff (ed.), *The Philosophy of History in our Time*, Doubleday, Garden City, 1959, p. 161).

[104]*Philosophy of History*, p. 26. He notes, however, the thesis of H.L.A. Hart that 'action' is an 'ascriptive' rather than a purely 'descriptive' concept, in 'The Ascription of Responsibility and Rights', in A. Flew (ed.), *Logic and Language* (First Series) (Blackwell, 1951), pp. 145-66, *Cf.* G. Pitcher's comments, 'Hart on Action and Responsibility', *PhR*, LXIX, no. 2, 1960, pp. 226-35.

[105]Reprinted in F. Stern (ed.), *The Varieties of History: From Voltaire to the Present*, pp. 315-28.

[106]*Ibid.*, pp. 323 ff.

[107]Quoted in W.H. Dray, *Philosophy of History*, p. 28; *cf.* J. Barzun's contention that 'exist in history' means 'are memorable' (in F. Stern, *op. cit.*, p. 397).

[108]*Cf.* E.H. Carr, *What is History?*, p. 29; R.G. Collingwood, *The Idea of History*, pp. 257 ff.; J.H. Hexter, *Reappraisals in History* (Longmans, 1961), pp. 1-13.

[109]*Annals*, XV. 44. 4.

[110]*Cf.* K. Heussi, *Die Krisis des Historismus*, p. 36; B. Lonergan, *Method in Theology*, pp. 214 ff.; D.M. Baillie, *God Was In Christ* (Faber, 1948), p. 109.

[111]*Cf.* the discussion of historical narrative in J.H. Hexter, 'The Rhetoric of History', in D.L. Sills (ed.), *The International Encyclopedia of the Social Sciences*, VI (Macmillan, New York, 1968), pp. 368-94; reprinted in Hexter's *Doing History*, pp. 15-76.

[112]*Cf.* F. Stern (ed.), *The Varieties of History: From Voltaire to the Present*, p. 379.

[113]M. *Manilii Astronomicon: Liber Primus*[2] (Cambridge University Press, 1937), p. 87.

[114]Hebrew uses the device of inserting *lē'mōr* (saying), and Greek the word *hoti* (that), before giving the contents of an utterance. This was the nearest equivalent to inverted commas (*cf.* R.W. Funk, *A Greek Grammar of the New Testament*, Cambridge University Press, 1961, ¶ 470, pp. 246 f.). Whilst their use, together with that of the first person in what follows, indicates the writer's intention of reporting the content of what was said, this cannot be taken to imply that he was consciously adopting the same conventions of verbatim quotation which quotation marks imply today. *Cf.* above, p. 128.

[115]*Cf.* J. Goldingay's discussion of different ways of writing history with reference to Job and Kings in ' "That You May Know that Yahweh is God": A Study in the Relationship between Theology and Historical Truth in the Old Testament', *TB* 23, 1972, pp. 58-93, especially pp. 81 ff.

[116]On the notion of models in scientific explanation, see R. B. Braithwaite, *Scientific Explanation* (Cambridge University Press, 1953); E.L. Mascall, *Christian Theology and Natural Science* (Longmans, 1956), pp. 65-76; and for the idea of models and language, see I.T. Ramsey, *Religious Language* (SCM Press, 1957), pp. 49-89; *idem, Christian Empiricism* (Sheldon Press, 1974); I.G. Barbour, *Myths, Models and Paradigms* (SCM Press, 1974).

[117]*Cf.* M. Bloch: 'When all is said and done, a single word, "Understanding", is the beacon light of our studies' (*The Historian's Craft*, Manchester University Press, 1954, p. 143).

[118]*The Idea of History*, pp. 282-302.

[119]Translated from W. Dilthey, 'Plan der Fortsetzung zum Aufbau der geschichtlichen Welt in den Geisteswissenschaften', in *Gesammelte Schriften*, VII (Teubner, Leipzig and Berlin, 1927), p. 215. See further the discussion in H.A. Hodges, *The Philosophy of Wilhelm Dilthey* (Routledge & Kegan Paul, 1952), pp. 275 ff.; and R.G. Collingwood, *The Idea of History*, pp. 171-6, 314 f.

Cf. also W. Pannenberg, *Basic Questions in Theology*, I, p. 8; H.-G. Gadamer, *Warheit und Methode: Grundzüge einer philosophischen Hermeneutik*[2] (Mohr, Tübingen, 1965), pp. 289 f., 356 f., 375.

The position that Dilthey advocates appears to be diametrically opposite to that of Bultmann, who concluded his Gifford Lectures by saying: 'The meaning in history always lies in the present, and when the present is conceived as the eschatological present by Christian faith the meaning in history is realised. Man who complains: "I cannot see meaning in history, and therefore my life, interwoven in history, is meaningless", is to be admonished: do not look around yourself into universal history, you must look into your own personal history. Always in your present lies the meaning in history, and you cannot see it as a spectator, but only in your responsible decisions. In every moment slumbers the possibility of being the eschatological moment.

You must awaken it' (*History and Eschatology*, p. 155).

[120]*God Who Acts: Biblical Theology as Recital* (SCM Press, 1952), p. 55.

[121]*Ibid.*, p. 55.

[122]*Ibid.*, p. 55.

[123]*Nature, Man and God* (Macmillan, 1934), p. 322.

[124]*Ibid.*, p. 317.

[125]*Existence and Faith* (Fontana, 1964), p. 100; *cf.* above, n. 119.

[126]*Ibid.*, p. 102.

[127]*Ibid.*, p. 106; *cf. idem, Jesus Christ and Mythology*, pp. 62, 64.

[128]*Existence and Faith*, p. 163; *cf.* Bultmann's strictures on his colleagues and scholars who have embarked on the new quest of the historical Jesus by trying to show how the kerygma of the early church is grounded in the history of Jesus: 'The Primitive Christian Kerygma and the Historical Jesus' (1962), in C.E. Braaten and R. A. Harrisville (eds.), *The Historical Jesus and the Kerygmatic Christ: Essays on the New Quest of the Historical Jesus* (Abingdon, New York, 1964), pp. 15-42.

[129]*Kerygma and Myth*, I, pp. 34-44. 'It is often said, most of the time in criticism, that according to my interpretation of the kerygma Jesus has risen in the kerygma. I accept this proposition. It is entirely correct, assuming that it is properly understood' (in *The Historical Jesus and the Kerygmatic Christ*, p. 42). *Cf.* O. Cullmann's comments in *Salvation in History*, pp. 50 ff.

[130]*Existence and Faith*, p. 64.

[131]*Has Christianity a Revelation?* (SCM Press, 1964), p. 238.

[132]*Salvation in History*, p. 321.

[133]*Church Dogmatics*, I. 1 (T. & T. Clark, 1936), p. 155.

[134]*Cf.* J. Barr, *Old and New in Interpretation: A Study of the Two Testaments* (SCM Press, 1966), pp. 77 f.

[135]*Church Dogmatics*, I, 1, p. 156.

[136]*Ibid.*, p. 136.

[137]*Ibid.*, pp. 149 f.

[138]For further discussion see C. Brown, *Karl Barth and the Christian Message*, pp. 31-44.

[139]*Cf. Jesus: God and Man*[2] (SCM Press, 1970); *idem, Basic Questions in Theology*, I-III (SCM Press, 1970-3); *idem, The Apostles' Creed in the Light of Today's Questions*; *idem*, 'Hermeneutics and Universal History', in R.W. Funk (ed.), *History and Hermeneutic*; *idem* (ed.), *Revelation as History* (Sheed & Ward, 1969); *cf.* also J.M. Robinson and J.B. Cobb (eds.), *Theology as History* (Harper & Row, New York, 1967).

[140]*Revelation as History*, p. 126; *cf.* Dt. 4:37-40; 7:7-11.

[41]*Ibid.*, p. 127; *cf.* U. Wilckens' essay 'The Understanding of Revelation within Primitive Christianity', in *Revelation as History*, pp. 55-121.

[143]W. Pannenberg, *ibid.*, p. 131.

[143]*Ibid.*, p. 131.

[144]*Cf.* A. Alt, 'Die Deutung der Weltgeschichte im Alten Testament', *AThK* 56, 1959, pp. 129 ff.

[145]W. Pannenberg, *Revelation as History*, p. 133. Pannenberg has offered a

clarification of his views on Hegel in 'The Significance of Christianity in the Philosophy of Hegel', *Basic Questions in Theology*, III, pp. 144-77.

[146]*Revelation as History*, p. 135; *cf.* 2 Cor. 4:4 which Pannenberg there discusses.

[147]*Revelation as History*, p. 137.

[148]*Cf.* R. Bultmann's position (see nn. 119, 129) with that of D.M. Baillie, *God Was in Christ*, pp. 30-58, and L.E. Keck, *A Future for the Historical Jesus* (SCM Press, 1972).

[149]*Revelation as History*, p. 138; *cf.* Pannenberg's strictures on the existentialist position: 'Whether the decision to believe has first to guarantee the truth of the facts on which trust in Jesus Christ and the God revealed in him depends, or whether faith is rendered independent of those facts, both come ultimately to the same thing: in both cases faith depends on the believer and this decision to believe, instead of on the factual substance in whose reliability he can trust. Where faith is understood and required in this sense—as a leap of blind "decision" without further justification—it is degraded to a work of self-redemption. A faith which does not find its justification outside itself—i.e., from the thing on which it relies—remains imprisoned in its own ego and cannot be sustained' (*The Apostles' Creed in the Light of Today's Questions*, p. 10).

[150]*Revelation as History*, p. 139.

[151]See above, pp. 164 n. 60, 172 f.

[152]*Revelation as History*, p. 142; *cf. The Apostles' Creed in the Light of Today's Questions*, pp. 96-115.

[153]*Revelation as History*, p. 152.

[154]*Ibid.*, p. 153. In discussing the idea of fulfilment, Pannenberg subsequently clarified his position in a way which avoids giving the impression that the fulfilment is like finding the missing piece of a jigsaw puzzle which fits exactly into the place formed by the existing pieces. 'Rather, history has "overtaken" promises understood in this sense' (J.M. Robinson and J.B. Cobb (eds.), *Theology as History*, p. 259; *cf.* p. 120; W. Pannenberg, *Basic Questions in Theology*, I, pp. xvii, 19. See also on this A.D. Galloway, *Wolfhart Pannenberg* (Allen & Unwin, 1973), pp. 53 ff.; J. Moltmann, *Theology of Hope*, pp. 110 ff.; J. Goldingay, in *TB* 23, 1972, p. 70; E. Schweizer, *Jesus* (SCM Press, 1971), pp. 13-51; and the discussion of fulfilment above, p. 176).

[155]*Revelation as History*, pp. 153 f.

[156]*Ibid.*, p. 154.

[157]*Ibid.*, p. 158; *cf.* 'Kerygma and History', in *Basic Questions in Theology*, I, pp. 81-95.

[158]H. Conzelmann, *An Outline Theology of the New Testament* (SCM Press, 1969), p. 236.

[159]*Revelation as History*, pp. 150 f. On the question of Gnosticism, see further E.M. Yamauchi, *Pre-Christian Gnosticism* (Inter-Varsity Press, 1973); and J.W. Drane, 'Gnosticism and the New Testament', *TSFB* 68, 1974, pp. 6-13, and 69, 1974, pp. 1-7.

[160]In a performative utterance the words themselves actually bring about the action; *e.g.* 'I name this ship the *Queen Elizabeth*'. Similarly the statement 'I promise that...' is not a mere description but the actual making of the promise. Statements such as 'I believe in God', 'I baptize you in the name of the Father, and of the Son, and of the Holy Spirit', are in themselves part of the action. It would seem that statements such as 'My son, your sins are forgiven... Rise, take up your pallet and walk' (Mk. 2: 5, 10) and 'The time is fulfilled, and the kingdom of God is at hand; repent, and believe in the gospel' (Mk. 1: 15) do not merely contain descriptions, but actually bring about a new state of affairs through being uttered. On this aspect of language, see J.L. Austin, *Philosophical Papers*, ed. by J.O. Urmson and G.J. Warnock, (Oxford University Press, 1961), pp. 222-39; D.D. Evans, *The Logic of Self-Involvement* (SCM Press, 1963).

[161]*New Testament Theology*, I, *The Proclamation of Jesus* (SCM Press, 1971), p. 96.

[162]The phrase is that of E. Haenchen, endorsed by C.H. Dodd and J. Jeremias (J. Jeremias, *The Parables of Jesus*[2], SCM Press, 1963, p. 230). *Cf.* also A.C. Thiselton, 'The Parables as Language-Event: Some Comments on Fuch's Hermeneutics in the Light of Linguistic Philosophy', *SJT*, vol. XXIII, no. 4, 1970, pp. 437-68; K. Kantzer, 'The Christ-Revelation as Act and Interpretation', in C.F. Henry (ed.), *Jesus of Nazareth: Saviour and Lord* (Inter-Varsity Press, 1967), pp. 243-64.

[163]*Cf.* I.T. Ramsey, *Religious Language*, pp. 11-48; *idem* (ed.), *Words about God* (SCM Press, 1971), pp. 202-23.

[164]E. Brunner, drawing on the work of F. Ebner and M. Buber, saw revelation as an I-Thou encounter, as opposed to an I-It relationship (*cf.* E. Brunner, *Truth as Encounter*, SCM Press, 1964). The application of this concept to revelation has been criticized, but not in my opinion convincingly, by J. Macquarrie in *Principles of Christian Theology* (SCM Press, 1966), p. 84.

[165]For a discussion of Barth's view see C. Brown, *Karl Barth and the Christian Message*, pp. 77-98.

[166]*Cf.* J.W. Wenham, *Christ and the Bible* (Inter-Varsity Press, 1972); B.B. Warfield, *The Inspiration and Authority of the Bible* (Marshall, Morgan & Scott, 1951).

[167]*Cf.* C. Brown, *Karl Barth and the Christian Message*, pp. 34, 111 f.; D.M. Baillie, *The Theology of the Sacraments and Other Papers* (Faber, 1956), pp. 42 ff.

[168]See above, pp. 174 ff.; *cf.* pp. 153 f.

[169]J. Hick, *Faith and Knowledge*[2] (Macmillan, 1967), pp. 141 f.; *cf.* L. Wittgenstein, *Philosophical Investigations*[3] (Blackwell, 1967), Part II, section xi, pp. 193-229.

[170]*Faith and Knowledge*, p. 103.

[171]Quoted from the reprint in I.T. Ramsey (ed.), *Christian Ethics and Contemporary Philosophy* (SCM Press, 1966), p. 68.

[172]*Ibid.*, p. 63.

[173]*Cf.* J. Jeremias, *The Parables of Jesus*, pp. 114-229.
[174]Ex. 12-15; 20:2; *cf.* Jdg. 6:8, 9, 13; 1 Sa. 12:6 ff.; 1 Ki. 8:51; 2 Ch. 7:22; Ne. 9:9 ff.; Pss. 77:14-20; 78:12-55; 80:8; 106:7-12; 114; Je. 7:21-4; 11:1-8; 34:13; Ho. 11:1; Dn. 9:15; 1 Cor. 10:1 ff.; Heb. 3:16 ff.; 13:13. *Cf.* also the covenant theme in the Last Supper (Mt. 26:28; Ex. 24:6-8; Heb. 9:20).
[175]*Cf.* J. McIntyre, *The Christian Doctrine of History* (Oliver & Boyd, 1957); E.C. Rust, *Towards a Theological Understanding of History* (Oxford University Press, New York, 1963); J. Moltmann, *Theology of Hope*; *idem, Hope and Planning* (SCM Press, 1971); and J.W. Montgomery, *History in Christian Perspective*, I, *The Shape of the Past* (Edwards Brothers, Ann Arbor, 1962), for discussion of the shape of history and the Christian future hope.
[176]On the interpretation of the early chapters of Genesis, see D. Kidner, *Genesis* (Tyndale Old Testament Commentaries, Inter-Varsity Press, 1967), pp. 43-112; N. Ridderbos, *Is there a Conflict between Genesis 1 and Natural Science?* (Eerdmans, Grand Rapids, 1957). On the controversies over science and religion, see R.E.D. Clark, *Darwin: Before and After* (Paternoster Press, 1948); A.O.J. Cockshut (ed.), *Religious Controversies in the Nineteenth Century: Selected Documents* (A. & C. Black, 1966), pp. 241-65; A. Symondson (ed.), *The Victorian Crisis of Faith* SPCK, 1970).
[177]On the interpretation of Revelation, see W. Hendriksen, *More than Conquerors* (Inter-Varsity Press, 1962); L. Morris, *Revelation* (Tyndale New Testament Commentaries, Inter-Varsity Press, 1969); G.B. Caird, *A Commentary on the Revelation of St John the Divine* (A. & C. Black, 1966); G.R. Beasley-Murray, *The Book of Revelation* (New Century Bible, Oliphants, 1974); and M. Wilcock, *I Saw Heaven Opened: The Message of Revelation* (Inter-Varsity Press, 1975).
[178]*Matthew Twenty-Four: An Exposition* (Presbyterian and Reformed Publishing Company, Philadelphia, 1948), pp. 71-7; *cf.* Is. 13:10; 34:4 f.; Ezk. 32:7 f.; Joel 2:28-32; Acts 2:16-21; Lk. 10:18; Jn. 12:31; 1 Thes. 4:16; 2 Pet. 3:10 ff.; Rev. 6:12-17; 18:1. The work has been reprinted in *An Eschatology of Victory* (Presbyterian and Reformed Publishing Company, Nutley, NJ, 1971). See also R.T. France, *Jesus and the Old Testament*, Appendix A, 'The Reference of Mark 13:24-27', pp. 227-39, especially 229 ff.
[179]*Criticism and Faith* (Hodder & Stoughton, 1953), p. 9; *cf. idem, The Church and the Reality of Christ* (Collins, 1963), p. 16.
[180]*Cf.* the discussion by A.R.C. Leaney in A.T. Hanson (ed.), *Vindications* (SCM Press, 1966), pp. 103 ff.
[181]In C. Braaten and R.A. Harrisville (eds.), *Kerygma and History: A Symposium on the Theology of Rudolf Bultmann* (Abingdon, New York, 1962), p. 107.
[182]In A.T. Hanson (ed.), *Vindications*, p. 72.

BIBLIOGRAPHY

The philosophy of history
Becker, C.L., *The Heavenly City of the Eighteenth-Century Philosophers* (Yale University Press, 1932).
Idem, Detachment and the Writing of History: Essays and Letters of Carl L. Becker, ed. by P. Snyder (Cornell University Press, 1958).
Berlin, I., *Historical Inevitability* (Oxford University Press, 1954).
Bloch, M., *The Historian's Craft* (Manchester University Press, 1954).
Butterfield, H., *History and Human Relations* (Collins, 1951).
Carr, E.H., *What is History?* (Oxford University Press, 1960; Pelican, 1964).
Collingwood, R.G., *The Idea of History* (Oxford University Press, 1946; reprinted with alterations, 1961).
Idem, Human Nature and Human History (Oxford University Press, for the British Academy, 1936).
Croce, B., *Theory and History of Historiography* (Harrap, 1921).
Danto, A.C., *Analytical Philosophy and History* (Cambridge University Press, 1965).
Donagan, A., *The Later Philosophy of R.G. Collingwood* (Oxford University Press, 1962).
Donagan, A. and B., *Philosophy of History* (Macmillan, 1965).
Dray, W.H., *Philosophy of History* (Prentice-Hall, Englewood Cliffs, 1964).
Idem (ed.), *Philosophical Analysis and History* (Harper & Row, New York, 1966).
Idem, 'History and Value Judgments', in P. Edwards (ed.), *Encyclopedia of Philosophy,* IV (Collier-Macmillan, 1967), pp. 26-30.
Idem, 'Philosophy of History', in P. Edwards (ed.), *Encyclopedia of Philosophy,* VI (Macmillan, 9167), pp. 247-54.
Elton, G.R., *The Practice of History* (Fontana, 1970).
Gadamer, H.-G., *Warheit und Methode: Grundzüge einer philosophischen Hermeneutik²* (Mohr, Tübingen, 1965).
Gallie, W.B., *Philosophy and the Historical Understanding* (Chatto & Windus, 1964).
Gardiner, P., *The Nature Of Historical Explanation* (Oxford University Press, 1961).
Idem (ed.), *Theories of History* (Free Press, Glencoe, 1959).
Geyl, P., *Debates with Historians* (Fontana, 1970).
Idem, Use and Abuse of History (Archon, Hamden, Connecticut, 1970).
Gooch, G.P., *History and Historians in the Nineteenth Century* (Longmans, 1913).
Halperin, S.W. (ed.), *Some 20th-Century Historians* (Chicago University Press, 1961).
Heussi, K., *Die Krisis des Historismus* (Mohr, Tübingen, 1932).
Hexter, J.H., *Reappraisals in History* (Longmans, 1961).
Idem, Doing History (Allen & Unwin, 1971).
Idem, The History Primer (Allen Lane, The Penguin Press, 1972).

Hook, S. (ed.), *Philosophy and History: A Symposium* (New York University Press, 1963).

Hume, D., *Enquiries Concerning the Human Understanding and Concerning Principles of Morals*, ed. by L.A. Selby-Bigge (2nd edn., Oxford University Press, 1902).

Klibansky, R., and Paton, H.J. (eds.), *Philosophy and History: Essays Presented to Ernst Cassirer* (Oxford University Press, 1936).

Krausz, M. (ed.), *Critical Essays on the Philosophy of R.G. Collingwood (Oxford University Press, 1972).*

Löwith, K., *Meaning in History* (Chicago University Press, 1949).

Mandelbaum, M., *The Problem of Historical Knowledge: An Answer to Relativism* (Harper & Row, New York, 1938).

Idem, 'Historicism', in P. Edwards (ed.), *Encyclopedia of Philosophy*, IV (Macmillan, 1967), pp. 22-5.

Marwick, A., *The Nature of History* (Macmillan, for the Open University, 1970).

Mazlish, B., *The Riddle of History: The Great Speculators from Vico to Freud* (Harper & Row, New York, 1966).

Mehta, V., *Fly and the Fly-Bottle: Encounters with British Intellectuals* (Pelican, 1965).

Meiland, J.W., *Scepticism and Historical Knowledge* (Random House, New York, 1965).

Meinecke, F., Historicism: *The Rise of a New Outlook* (Routledge & Kegan Paul, 1972).

Idem, Zur Theorie und Philosophie der Geschichte[2] (Koehler, Munich, 1965).

Idem, Zur Geschichte der Geschichtsschreibung (Koehler, Munich, 1968).

Meyerhoff, H. (ed.), *The Philosophy of History in our Time* (Doubleday, Garden City, 1959).

Mohan, R.P., *Philosophy of History: An Introduction* (Bruce Publishing Company, New York, 1970).

Namier, L., *Avenues of History* (Hamish Hamilton, 1952).

Idem, Personalities and Powers (Hamish Hamilton, 1955).

Oakeshott, M., *Experience and its Modes* (Cambridge University Press, 1933).

Plumb, J.H., *The Death of the Past* (Pelican, 1973).

Polanyi, M., *Personal Knowledge: Towards a Post-Critical Philosophy* (Routledge & Kegan Paul, 1958).

Idem, The Tacit Dimension (Routledge & Kegan Paul, 1967).

Popper, K., *The Poverty of Historicism* (Routledge & Kegan Paul, 1957).

Price, H.H., *Thinking and Experience* (Hutchinson, 1953).

Idem, Belief (Allen & Unwin, 1969).

Rowse, A.L., *The Use of History* (Pelican, 1963).

Schlipp, P.A. (ed.), *The Philosophy of Ernst Cassirer* (Open Court, La Salle, Illinois, 1949).

Stern, F. (ed.), *The Varieties of History: From Voltaire to the Present* (Macmillan, 1970).

Stover, R., *The Nature of Historical Thinking* (University of North Carolina, 1967).

Wagner, F. (ed.), *Geschichtswissenschaft* (Karl Alber Verlag, Munich, 1966).

Walsh, W.H., *An Introduction to Philosophy of History* (Hutchinson, 1951).

White, M., *Foundations of Historical Knowledge* (Harper & Row, New York, 1956).

Widgery, A.G., *The Meanings in History* (Allen & Unwin, 1967).

History and Christianity

Arbaugh, G.E. and G.B., *Kierkegaard's Authorship: A Guide to the Writings of Kierkegaard* (Allen & Unwin, 1968).

Albright, W.F., *History, Archaeology and Christian Humanism* (McGraw-Hill, New York, 1964).

Anderson, H., *Jesus and Christian Origins: A Commentary on Modern Viewpoints* (Oxford University Press, New York, 1964).

Anderson, J.N.D., *Christianity: The Witness of History* (Inter-Varsity Press, 1969).

Baillie, D.M., *God Was In Christ* (Faber, 1948).

Idem, The Theology of the Sacraments and Other Papers (Faber, 1957).

Barr, J., *Old and New in Interpretation: A Study of the Two Testaments* (SCM Press, 1966).

Barth, K., *Church Dogmatics* I. 1 (T. & T. Clark, 1936).

Idem, Protestant Theology in the Nineteenth Century: Its Background and History (SCM Press, 1972).

Bartsch, H.-W., (ed.), *Kerygma and Myth*, vols. I and II combined with enlarged bibliography (SPCK, 1972).

Berkhof, H., *Christ, the Meaning of History* (SCM Press, 1966).

Bodenstein, W., *Neige des Historismus: Ernst Troeltschs Entwicklungsgang* (Gütersloher Verlagshaus, Gütersloh, 1959).

Braaten, C.E., *History and Hermeneutics* (Lutterworth, 1968).

Idem, and Harrisville, R.A. (eds.), *Kerygma and History* (Abingdon, New York and Nashville, 1962).

Idem, The Historical Jesus and the Kerygmatic Christ: Essays on the New Quest of the Historical Jesus (Abingdon, New York and Nashville, 1964).

Brown, C., *Karl Barth and the Christian Message* (Inter-Varsity Press, 1967).

Idem, Philosophy and the Christian Faith (Inter-Varsity Press, 1969).

Bruce, F.F., 'History and the Gospel', *Faith and Thought*, XCIII, no. 3, 1964, pp. 121-45.

Idem, New Testament History (Nelson, 1969).

Idem, Jesus and Christian Origins Outside the New Testament (Hodder & Stoughton, 1974).

Bultmann, R., *Essays Philosophical and Theological* (SCM Press, 1955).

Idem, Existence and Faith: Shorter Writings (Fontana, 1964).

Idem, Faith and Understanding: Collected Essays (SCM Press, 1969).

Idem, Jesus Christ and Mythology (SCM Press, 1960).

Idem, Primitive Christianity in its Contemporary Setting (Fontana, 1962).

Idem, History and Eschatology: The Presence of Eternity (Harper & Row, New York, 1957).

Butterfield, H., *Christianity and History* (Bell, 1949).
Campbell, R., 'Lessing's Problem and Kierkegaard's Answer', *SJT* 19, 1966, pp. 35-54, reprinted in J. Gill (ed.), *Essays on Kierkegaard* (Burgess, Minneapolis, 1968).
Idem, 'History and Bultmann's Structural Inconsistency', *RS* 9, 1973, pp. 63-79.
The Cambridge History of the Bible (Cambridge University Press; vol. I, ed. by P.R. Ackroyd and C.F. Evans, 1970; vol. II, ed. by G.W.H. Lampe, 1969; vol. III, ed. by S.L. Greenslade, 1963).
Carnell, E.J., *The Burden of Søren Kierkegaard* (Paternoster Press, 1965).
Casserley, J.V.L., *Towards a Theology of History* (Faber, 1965).
Cullmann, O., *Salvation in History* (SCM Press, 1967).
Dilthey, W., *Gesammelte Schriften, VII, Der Aufbau der geschichtlichen Welt in den Geisteswissenschaften* (Teubner, Leipzig, 1927).
Idem, Gesammelte Schriften, VIII, Weltanschauungslehre: Abhandlungen zur Philosophie der Philosophie (Teubner, Leipzig, 1931).
Dodd, C.H., *History and the Gospel*[2] (Hodder & Stoughton, 1964).
Idem, The Founder of Christianity (Fontana, 1973).
Dupré, L., *Kierkegaard as Theologian* (Sheed & Ward, 1964).
Dyson, A.O., *The Immortality of the Past* (SCM Press, 1974).
Ebeling, G., *The Nature of Faith* (Fontana, 1966).
Idem, Word and Faith (SCM Press, 1963).
Evans, C.F., *Resurrection and the New Testament* (SCM Press, 1970).
Farmer, W.R., Moule, C.F.D., and Niebuhr, R.R. (eds.), *Christian History and Interpretation: Studies Presented to John Knox* (Cambridge University Press, 1967).
Forbes, D., *The Liberal Anglican Idea of History* (Cambridge University Press, 1962).
Flückiger, F., *Theologie der Geschichte: Die biblische Rede von Gott und die neuere Geschichtstheologie* (Brockhaus, Wuppertal, 1970).
Fuchs, E., *Hermeneutik*[4] (Mohr, Tübingen, 1970).
Idem, Zum hermeneutischen Problem in der Theologie: Die existentiale Interpretation[2] (Mohr, Tübingen, 1965).
Idem, Studies of the Historical Jesus (SCM Press, 1964).
Fuller, D., *Easter Faith and History* (Inter-Varsity Press, 1968).
Funk, R.W. (ed.), *History and Hermeneutic (Journal for Theology and the Church*, 4, Harper & Row, New York, 1967).
Galloway, A., *Wolfhart Pannenberg* (Allen & Unwin, 1973).
Gerdes, H., *Das Christusbild Sören Kierkegaards* (Diederichs, Düsseldorf and Cologne, 1960).
Idem, Sören Kierkegaard (de Gruyter, Berlin, 1966).
Goldingay, J., ' "That You May Know that Yahweh is God": A Study in the Relationship between Theology and Historical Truth in the Old Testament', *TB* 23, 1972, pp. 58-93.
Harvey, V.A., *The Historian and the Believer* (SCM Press, 1967).
Helm, P., *The Varieties of Belief* (Allen & Unwin, 1973).
Henry, C.F. (ed.), *Revelation and the Bible: Contemporary Evangelical*

Thought (Inter-Varsity Press, 1959).

Idem (ed.), *Jesus of Nazareth: Saviour and Lord* (Inter-Varsity Press, 1967).

Hick, J., *Faith and the Philosophers* (Macmillan, 1964).

Idem, Faith and Knowledge[2] (Macmillan, 1967).

Hodges, H.A., *The Philosophy of Wilhem Dilthey* (Routledge & Kegan Paul, 1952).

Holland, R.F., 'The Miraculous', *APhQ*, II, 1965; reprinted in D.Z. Phillips (ed.), *Religion and Understanding* (Blackwell, 1967).

Hordern, W., *Introduction to Theology* (Lutterworth, 1968).

Hünermann, P., *Der Durchbruch geschichtlichen Denkens im 19. Jahrhundert* (Herder, Freiburg, Basel and Vienna, 1967).

Jeremias, J., *The Parables of Jesus*[2] (SCM Press, 1963).

Idem, New Testament Theology, I, *The Proclamation of Jesus* (SCM Press, 1971).

Johnson, R.A., *The Origins of Demythologizing: Philosophy and Historiography in the Theology of Rudolf Bultmann* (Brill, Leiden, 1974).

Kierkegaard, S., *Philosophical Fragments*, ed. by N. Thulstrup (Princeton University Press, 2nd edn. 1962).

Idem, Concluding Unscientific Postscript to the Philosophical Fragments (Princeton University Press, 1941).

Idem, Training in Christianity (Princeton University Press, 1944).

Kegley, C.W. (ed.), *The Theology of Rudolf Bultmann* (SCM Press, 1966).

Keller, E. and M.-L., *Miracles in Dispute: A Continuing Debate* (SCM Press, 1969).

Knox, J., *Criticism and Faith* (Hodder & Stoughton, 1953).

Kümmel, W.G., *The New Testament: The History of the Investigation of its Problems* (SCM Press, 1973).

Künneth, W., *The Theology of the Resurrection* (SCM Press, 1965).

Ladd, G.E., *The New Testament and Criticism* (Hodder & Stoughton, 1970).

Lawton, J.S., *Miracles and Revelation* (Lutterworth, 1959).

Lessing, G.E., *Theological Writings*, ed. by H. Chadwick (A. & C. Black, 1956).

Lewis, C.S., *Miracles: A Preliminary Study* (Bles, 1947).

Lewis, H.D., *Freedom and History* (Allen & Unwin, 1962).

Locke, J., *The Reasonableness of Christianity with a Discourse of Miracles*, ed. by I.T. Ramsey (A. & C. Black, 1958).

Lonergan, B., *Method in Theology* (Darton, Longman & Todd, 1972).

Loos, H. van der, *The Miracles of Jesus* (Brill, Leiden, 1965).

McArthur, H.K. (ed.), *In Search of the Historical Jesus* (SPCK, 1969).

McIntyre, J., *The Christian Doctrine of History* (Oliver & Boyd, 1957).

Idem, The Shape of Christology (SCM Press, 1966).

Malet, A., *The Thought of Rudolf Bultmann* (Irish University Press, Shannon, 1969).

Marrou, H.I., *The Meaning in History* (Helicon, Baltimore-Dublin, 1966).

Marxsen, W., *The Resurrection of Jesus of Nazareth* (SCM Press, 1970).

Mascall, E.L., *Christian Theology and Natural Science: Some Questions in their Relations (Longmans, 1956).*

Idem, Theology and Images (Mowbray, 1963).
Idem, The Christian Universe (Darton, Longman & Todd, 1966).
Idem, Theology and the Future (Darton, Longman & Todd, 1968).
Idem, The Openness of Being: Natural Theology Today (Darton, Longman & Todd, 1971).
Meinhold, P., Geschichte der kirchlichen Historiographie, I and II (Karl Aber Verlag, Munich, 1967).
Moltmann, J., Theology of Hope (SCM Press, 1967).
Idem, Hope and Planning (SCM Press, 1971).
Montgomery, J.W., History in Christian Perspective, I, The Shape of the Past: An Introduction to Philosophical Historiography (Edwards Brothers, Ann Arbor, 1962).
Moule, C.F.D., The Phenomenon of the New Testament (A. & C. Black, 1967).
Idem (ed.), Miracles: Cambridge Studies in their Philosophy and History (Mowbray, 1965).
Idem (ed.), The Significance of the Message of the Resurrection for Faith in Jesus Christ (SCM Press, 1968).
Navone, J.J., History and Faith in the Thought of Alan Richardson (SCM Press, 1966).
Neill, S., The Interpretation of the New Testament, 1861-1961 (Oxford University Press, 1964).
Niebuhr, R.R., Beyond Tragedy: Essays on the Christian Interpretation of History (Charles Scribner's Sons, New York, 1937).
Idem, The Nature and Destiny of Man: A Christian Interpretation, I and II (Nisbet, 1941-3).
Idem, Faith and History (Charles Scribner's Sons, New York, 1949).
Idem, The Irony of American History (Charles Scribner's Sons, New York, 1952).
Idem, The Self and the Dramas of History (Charles Scribner's Sons, New York, 1955).
Idem, Resurrection and Historical Reason: A Study of Theological Method (Charles Scribner's Sons, New York, 1957).
Nygren, A., Meaning and Method: Prolegomena to a Scientific Philosophy of Religion and a Scientific Theology (Epworth, 1972).
Orr, J., The Resurrection of Jesus (Hodder & Stoughton, 1908).
Owen, H.P., Revelation and Existence (University of Wales Press, 1957).
Idem, The Christian Knowledge of God (Athlone Press, 1969).
Idem, Concepts of Deity (Macmillan, 1971).
Palmer, H., The Logic of Gospel Criticism (Macmillan, 1968).
Pannenberg, W., Jesus—God and Man² (SCM Press, 1970).
Idem, Basic Questions in Theology, I-III (SCM Press, 1970-3).
Idem, The Apostles' Creed in the Light of Today's Questions (SCM Press, 1972).
Idem (ed.), Revelation as History (Sheed & Ward, 1969).
Pauck, W., Harnack and Troeltsch: Two Historical Theologians (Oxford University Press, New York, 1968).
Ramsey, A.M., The Resurrection of Christ: A Study of the Event and its Meaning for the Christian Faith (Fontana, 1961).

Ramsey, I.T., *Religious Language: An Empirical Placing of Theological Phrases* (SCM Press, 1957).

Idem, *Christian Empiricism*, ed. by J.H. Gill (Sheldon Press, 1974).

Idem (ed.), *Christian Ethics and Contemporary Philosophy* (SCM Press, 1966).

Idem (ed.), *Words about God: The Philosophy of Religion* (SCM Press, 1971).

Reist, B.A., *Towards a Theology of Involvement: A Study of Ernst Troeltsch* (SCM Press, 1966).

Reumann, J., *Jesus in the Church's Gospels: Modern Scholarship and the Earliest Sources* (SPCK, 1970).

Richardson, A., *The Miracle Stories of the Gospels* (SCM Press, 1941).

Idem, *Christian Apologetics* (SCM Press, 1947).

Idem, *Introduction to the Theology of the New Testament* (SCM Press, 1958).

Idem, *The Bible in the Age of Science* (SCM Press, 1961).

Idem, *History: Sacred and Profane* (SCM Press, 1964).

Ristow, H., and Matthiae, K., *Der historische Jesus und der kerygmatische Christus*[2] (Evangelische Verlaganstalt, Berlin, 1962).

Roberts, T.A., *History and Christian Apologetic* (SPCK, 1960).

Idem, 'The Historian and the Believer', *RS* 7, 1971, pp. 251-7.

Robinson, J.A.T., 'Resurrection in the NT', in G.A. Buttrick (ed.), *The Interpreter's Dictionary of the Bible*, IV (Abingdon, New York and Nashville, 1962), pp. 43-53.

Robinson, J.M., *A New Quest of the Historical Jesus* (SCM Press, 1959).

Idem (ed.), *The Future of our Religious Past: Essays in Honour of Rudolf Bultmann* (SCM Press, 1971).

Idem, and Cobb, J.B., Jr (eds.), *The New Hermeneutic* (Harper & Row, New York, 1964).

Idem, *Theology as History* (Harper & Row, New York, 1967).

Rust, E.C., *Towards a Theological Understanding of History* (Oxford University Press, New York, 1963).

Sanders, E.P., *The Tendencies of the Gospel Tradition* (Cambridge University Press, 1965).

Schaeffer, F., *Escape from Reason* (Inter-Varsity Press, 1968).

Idem, *The God who is There* (Hodder & Stoughton, 1968).

Idem, *He is There and He is not Silent* (Hodder, 1972).

Schmitthals, W., *An Introduction to the Theology of Rudolf Bultmann* (SCM Press 1968).

Schweitzer, A., *The Quest of the Historical Jesus: A Critical Study of its Progress from Reimarus to Wrede* (1910; A. & C. Black, 3rd edn., 1954).

Sponheim, P., *Kierkegaard on Christ and Christian Coherence* (SCM Press, 1968).

Swinburne, R., *The Concept of Miracle* (Macmillan, 1970).

Sykes, S.W., and Clayton, J.P. (eds.), *Christ, Faith and History: Cambridge Studies in Christology* (Cambridge University Press, 1972).

Thiselton, A.C., 'Kierkegaard and the Nature of Truth', *The Churchman* 89, 1975, pp. 85-105.

Tillich, P., *The Interpretation of History* (Charles Scribner's Sons, New York, 1936).

Idem, *Systematic Theology*, I-III (Nisbet, 1953-64).

Torrance, T.F., *Theology in Reconstruction* (SCM Press, 1965).

Idem, *Theological Science* (Oxford University Press, 1969).

Idem, *Space, Time and Incarnation* (Oxford University Press, 1969).

Idem, *God and Rationality* (Oxford University Press, 1971).

Idem, 'Newton, Einstein and Scientific Theology', *RS* 8, 1972, pp. 233-50.

Troeltsch, E., *Gessammelte Schriften*, II, *Zur religiösen Lage, Religionsphilosophie und Ethik*[2] (Mohr, Tübingen, 1922).

Idem, *The Absoluteness of Christianity and the History of Religions* (SCM Press, 1972).

Idem, *Christian Thought: Its History and Application*, ed. Baron F. von Hügel (1923; Meridian Books, New York, 1957).

Trotter, T.F. (ed.), *Jesus and the Historian* (Westminster Press, Philadelphia, 1968).

Tupper, E.F., *The Theology of Wolfhart Pannenberg* (SCM Press, 1974).

Tuttle, H.N., *Wilhelm Dilthey's Philosophy of Historical Understanding: A Critical Analysis* (Brill, Leiden, 1969).

Warfield, B.B., *The Inspiration and Authority of the Bible* (Marshall, Morgan & Scott, 1951).

Idem, *Miracles: Yesterday and Today, True and False* (Eerdmans, Grand Rapids, 1954; first published under the title *Counterfeit Miracles*).

Wenham, J.W., *Christ and the Bible* (Inter-Varsity Press, 1972).

Wright, G.E., *God who Acts: Biblical Theology as Recital* (SCM Press, 1952).

Young, W., *History and Existential Theology: The Role of History in the Thought of Rudolf Bultmann* (Westminster Press, 1969).

Zahrnt, H., *The Historical Jesus* (Collins, 1963).

Idem, *The Question of God: Protestant Theology in the Twentieth Century* (Collins, 1969).

INDEX OF NAMES

In this and the following index, n. denotes that the reference occurs in a note. The names given below occur in the text of the articles and notes but the bibliographies are not included.

Ackroyd, P.R., 67 n., 68 n.
Albright, W.F., 56, 57, 64, 71 n., 72 n., 168, 207 n.
Alt, A., 57, 213 n.
Anderson, F.I., 70 n.
Anderson, G.W., 70 n.
Augustine, 65, 73 n.
Austin, J.L., 215 n.

Baillie, D.M., 211 n., 214 n., 215 n.
Baird, J.A., 137 n., 138 n., 140 n.
Baltzer, K., 69
Barbour, I.G., 204 n., 212 n.
Barbour, R.S., 134 n., 135 n., 136 n., 137 n.
Barr, J., 213 n.
Barth, K., 187 f., 193, 201 n., 215 n.
Bartsch, H.-W., 209 n.
Barzun, J., 211 n.
Beard, C.A., 179 f.
Beasley-Murray, G.R., 216 n.
Becker, C.L., 209 n., 211 n.
Berlin, I., 178
Beyerlin, W., 69 n.

Beyschlag, W., 99 n.
Birkeland, H., 140 n.
Black, M., 123, 139 n.
Bloch, M. 212 n.
Böhlig, A., 98 n.
Bornkamm, G., 165, 205 n.
Braaten, C.E., 209 n., 210 n., 213 n., 216 n.
Braithwaite, R.B., 197 f., 212 n.
Bright, J., 15 ff., 22, 52 ff., 55, 67 n., 68 n., 71 n.
Burckhardt, J., 180
Brown, C., 201 n., 202 n., 209 n., 213 n., 215 n.
Brown, P., 73 n.
Brown, R.E., 68 n.
Bruce, F.F., 140 n., 210 n.
Brunner, E., 215 n.
Buber, M., 215 n.
Bultmann, R., 85-9, 91, 97 n., 98 n., 101 ff., 105, 108, 113, 115, 117 f., 120, 134 n., 135 n., 138 n., 139 n., 171, 174, 186 f., 209 n., 212 n., 213 n., 214 n.
Burkitt, F.C., 97 n., 98 n.
Burney, C.F., 98 n., 139 n.
Butterfield, H., 178

Cairns, D., 209 n.
Callaway, J.P., 72 n.
Calvert, D.G.A., 136 n.
Calvin, J., 203 n.
Cambier, J., 139 n.
Campenhausen, H. von, 204 n.
Carlston, C.E., 135 n.
Carnley, P., 202 n.
Carr, E.H., 208 n., 211 n.
Carrington, P., 139 n., 140 n.
Cerfaux, L., 138 n., 139 n.
Childs, B.S., 54, 71 n.
Clines, D.J.A., 69 n.
Cobb, J.B., 209 n., 214 n.
Cockshut, A.O.J., 216 n.
Collingwood, R.G., 166, 192, 206 n., 208 n., 209 n., 211 n., 212 n.
Conzelmann, H., 192, 214 n.
Craigie, P.C., 53
Creed, J.M., 97 n.
Cross, F.M., 68 n., 70 n., 71 n.
Cullman, O., 124, 139 n., 140 n., 187, 207 n., 213 n.
Cuppitt, D., 205 n.

Dahl, N.A., 139 n.
Danto, A.C., 206 n.
Davies, W.D., 121, 139 n., 140
Dibelius, M., 89, 97 n., 139 n.
Dilthey, W., 184, 212 n.
Dodd, C.H., 137 n., 138 n., 215 n.
Doeve, J.W., 139 n.
Downing, F.G., 135 n., 136 n., 187, 213 n.
Drane, J.W., 214 n.
Dray, W.H., 178, 206 n., 211 n.
Drower, E.S., 97 n., 98 n.

Ebner, F., 215 n.
Eichrodt, W., 24 f., 28, 31, 67 n., 68 n.
Eissfeldt, O., 70 n.
Elderen, B. Van, 141 n.

Ellis, E.E., 210 n.
Emerton, J.A., 140 n.
Erlandsson, S., 70 n.
Eusebius, 98 n.
Evans, C.F., 67 n., 68 n.
Evans, D.D., 215 n.
Evans, P.W., 141 n.

Farmer, H.H., 203 n.
Fitzmyer, J.A., 140 n.
Fohrer, G., 70 n.
France, R.T., 135 n., 210 n., 216 n.
Freedman, D.N., 70 n., 71 n.
Fuller, R.H., 110, 135 n.
Funk, R.W., 209 n., 212 n.

Gadamer, H.-G., 212 n.
Galloway, A., 214 n.
Gaster, T.H., 80
Gerhardsson, B., 120 ff., 123, 134 n., 139 n., 140 n.
Glasson, T.F., 135 n.
Glasswell, M.E., 204 n.
Goldingay, J., 212 n., 214 n.
Golka, F., 71 n.
Gordon, C.H., 97 n.
Gray, J., 68 n.
Greenberg, M., 69 n.
Greenslade, S.L., 67 n.
Gundry, R.H., 128, 137 n., 138 n., 140 n., 211 n.
Guthrie, D., 137 n.

Haenchen, E., 215 n.
Hanson, A.T., 134 n., 136 n., 216 n.
Hanson, R.P.C., 67 n., 114, 136 n., 137 n., 138 n., 199
Harris, J.R., 98 n.
Harrison, E.F., 140 n.
Harrison, R.K., 69 n.
Harrisville, R.A., 213 n., 216 n.
Hart, H.L.A., 211 n.

Harvey, Van A., 31 ff., 68 n., 166 f., 207 n.
Hasel, G.F., 67 n.
Hegel, G.W.F., 214 n.
Heidegger, M., 97 n.
Hempel, C.G., 203 n., 206 n., 208 n.
Hendrikson, W., 216 n.
Henry, C.F., 215 n.
Herrmann, S., 71 n.
Hesse, M., 204 n.
Heussi, K., 202 n., 211 n.
Hexter, J.H., 206 n., 211 n.
Hick, J., 195 f., 215 n.
Hill, D., 103 n.
Hodges, H.A., 212 n.
Hodgson, P.C., 96 n., 136 n.
Holland, R.F., 157, 203 n.
Hooke, S.H., 96 n.
Hooker, M.D., 136 n.
Housman, A.E., 181
Hume, D., 159-62, 204 n.
Hyatt, J.P., 67 n.

Jeremias, J., 116, 123, 139 n., 140 n., 193, 215 n., 216 n.
Jerome, 65
Julian, 96 n.

Kaiser, O., 67 n.
Kantzer, K., 215 n.
Käsemann, E., 96 n., 98 n., 134 n.
Kaufmann, W., 39, 65, 69 n.
Kaufmann, Y., 69 n., 70 n.
Keck, L.E., 214 n.
Kidner, D., 216 n.
Kierkegaard, S.A., 148-53, 201 n.
Kik, J.M., 198, 216 n.
Kilian, R., 67 n.
Kitchen, K.A., 69 n., 80 n.
Klein, R.W., 68 n.
Knox, J., 136, 199
Knox, W.L., 138 n.

Koch, K., 68 n.
Kraus, H.-J., 69 n.
Künneth, W., 199, 205 n.

Ladd, G.E., 96 n., 116, 129, 134 n., 209 n.
Lampe, G.W.H., 67 n., 204 n.
Lapp, P.W., 58 ff., 60 f., 72 n.
Leaney, A.R.C., 216 n.
Lemke, W.E., 69 n.
Lewis, C.S., 37 f., 65, 69 n.
Lietzmann, H., 97 n.
Lightfoot, R.H., 139 n.
Lindars, B., 135 n., 210 n.
Liver, J., 68 n.
Locke, J., 156 f., 160, 203 n.
Loersch, S., 69 n.
Lohfink, N., 68 n., 69 n., 70 n.
Lonergan, B., 202 n., 209 n., 211 n.
Longenecker, R.N., 211 n.
Luther, M., 87, 184

McArthur, H.K., 115
McCarthy, D.J., 69 n.
McCullough, W.S., 69 n.
McEleney, N.J., 134 n., 135 n., 137 n.
Mackenzie, R.A.F., 69 n.
McKinnon, A., 204 n.
McIntyre, J., 216 n.
McNamara, M., 140 n.
Macquarrie, J., 215 n.
Macuch, R., 98 n.

Malamat, A., 72 n.
Manson, T.W., 90, 97 n., 124, 137 n., 139 n.
Marshall, I.H., 104 n.
Martin, R.P., 96 n.
Mascall, E.L., 204 n., 212 n.
Mettinger, T.N.D., 68 n.
Miegge, G., 97 n.
Moltmann, J., 210 n., 214 n.

Montgommery, J.W., 216 n.
Morris, L., 204 n., 216 n.
Mosley, A.W., 138 n.
Motyer, J.A., 67 n.
Moule, C.F.D., 96 n., 138 n.,
140 n., 204 n., 205 n., 206 n.
Mowinckel, S., 69 n.
Myers, J.M., 69 n.
Mylonas, G.E., 96 n.

Nagel, E., 211 n.
Namier, L., 167, 173, 181 f.,
210 n.
Navone, J., 202 n.
Neugebauer, F., 103 n.
Nicholson, E.W., 68 n.
Nielson, E., 70 n.
Nineham, D.E., 106, 134 n.,
137 n.
Norden, E., 96 n.
Noth, M., 49-53, 55 f., 57 ff.,
64, 68 n., 70 n., 71 n.
Nowell-Smith, P., 204 n.

Ogden, S.M., 209 n.
Orr, J., 204 n.

Pallis, S.A., 98 n.
Pannenberg, W., 96 n., 172 f.,
176, 188-92, 205 n., 211 n.,
212 n., 213 n., 214 n.
Paul, S.M., 69 n.
Peacocke, A.R., 204 n.
Peake, A.S., 76
Perrin, N., 101, 103 ff., 108 ff.,
112 f., 134 n., 135 n., 137 n.,
139 n.
Phillips, D.Z., 203 n.
Pitcher, G., 211 n.
Porten, B., 68 n.
Polanyi, M., 207 n.

Rad, G. von, 17, 22 ff., 25 f., 28,
31, 67 n.
Ramsey, A.M., 139 n.

Ramsey, I.T., 203 n., 212 n.,
215 n.
Ranke, L. von, 97 n., 177, 180
Redford, D.B., 69 n.
Rehm, M., 67 n.
Reimarus, H.S., 201 n.
Reitzenstein, R., 90, 97 n.
Richardson, A., 134 n., 154 ff.,
164 f., 202 n., 203 n., 204 n.,
205 n., 208 n.
Ridderbos, N., 216 n.
Riesenfeld, H., 120, 137 n., 139 n.
Robinson, J.A., 98 n.
Robinson, J.A.T., 86, 99 n.
Robinson, J.M., 96 n., 97 n.,
119, 209 n., 213 n., 214 n.
Routley, E., 96 n.
Rowley, H.H., 89, 97 n.
Rudolph, K., 97 n.
Rust, E.C., 216 n.

Sanders, E.P., 135 n., 141 n.
Sanders, J.T., 98 n.
Schaeffer, F., 154, 202 n.
Schlier, H., 93, 98 n.
Schmiedel, P.W., 108
Schmithals, W., 209 n.
Schweizer, E., 214 n.
Scott, E.F., 138 n.
Sherwin-White, A.N., 138 n.
Schmiedel, P.W., 108
Schmithals, W., 209 n.
Schweizer, E., 214 n.
Scott, E.F., 138 n.
Sherwin-White, A.N., 138 n.
Skehan, P.W., 68 n.
Smith, D.M., 211 n.
Smith, M., 139 n.
Stamm, J.J., 70 n.
Stanton, G.N., 134 n., 139 n.,
140 n.
Stendahl, K., 210 n.
Stern, F., 207 n., 210 n., 211 n.,
212 n.

Strauss, D.F., 79, 96 n.
Suetonius, 209 n.
Swinburne, R., 160 f., 163, 165, 203 n., 204 n., 207 n.
Symondson, A., 216 n.

Tacitus, 180, 209 n.
Talmon, S., 68 n.
Tasker, R.V.G., 141 n.
Taylor, V., 136 n., 137 n.
Teeple, H.M., 136 n.
Temple, W., 186 f., 213 n.
Thiselton, A.C., 215 n.
Thompson, R.J., 69 n.
Torrance, T.F., 174 f., 210 n.
Troeltsch, E., 171 f., 175, 210 n., 211 n.
Turner, H.E.W., 114 f., 140 n.
Turner, N., 140 n.

Vaux, R. de, 17, 26 ff., 29, 31, 54, 62, 67 n., 68 n., 71 n., 72 n.
Vincent, J.J., 139 n.

Wainwright, A.W., 140 n.
Walker, W.O., 134 n.
Walsh, W.H., 206 n.
Warfield, B.B., 215 n.
Watts, I., 83
Weinfeld, M., 68 n., 70 n.
Weipert, M., 56 f., 72 n.
Wellhausen, J., 69 n.
Wells, G.A., 96 n.
Wenham, G.J., 70 n., 73 n.
Wenham, J.W., 67 n., 209 n., 215 n.
White, M., 206 n.
Whybray, R.N., 68 n.
Wilckens, U., 213 n.
Wijngaards, J.N.M., 70 n.
Wilcock, M., 216 n.
Wildberger, H., 67 n.
Williams, C.S.C., 137 n., 140 n.
Wilson, R. McL., 98 n., 99 n.

Wittgenstein, L., 195, 215 n.
Wood, H.G., 139 n.
Wright, G.E., 70 n., 185 f., 213 n.

Yadin, Y., 72 n.
Yammauchi, E., 97 n., 98 n., 214 n.
Yeivin, S., 71 n.

INDEX OF SUBJECTS

Achin, 57
Aetiology, 52, 61
Ahaz, 18
Ai, 51, 55 ff., 60 f., 72 n., 73 n.
Analogy, 27, 68 n., 117, 171-7, 210 n.
Antichrist, 88
Apocalyptic, 88 ff., 92, 189, 198
Apostles, 132 f., 191
Aramaic, 109
Archaeology, 42, 53, 55-62, 71 n.
Assyria, 18 f., 41
Avesta, 90
Authenticity, 101 ff., 108 ff., 130
Authority, 15 ff., 101, 191, 193

Balaam, 24
Baptismal formula, 130 f., 141 n.
Beliar, 89
Bethel, 47, 58, 72 n.
Biblical realism, 116
Biblical theology and history, 13-34

Canaan, 48 ff., 53 f., 55-62, 71 n., 72 n.
Chronicles, Books of, 35 ff., 41
Church, 164 f.
Coherence, 108

Coincidence concept of miracles, 157 f.
Contemporaneity, 149 f., 152, 170
Contingency concept of miracles 157 f.
Cosmic victory, 92 ff.
Covenant, 22, 40, 69 n., 216 n.
Creation, 21, 182, 198, 216 n.
Creeds, 81 ff.
Criteria, 108-14, 134 n., 135 n., 136 n., 137 n., 138 n., 139 n., 140 n., 159 ff., 165-77
Crucifixion, 82 ff., 166 ff., 207 n.

Dan, 47
David, 45
Deduction, 208 n.
Demythologization, 85 f.
Deuteronomy, 36, 41, 44, 48, 69 n.
Dialectical theology, 149, 201 n.
Direct speech, 128 f., 182, 212 n.
Dispersion, 175
Dissimilarity, principle of, 108, 110 f., 124 f.
Docetism, 193

Eleusis, 79, 96 n.
Elisha, 30

Empty tomb, 164, 204 n.
Eschatology, 82 ff., 86, 88, 198 f., 212 n.
Et-Tell, 55, 60 f.
Evidence, 159-65, 165-77, 207 n.
Existentialism, 85, 97 n., 148 f., 151, 214 n.
Exodus, Book of, 42 ff., 46
Exodus, the, 15 f., 22, 31, 50, 176, 185

Facts, 164 f., 169, 177 ff., 208 n.
Faith, 17 ff., 66, 84 ff., 165, 175 f., 187, 190, 195, 210 n., 214 n.
Form criticism, 39 f., 89 f.
Fulfilment, 176 ff., 198 f., 214 n., 216 n.

Gayomart, 90 f.
Geschichte, 103, 119, 134 n.
Genesis, 21, 46, 198, 216 n.
Gnosticism, 90, 94, 98 n., 192, 214 n.

Hazor, 58 f.
Hermeneutics, 81-9, 170-7, 212 n., 213 n.
Hermes, 162
Hezekiah, 47
Historical criticism, 42
Historical event and interpretation, 84 ff., 170-7, 178 ff.
Historicism, 114-7, 132
Historie, 103 f., 119, 134 n.
History of religions school, 90 ff.
Holy war, 44
Homer, 79 f.
Hypothesis, 61, 66, 147, 154 f., 164 f., 169, 203 n., 209 n.

Image of God, 95
Immanuel prophecy, 18 ff.
Incarnation, 82 f., 94 f., 150, 174 ff.

Incognito, divine, 150 f., 208 n.
Iranian myth, 90, 97 n.

Jehoichin, 35
Jeremiah, 29, 195
Jericho, 56, 60 f.
Jerusalem, 30, 47, 81, 93, 195, 199
Jesus as a teacher, 15 f., 32 ff., 101-33, 150 f.
John the Baptist, 81, 91
Joshua, 41, 55, 61, 70 n.
Josiah, 36, 47
Judges, Book of, 45
Judgments in history, 166 f., 168 f., 177 ff.
Justification, 87

Kerygma, 28, 191, 213 n.
Kingdom of God, 112 f.
Kings, Books of, 22, 35 ff., 41

Laws in history, 166 ff., 206 n.
Laws in science, 86 ff., 155, 156-65, 165 ff., 174 f., 197, 203 n., 206 n., 208 n., 210 n.
Laws of God, 37, 47, 70 n., 191
Leviathan, 88
Logos, 79 ff., 93, 99 n.
Lord's Supper, 80, 216 n.

Mandaean literature, 91, 97 n., 98 n.
Manichaeism, 91, 97 n.
Miracles, 24, 156-65, 171 ff.
Models, 183 ff., 200, 212 n.
Monophysitism, 193
Moral Judgments, 29, 178 ff., 211 n.
Moses, 42 f., 47, 50
Multiple attestation, 108 f., 135 n., 207 n.
Myth, 79-99, 172, 174 ff.
Myth and ritual school, 80, 96 n.
mythos, 79 ff.

Nature, 194 f. (see also Laws in science, Miracles, Science)

Oral tradition, 52, 118, 120 ff.

Palaeography, 42
Paradigms, 153 f., 175 f.
Paradox, 27, 148-52
Pentateuch, 39, 42, 45-55, 69 n., 70 n., 71 n.
Performative utterances, 192, 215 n.
Perspectivism, 177, 179 f., 202 n., 211 n.
Peshitta, 91
Poetry, 53, 79 f.
Pontius Pilate, 82, 180
Presuppositions, 103-7, 115 f., 153 f.
Probability, 163 (see also Hypothesis)
Prophecy, 18 ff., 29, 103 f., 137 n. (see also Fulfilment)
Psalms, 19, 33, 40, 69 n., 135 n., 175, 194

Q material, 135 n.
Quotation, 128 f., 132, 182, 212 n.

Rabbinic teaching methods, 119 ff.
Rationalism, 202 n.
Reason, 156 f., 210 n.
Reconstruction, 181 ff.
Redaction criticism, 41 ff., 104 f., 134 n.
Relativism, 177, 179 f., 211 n.
Resurrection, 82 ff., 84 ff., 158, 164 f., 187, 190, 205 n., 206 n.
Revelation, 176, 185-97, 199, 201 n.
Revelation, Book of, 198, 216 n.
Roman authorities, 81 ff., 166, 180

Rules, 165 ff., 206 n., 207 n. (see also Laws in history)

Sacred history and secular history, 14 ff., 16 ff., 23 ff., 27 ff., 31 ff., 84 ff., 151 f., 152-6, 171 ff., 185 ff., 189 ff.
Sacrifice, 47
Samaria, 30
Saul, 45
Sayings of Jesus, 101-43
Sayings tradition, 117 ff.
Science, 147, 153, 174 f., 203 n., 204 n., 206 n., 208 n., 210 n. (see also Laws in science)
Solomon, 30, 35 f., 68 n.
Son of man, 113, 136 n., 207 n.
Source criticism, 35 f.
Space, 174 ff.
Style, 123
Supernatural, 87 ff., 106 ff., 156-65

Terminology of tradition, 123
Testimony, 107 n.
Textual criticism, 34 f., 68 n.
Three-decker universe, 85
Time, 175 ff.
Tradition criticism, 40 f.
Transcendence of God, 87 f., 149 ff., 201 n.
Truth, 177, 179, 201 f.

Value judgments, 177 f., 211 n.
Verification, 166 ff., 197
Violation concept of miracle, 157 ff., 163 f.

Wisdom, 94 f., 210 n.
Wolfenbüttel Fragments, 201 n.
Word of God, 185, 187 ff., 191 f., 193

Zeus, 162
Zoroastrianism, 90